Async Rust
Unleashing the Power of Fearless Concurrency

Maxwell Flitton and Caroline Morton

O'REILLY®

Async Rust

by Maxwell Flitton and Caroline Morton

Published by O'Reilly Media, Inc., 1005 Gravenstein Highway North, Sebastopol, CA 95472.

O'Reilly books may be purchased for educational, business, or sales promotional use. Online editions are also available for most titles (*http://oreilly.com*). For more information, contact our corporate/institutional sales department: 800-998-9938 or *corporate@oreilly.com*.

Acquisitions Editor: Brian Guerin	**Indexer:** Sue Klefstad
Development Editor: Melissa Potter	**Interior Designer:** David Futato
Production Editor: Jonathon Owen	**Cover Designer:** Karen Montgomery
Copyeditor: Sharon Wilkey	**Illustrator:** Kate Dullea
Proofreader: Heather Walley	

November 2024:   First Edition

Revision History for the First Edition

2024-11-12:   First Release
2025-01-31:   Second Release

See *http://oreilly.com/catalog/errata.csp?isbn=9781098149093* for release details.

978-1-098-14909-3

[LSI]

Table of Contents

Preface. vii

1. Introduction to Async. 1
   What Is Async?   2
   Introduction to Processes   5
   What Are Threads?   10
   Where Can We Utilize Async?   16
      Using Async for File I/O   17
      Improving HTTP Request Performance with Async   20
   Summary   22

2. Basic Async Rust. 23
   Understanding Tasks   23
   Futures   29
      Pinning in Futures   30
      Context in Futures   32
   Waking Futures Remotely   35
   Sharing Data Between Futures   37
      High-Level Data Sharing Between Futures   41
      How Are Futures Processed?   43
   Putting It All Together   44
   Summary   48

3. Building Our Own Async Queues. 49
   Building Our Own Async Queue   50
   Increasing Workers and Queues   57
   Passing Tasks to Different Queues   59
   Task Stealing   61

Refactoring Our spawn_task Function   63
Creating Our Own Join Macro   65
Configuring Our Runtime   66
Running Background Processes   68
Summary   69

4. Integrating Networking into Our Own Async Runtime..................... **71**
Understanding Executors and Connectors   72
Integrating hyper into Our Async Runtime   73
Building an HTTP Connection   74
Implementing the Tokio AsyncRead Trait   77
Implementing the Tokio AsyncWrite Trait   79
Connecting and Running Our Client   81
Introducing mio   82
    Polling Sockets in Futures   83
    Sending Data over the Socket   86
Summary   88

5. Coroutines... **89**
Introducing Coroutines   90
    What Are Coroutines?   90
    Why Use Coroutines?   91
Generating with Coroutines   94
    Implementing a Simple Generator in Rust   95
    Stacking Our Coroutines   96
    Calling a Coroutine from a Coroutine   98
Mimicking Async Behavior with Coroutines   100
Controlling Coroutines   104
Testing Coroutines   109
Summary   113

6. Reactive Programming... **115**
Building a Basic Reactive System   115
    Defining Our Subjects   116
    Building Our Display Observer   118
    Building Our Heater and Heat-Loss Observer   121
    Getting User Input via Callbacks   124
Enabling Broadcasting with an Event Bus   127
    Building Our Event Bus Struct   128
    Building Our Event Bus Handle   131
    Interacting with Our Event Bus via Async Tasks   132
Summary   135

7. Customizing Tokio. **137**
Building a Runtime   137
Processing Tasks with Local Pools   142
Getting Unsafe with Thread Data   147
Graceful Shutdowns   149
Summary   154

8. The Actor Model. **155**
Building a Basic Actor   155
Working with Actors Versus Mutexes   157
Implementing the Router Pattern   160
Implementing State Recovery for Actors   165
Creating Actor Supervision   170
Summary   176

9. Design Patterns. **179**
Building an Isolated Module   179
Waterfall Design Pattern   185
The Decorator Pattern   186
The State Machine Pattern   190
The Retry Pattern   193
The Circuit-Breaker Pattern   194
Summary   196

10. Building an Async Server with No Dependencies. **197**
Setting Up the Basics   197
Building Our std Async Runtime   199
  Building Our Waker   200
  Building Our Executor   202
  Running Our Executor   205
  Building Our Sender   207
  Building Our Receiver   208
  Building Our Sleep   209
Building Our Server   210
  Accepting Requests   211
  Handling Requests   214
Building Our Async Client   215
Summary   216

11. Testing. **219**
Performing Basic Sync Testing   219
Mocking Async Code   222

Testing For Deadlocks   224
Testing for Race Conditions   227
Testing Channel Capacity   229
Testing Network Interactions   231
Fine-Grained Future Testing   233
Summary   235

Index.   237

Preface

What Is Async Rust?

Asynchronous programming in Rust, often referred to as *Async Rust*, is a powerful paradigm that allows developers to write concurrent code that is more efficient and scalable. In contrast to traditional synchronous programming, where tasks are executed one after another, async programming enables tasks to run concurrently, which is particularly useful when dealing with I/O-bound operations like network requests or file handling. This approach allows for the efficient use of system resources and can lead to significant performance improvements in applications that need to handle multiple tasks at once without the need for additional cores.

Rust's type system and ownership model provide the safety guarantees that we all love. However, mastering async Rust requires an understanding of specific concepts, such as futures, pinning, and executors. This book will guide you through these concepts, equipping you with the knowledge needed to apply async to your own projects and programs.

Who Is This Book For?

This book is aimed at intermediate Rust developers who want to learn how to improve their applications and programs by using the range of asynchronous functionality available to them.

If you are new to Rust or programming in general, this book may not be the best starting point. Instead, we recommend the following resources for learning Rust from the ground up:

- *The Rust Programming Language* (*https://oreil.ly/3M49T*) by Steve Klabnik and Carol Nichols (No Starch Press, 2022).
- *Rust Web Programming* by Maxwell Flitton (Packt Publishing, 2023)

- Rust by Example (*https://oreil.ly/w_CHT*), a collection of online runnable examples written by the Rust community

Overview of the Chapters

Chapter 1, "Introduction to Async", gives a high-level overview of what async programming is and how it can be useful in particular types of programs—for example, for I/O operations. This chapter also explores threads and processes to explain the context in which async programming is implemented in relation to the operating system.

Chapter 2, "Basic Async Rust", delves into the basics of async programming in Rust, looking at what a future is and why pinning and context are needed to implement async Rust. We'll finish off with examples of basic data sharing between futures. This chapter will enable you to write basic async futures, implement the Future trait, and run async code.

Chapter 3, "Building Our Own Async Queues", puts together the information from the previous two chapters to create our own queue, where we implement passing tasks to different queues and stealing tasks. We create our own join macros and do some basic configuration of our runtime. This chapter shows how async tasks are passed through an async runtime and processed.

Chapter 4, "Integrating Networking into Our Own Async Runtime", is a relatively complicated chapter that drills down into what an executor and connector are and how to create a program that can do networking. We also get into *mio* and how to use sockets. This builds on the previous chapter, but feel free to skip this chapter if it is too challenging early on and come back to it later. This chapter shows how to integrate networking primitives into an async runtime.

Chapter 5, "Coroutines", introduces coroutines and how to implement them in Rust. We draw the parallels between async/await and coroutines and implement a basic generator in Rust. This chapter also shows how async tasks are essentially coroutines by building async functionality without any extra threads.

Chapter 6, "Reactive Programming", introduces reactive programming within the context of async Rust. We look at a heater system and build a simple example of a reactive system. We end the chapter learning how to create an event bus.

Chapter 7, "Customizing Tokio", does what it says on the tin. This chapter guides you through customizing your *Tokio* setup to solve your particular problem. We cannot cover the whole of *Tokio*, which is an extensive library, but we do go through building a runtime, local pools, and graceful shutdowns. With this chapter, you get to achieve fine-grained control of how your *Tokio* async tasks are processed, including pinning async tasks to specific threads so those tasks can reference the state of that thread when being polled to completion.

Chapter 8, "The Actor Model", illustrates the power of async as we build our own actor system. We look at the differences between actors and mutuxes and why actors are a helpful design pattern to know. We build a basic key-value storage mechanism using actors so you can get a feel for the design and monitoring of actors.

Chapter 9, "Design Patterns", is a brief overview of some of the common design patterns that work well within an async system. We take an isolated modular approach and apply various design patterns to highlight their benefits and pitfalls. This chapter enables you to integrate async code with existing synchronous codebases.

Chapter 10, "Building an Async Server with No Dependencies", brings together a lot of the content from the preceding chapters. We get into building our own async system, including our own executor and waker, using the standard library only. It is always helpful to be able to build from scratch if needed, and this chapter highlights some of the benefits and downsides of using a library.

Chapter 11, "Testing", introduces testing an async system. We look at mocking, standard testing, and *Tokio* testing capabilities. We also consider what are we testing for—deadlocks and data races—so we can write clearer and useful tests.

Conventions Used in This Book

The following typographical conventions are used in this book:

Italic
:   Indicates new terms, URLs, email addresses, filenames, and file extensions.

`Constant width`
:   Used for program listings, as well as within paragraphs to refer to program elements such as variable or function names, databases, data types, environment variables, statements, and keywords.

> This element signifies a tip or suggestion.

> This element signifies a general note.

This element indicates a warning or caution.

O'Reilly Online Learning

O'REILLY®
For more than 40 years, *O'Reilly Media* has provided technology and business training, knowledge, and insight to help companies succeed.

Our unique network of experts and innovators share their knowledge and expertise through books, articles, and our online learning platform. O'Reilly's online learning platform gives you on-demand access to live training courses, in-depth learning paths, interactive coding environments, and a vast collection of text and video from O'Reilly and 200+ other publishers. For more information, visit *https://oreilly.com*.

How to Contact Us

Please address comments and questions concerning this book to the publisher:

> O'Reilly Media, Inc.
> 1005 Gravenstein Highway North
> Sebastopol, CA 95472
> 800-889-8969 (in the United States or Canada)
> 707-827-7019 (international or local)
> 707-829-0104 (fax)
> *support@oreilly.com*
> *https://oreilly.com/about/contact.html*

We have a web page for this book, where we list errata, examples, and any additional information. You can access this page at *https://oreil.ly/async-rust*.

For news and information about our books and courses, visit *https://oreilly.com*.

Find us on LinkedIn: *https://linkedin.com/company/oreilly-media*.

Watch us on YouTube: *https://youtube.com/oreillymedia*.

Acknowledgments

We have had a huge amount of support from so many people through the process of writing this book. Thank you so much to everyone who helped us to make it a reality. We would like to give an especially big thanks to the following people:

First, the people of O'Reilly—in particular, Melissa Potter, Jonathon Owen, and Brian Guerin—for your feedback and encouragement throughout the whole book cycle.

Thank you to our technical reviewers, Glen De Cauwsemaecker, Allen Wyma, and Julio Merino. Thanks for the hours you put in to make this book better for our audience.

We would both like to thank the people at SurrealDB who have supported both of us during the writing of this book. In particular, thank you to Tobie Morgan Hitchcock, Jaime Morgan Hitchcock, Kirstie Marsh, Lizzie Holmes, Charli Baptie, Ned Rudkins-Stow, Meriel Cunningham, and many others for support on this journey.

Thank you to Harry Tsiligiannis, an amazing DevOps engineer who took the time to teach both of us about how to build a robust system. We learned a lot from you, and your knowledge has immensely improved our programming skills and our approach to problems.

Maxwell

My output would not have been possible without the extensive support I get from my family. My wife, Melanie Zhang, has been an amazing supportive partner in this journey, alongside raising our son, Henry Flitton, together. My mother, Allison Barson, and Mel's mother, Ping Zhang, have also been incredible in the amount of support they have given me when writing my books. They are mentioned here because without them, I would not have been able to write this book.

The engineering team at SurrealDB has been amazing, and I have learned so much from them. Emmanuel Keller has never ceased to teach me something new and has not held back on the time spent to help me. Hugh Kaznowski has always been open in bouncing around ideas over coffee and has pushed me to think deeply about approaches. Mees Delzenne has shown me innovative ways to structure Rust code. Alexander Fridriksson and Obinna Ekwuno have shown me again and again how to structure a message and convey information to developers. Ignacio Paz has been invaluable at showing me how to collaborate with people who have different perspectives and priorities. Corrado Bogni has never hesitated to show me how to carry out a task in style. Ned Rudkins-Stow taught me how to keep refining something until it's ready to be presented. Micha de Vries has repeatedly demonstrated that you can never have too much energy when approaching work. Jaime Morgan Hitchcock has shown me that sleep is essential for a human to function properly and succeed; in short, don't follow Jaime's example. Salvador Girones Gil has taught me that if you break a huge task into small jobs, you can achieve the unthinkable in a short time, as he has led the cloud development at SurrealDB at a shocking pace. Raphael Darley has been a reminder that you can juggle multiple things at once, as he studies computer science full-time at Oxford University, while working with us at SurrealDB and running his own company. I'm also grateful to Mark Gyles and Paz Macdonald, who remind me of the human element when communicating and engaging with developers and communities. Finally, Tobie Morgan Hitchcock has been an inspiration in coming up with an idea, fleshing out the details, and delivering on that idea as he turned his Oxford University thesis into the basis of SurrealDB.

And a special thanks to Caroline Morton for always having my back on all the projects we tackle together, and Professor Christos Bergeles for supporting my studies and projects in bioengineering with Rust.

Caroline

To my mum, Margaret Morton, and her partner, Jacques Lumb, thank you for your incredible support and constant care throughout this process. Your kindness has been a source of strength for me.

This book would not have been possible without the companionship and encouragement of my wonderful friends. In no particular order, I am deeply grateful to Tabitha Grimshaw and Emma Laurence, who have cheered me on and taken me out for much-needed breaks. I would also like to thank Professor Rohini Mathur and Dr. Kate Mansfield for their company, guidance, and support and Dr. Marie Spreckley for being a trusted sounding board. A special thank you to Dr. Rob Johnson, a great longtime friend, who has always encouraged me to think clearly and articulate my thoughts. Dr. Jo Horsburgh, thank you for your unwavering support; and Kristen Petit, one of my oldest friends, your boundless enthusiasm has always lifted my spirits. I am immensely grateful to Professor Sue Smith, who took a chance and gave me my first academic job, setting me on this path. You embody what a great leader should be—kind, knowledgeable, and without ego.

This book is dedicated to my dad, Michael Frank Morton, who was taken from us too soon. I also want to remember my dear aunt, Marilyn Bickerton, who we lost too early. In her memory, I encourage everyone to support ALS research.

Finally, thank you to Maxwell for inviting me on this journey! It would not have been possible without you. Your depth of knowledge and expertise continue to surprise and amaze me. Thank you for all your hard work!

CHAPTER 1

Introduction to Async

For years, software engineers have been spoiled by the relentless increase in hardware performance. Phrases like "just chuck more computing power at it" or "write time is more expensive than read time" have become popular one-liners when justifying using a slow algorithm, rushed approach, or slow programming language. However, at the time of this writing, multiple microprocessor manufacturers have reported that the semiconductor advancement has slowed since 2010, leading to the controversial statement from NVIDIA CEO Jensen Huang in 2022 that "Moore's law is dead." With the increased demand on software and increasing number of I/O network calls in systems such as microservices, we need to be more efficient with our resources.

This is where *async programming* comes in. With async programming, we do not need to add another core to the CPU to get performance gains. Instead, with async, we can effectively juggle multiple tasks on a single thread if there is some dead time in those tasks, such as waiting for a response from a server.

We live our lives in an async way. For instance, when we put the laundry into the washing machine, we do not sit still, doing nothing, until the machine has finished. Instead, we do other things. If we want our computer and programs to live an efficient life, we need to embrace async programming.

However, before we roll up our sleeves and dive into the weeds of async programming, we need to understand where this topic sits in the context of our computers. This chapter provides an overview of how threads and processes work, demonstrating the effectiveness of async programming in I/O operations.

After reading this chapter, you should understand what async programming is at a high level, without knowing the intricate details of an async program. You will also understand some basic concepts around threads and Rust; these concepts pop up in async programming due to async runtimes using threads to execute async tasks. You should be ready to explore the details of how async programs work in the following chapter, which focuses on more concrete examples of async programming. If you are familiar with processes, threads, and sharing data between them, feel free to skip this chapter. In Chapter 2, we cover async-specific concepts like futures, tasks, and how an async runtime executes tasks.

What Is Async?

When we use a computer, we expect it to perform multiple tasks at the same time. Our experience would be pretty bad otherwise. However, think about all the tasks that a computer does at one time. As we write this book, we've clicked onto the activity monitor of our Apple M1 MacBook with eight cores. The laptop at one point was running 3,118 threads and 453 processes while only using 7% of the CPU.

Why are there so many processes and threads? The reason is that there are multiple running applications, open browser tabs, and other background processes. So how does the laptop keep all these threads and processes running at the same time? Here's the thing: the computer is not running all 3,118 threads and 453 processes at the same time. The computer needs to schedule resources.

To demonstrate the need for scheduling resources, we can run some computationally expensive code to see how the activity monitor changes. To stress our CPU, we employ a recursion calculation like this Fibonacci number calculation:

```
fn fibonacci(n: u64) -> u64 {
    if n == 0 || n == 1 {
        return n;
    }
    fibonacci(n-1) + fibonacci(n-2)
}
```

We can then spawn eight threads and calculate the 4,000th number with the following code:

```
use std::thread;


fn main() {
    let mut threads = Vec::new();


    for i in 0..8 {
        let handle = thread::spawn(move || {
            let result = fibonacci(4000);
            println!("Thread {} result: {}", i, result);
        });
        threads.push(handle);
    }
    for handle in threads {
```

```
        handle.join().unwrap();
    }
}
```

If we then run this code, our CPU usage jumps to 99.95%, but our processes and threads do not change much. From this, we can deduce that most of these processes and threads are not using CPU resources all the time.

Modern CPU design is very nuanced. What we need to know is that a portion of CPU time is allocated when a thread or process is created. Our task in the created thread or process is then scheduled to run on one of the CPU cores. The process or thread runs until it is interrupted or yielded by the CPU voluntarily. Once the interruption has occurred, the CPU saves the state of the process or thread, and then the CPU switches to another process or thread.

Now that you understand at a high level how the CPU interacts with processes and threads, let's see basic asynchronous code in action. The specifics of the asynchronous code are covered in the following chapter, so right now it's not important to understand exactly how every line of code works but instead to appreciate how asynchronous code is utilizing CPU resources. First, we need the following dependencies:

```
[dependencies]
reqwest = "0.11.14"
tokio = { version = "1.26.0", features = ["full"] }
```

The Rust library *Tokio* is giving us a high-level abstraction of an async runtime, and *reqwest* enables us to make async HTTP requests. HTTP requests are a good, simple real-world example of using async because of the latency through the network when making a request to a server. The CPU doesn't need to do anything when waiting on a network response. We can time how long it takes to make a simple HTTP request when using *Tokio* as the async runtime with this code:

```
use std::time::Instant;
use reqwest::Error;


#[tokio::main]
async fn main() -> Result<(), Error> {
    let url = "https://jsonplaceholder.typicode.com/posts/1";
    let start_time = Instant::now();

    let _ = reqwest::get(url).await?;

    let elapsed_time = start_time.elapsed();
    println!("Request took {} ms", elapsed_time.as_millis());

    Ok(())
}
```

Your time may vary, but at the time of this writing, it took roughly 140 ms to make the request. We can increase the number of requests by merely copying and pasting the request another three times, like so:

```
let first = reqwest::get(url);
let second = reqwest::get(url);
let third = reqwest::get(url);
let fourth = reqwest::get(url);

let first = first.await?;
let second = second.await?;
let third = third.await?;
let fourth = fourth.await?;
```

Running our program again gave us 656 ms. This makes sense, since we have increased the number of requests by four. If our time was less than 140×4, the result would not make sense, because the increase in total time would not be proportional to increasing the number of requests by four.

Note that although we are using async syntax, we have essentially just written synchronous code. This means we are executing each request after the previous one has finished. To make our code truly asynchronous, we can join the tasks together and have them running at the same time with the following code:

```
let (_, _, _, _) = tokio::join!(
    reqwest::get(url),
    reqwest::get(url),
    reqwest::get(url),
    reqwest::get(url),
);
```

Here we are using `tokio::join!`, a macro provided by *Tokio*. This macro enables multiple tasks to run concurrently. Unlike the previous example, where requests were awaited one after another, this approach allows them to progress simultaneously. As expected, running this code gives us a duration time of 137 ms. That's a 4.7 times increase in the speed of our program without increasing the number of threads! This is essentially async programming. Using async programming, we can free up CPU resources by not blocking the CPU with tasks that can wait. See Figure 1-1.

To help you understand the context around async programming, we need to briefly explore how processes and threads work. While we will not be using processes in asynchronous programming, it is important to understand how they work and communicate with each other in order to give us context for threads and asynchronous programming.

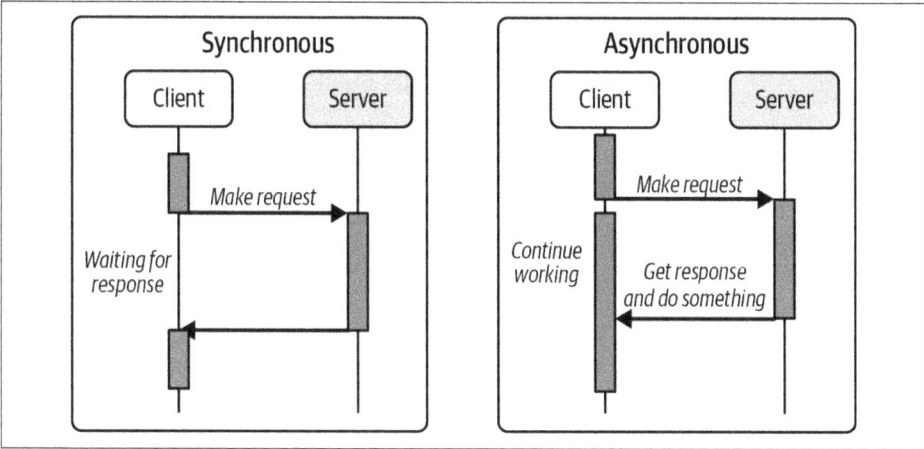

Figure 1-1. Blocking synchronous timeline compared to asynchronous timeline

Introduction to Processes

Standard async programming in Rust does not use multiprocessing; however, we can achieve async behavior by using multiprocessing. For this to work, our async systems must sit within a *process*.

Let's think about the database PostgreSQL. It spawns a process for every connection made. These processes are single-threaded. If you have ever looked at Rust web frameworks, you might have noticed that the functions defining the endpoints of the Rust web servers are async functions, which means that processes are not spawned per connection for Rust servers. Instead, the Rust web server usually has a thread pool, and incoming HTTP requests are async tasks that are run on this thread pool. We cover how async tasks interact with a thread pool in Chapter 3. For now, let's focus on where processes fit within async programming.

A *process* is an abstraction provided by an operating system that is executed by the CPU. Processes can be run by a program or application. The instructions of the program are loaded into memory, and the CPU executes these instructions in a sequence to perform a task or set of tasks. Processes are like threads for external inputs (like those from a user via a keyboard or data from other processes) and can generate output, as seen in Figure 1-2.

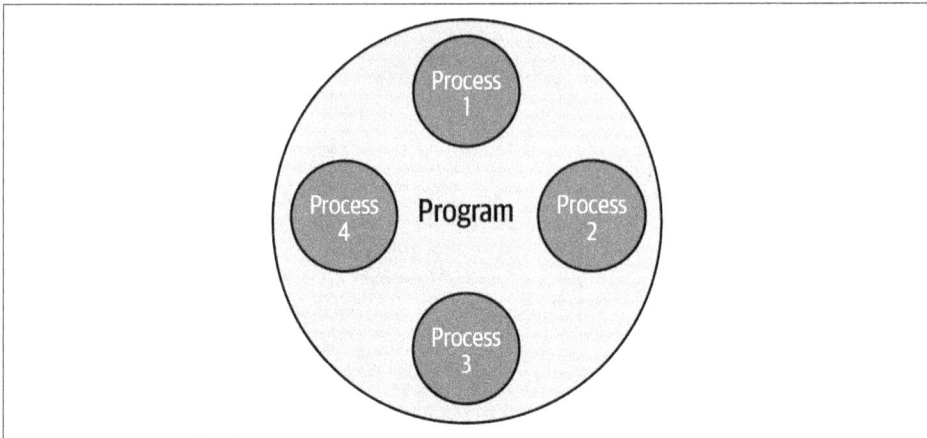

Figure 1-2. How processes relate to a program

Processes differ from threads in that each process consists of its own memory space, and this is an essential part of how the CPU is managed because it prevents data from being corrupted or bleeding over into other processes.

A process has its own ID called a *process ID* (PID), which can be monitored and controlled by the computer's operating system. Many programmers have used PIDs to kill stalled or faulty programs by using the command kill *PID* without realizing exactly what this PID represents. A PID is a unique identifier that the OS assigns to a process. It allows the OS to keep track of all the resources associated with the process, such as memory usage and CPU time.

Going back to PostgreSQL, while we must acknowledge that historical reasons do play a role in spawning a process per connection, this approach has some advantages. If a process is spawned per connection, then we have true fault isolation and memory protection per connection. This means that a connection has zero chance of accessing or corrupting the memory of another connection. Spawning a process per connection also has no shared state and is a simpler concurrency model. However, shared state can lead to complications. For instance, if two async tasks representing individual connections each rely on data from shared memory, we must introduce synchronization primitives such as locks. These synchronization primitives are at risk of adding complications such as deadlocks, which can end up grinding all connections that are relying on that lock to a halt. These problems can be hard to debug, and we cover concepts such as testing for deadlocks in Chapter 11. The simpler concurrency model of processes reduces the risk of sync complications, but the risk is not completely eliminated; acquiring external locks such as file locks can still cause complications regardless of state isolation. The state isolation of processes can also protect against memory bugs. For instance, in a language like C or C++, we could have code that does not deallocate the memory afterwards, resulting in an ever-growing consumption of memory until the computer runs out of it. (We cover memory leaks in Chapter 6.) If certain functions that connections run have memory leaks, the memory can run out for the entire program. However, we can run processes with memory limits, isolating the worst offenders.

To illustrate how processes fit in relation to async programming in Rust, we can recreate the async nature of our four HTTP requests with the following layout:

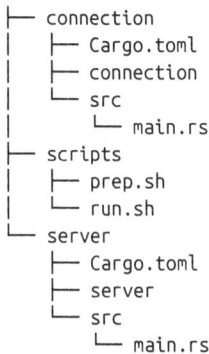

```
├── connection
│   ├── Cargo.toml
│   ├── connection
│   └── src
│       └── main.rs
├── scripts
│   ├── prep.sh
│   └── run.sh
└── server
    ├── Cargo.toml
    ├── server
    └── src
        └── main.rs
```

Here, we call our server package *server_bin* and the connection package *connection_bin*. Our connection binary has the same *Tokio* and *reqwest* dependencies as in the previous section. In our connection *main.rs* file, we merely make a request and print out the result with the following code:

```
use reqwest::Error;

#[tokio::main]
async fn main() -> Result<(), Error> {
    let url = "https://jsonplaceholder.typicode.com/posts/1";
    let response = reqwest::get(url).await?;

    if response.status().is_success() {
        let body = response.text().await?;
        println!("{}", body);
    } else {
        println!(
            "Failed to get a valid response. Status: {}",
            response.status()
        );
    }
    Ok(())
}
```

For the server, we create a process that makes the HTTP request every time we run the binary with the following *server/main.rs* file:

```
use std::process::{Command, Output};

fn main() {
```

```rust
    let output: Output = Command::new("./connection_bin")
        .output()
        .expect("Failed to execute command");
    if output.status.success() {
        let stdout = String::from_utf8_lossy(&output.stdout);
        println!("Output: {}", stdout);
    } else {
        let stderr = String::from_utf8_lossy(&output.stderr);
        eprintln!("Error: {}", stderr);
    }
}
```

Here, we can see that our command is running the binary of the connection. We can also see that we can handle the output of a process. If the process exits with a 0, then the process exited without any errors. If the process exits with 1, then the process did error. Whatever the outcome, we serialize the output and print it. We now have to build out our *scripts/prep.sh* file, which has the following code:

```bash
#!/usr/bin/env bash

SCRIPTPATH="$( cd "$(dirname "$0")" ; pwd -P )"
cd $SCRIPTPATH
cd ..
cd connection && cargo build --release && cd ..
cd server && cargo build --release && cd ..
cp connection/target/release/connection_bin ./
cp server/target/release/server_bin ./
```

Here, we are compiling the binaries and moving them into the root directory. We now need to code our *scripts/run.sh* to run four connections at the same time. First, we navigate to the root directory as follows:

```bash
#!/usr/bin/env bash

SCRIPTPATH="$( cd "$(dirname "$0")" ; pwd -P )"
cd $SCRIPTPATH
cd ..
```

We then run all four processes in the background, getting the PIDs of each one:

```bash
./server_bin &
pid1=$!
./server_bin &
pid2=$!
./server_bin &
pid3=$!
./server_bin &
pid4=$!
```

We then wait for the results and print out the exit codes:

```bash
wait $pid1
exit_code1=$?
```

```
wait $pid2
exit_code2=$?
wait $pid3
exit_code3=$?
wait $pid4
exit_code4=$?
echo "Task 1 (PID $pid1) exited with code $exit_code1"
echo "Task 2 (PID $pid2) exited with code $exit_code2"
echo "Task 3 (PID $pid3) exited with code $exit_code3"
echo "Task 4 (PID $pid4) exited with code $exit_code4"
```

After running the prep script and timing the run script using the `time sh scripts/run.sh` command, we found that our time was 123 ms, which is just slightly quicker than our async example. This shows that we can achieve async behavior by waiting on processes. However, this is not a demonstration that processes are better. We will be using more resources because processes are more resource heavy. Our standard async program is one process with multiple threads. This could lead to some contention on scheduling async tasks by the CPU due to shared memory. However, processes are simple to schedule by the CPU because they are isolated.

Before we run off spawning processes for everything, we need to consider some drawbacks. There can be limits to the number of threads we can spawn in an OS, and spawning processes is more expensive and will not scale as well. Once we start using all our cores, the extra spawned processes will start to get blocked. We also must appreciate the number of moving parts; interprocess communication can be expensive because of the need for serialization. What is interesting is that we also had async code in our process, and this is a nice demonstration of where processes sit. In PostgreSQL, a connection is a process, but that process contains async code that runs the command and accesses data storage.

To reduce the number of moving parts, we could use *Tokio*'s async tasks to point to processes that we spin up:

```
let mut handles = vec![];
for _ in 0..4 {
    let handle = tokio::spawn(async {
        let output = Command::new("./connection_bin")
            .output()
            .await;
        match output {
            Ok(output) => {
                println!(
                    "Process completed with output: {}",
                    String::from_utf8_lossy(&output.stdout)
                );
                Ok(output.status.code().unwrap_or(-1))
            }
            Err(e) => {
                eprintln!("Failed to run process: {}", e);
```

```
                Err(e)
            }
        }
    });
    handles.push(handle);
}
```

We then handle the process outcomes:

```
let mut results = Vec::with_capacity(handles.len());
for handle in handles {
    results.push(handle.await.unwrap());
}
for (i, result) in results.into_iter().enumerate() {
    match result {
        Ok(exit_code) => println!(
            "Process {} exited with code {}",
            i + 1, exit_code
        ),
        Err(e) => eprintln!(
            "Process {} failed: {}",
            i + 1, e
        ),
    }
}
```

While this reduces the number of moving parts, we still have the scaling issues of processes combined with the overhead of having to serialize data between the process and our main program. Because Rust is memory safe and we can handle errors as values, the isolation benefits behind processes are not as strong. For instance, unless we are actively producing unsafe Rust code, we are not going to get a memory leak in one of our threads.

Remember what we want to do with asynchronous programming: We want to spin off lightweight, nonblocking tasks and wait for them to finish. In a lot of cases, we will want to get the data from those tasks and use them. We also want the option of sending the task to the async runtime with data. Threads seem like a much better choice over processes for asynchronous programming due to the ease of sharing data between threads. We will cover threads next.

What Are Threads?

A *thread* of execution is the smallest sequence of programmed instructions that can be executed by the CPU. A thread can be independently managed by a scheduler. Inside a process, we can share memory across multiple threads (Figure 1-3).

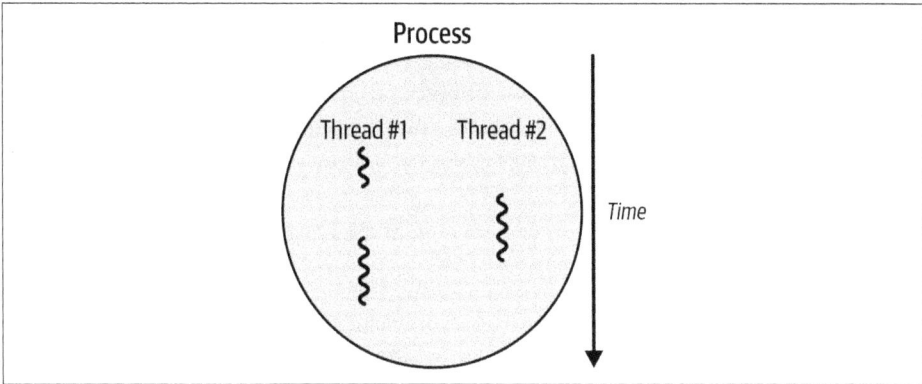

Figure 1-3. How threads relate to a process

While both threads and async tasks are managed by a scheduler, they are different. Threads can run at the same time on different CPU cores, while async tasks usually wait their turn to use the CPU. We will cover async tasks in much more detail in Chapter 2.

To spin up threads, we can revisit our Fibonacci number recursive function and spread the calculations of Fibonacci numbers over four threads. First, we need to import the following:

```
use std::time::Instant;
use std::thread;
```

We can then time how long it takes to calculate the 50th Fibonacci number in the main function:

```
let start = Instant::now();
let _ = fibonacci(50);
let duration = start.elapsed();
println!("fibonacci(50) in {:?}", duration);
```

Next, we can reset the timer and calculate the time taken to calculate four 50th Fibonacci numbers over four threads. We achieve the multithreading by iterating four times to spawn four threads and attach each JoinHandle into a vector:

```
let start = Instant::now();
let mut handles = vec![];
for _ in 0..4 {
    let handle = thread::spawn(|| {
        fibonacci(50)
    });
    handles.push(handle);
}
```

A JoinHandle allows you to wait for a thread to finish, pausing the program until that thread completes. Joining the thread means blocking the program until the thread is terminated. A `JoinHandle` implements the `Send` and `Sync` traits, which means that it can be sent between threads. However, a `JoinHandle` does not implement the `Clone` trait. This is because we need a unique `JoinHandle` for each thread. If there are multiple +JoinHandle+s for one thread, you can run the risk of multiple threads trying to join the running thread, leading to data races.

> If you have used other programming languages, you may have come across *green threads*. These threads are scheduled by something other than the operating system (for example, a runtime or a virtual machine). Rust originally implemented green threads before pulling them prior to version 1. The main reason for removing them and moving to a native thread, with green threads in libraries, is that in Rust, threads and I/O operations are coupled, which forced native threads and green threads to have and maintain the same API. This resulted in various problems in using I/O operations and designating allocation. See the Rust documentation on green threads (*https://oreil.ly/ghxQr*) for more information. Note that while Rust itself does not implement green threads, runtimes like *Tokio* do.

Now that we have our vector of `JoinHandle`, we can wait for them to execute and then print the time taken:

```
for handle in handles {
    let _ = handle.join();
}
let duration = start.elapsed();
println!("4 threads fibonacci(50) took {:?}", duration);
```

Running our program gives the following output:

```
fibonacci(50) in 39.665599542s
4 threads fibonacci(50) took 42.601305333s
```

We can see that when using threads in Rust, multiple CPU-intensive tasks can be handled at the same time. Therefore, we can deduce that multiple threads can also handle waiting concurrently. Even though we do not use the results of the Fibonacci calculations, we could use the results of the threads in our main program if we wanted to. When we are calling a join on a `JoinHandle` in this example, we are returning a `Result<u64, Box<dyn Any + Send>>`. The `u64` is the result of the calculated Fibonacci number from the thread. The `Box<dyn Any + Send>` is a dynamic trait object that provides flexibility in handling various types of errors. These error types need to be sent over, but there could be a whole host of reasons why a thread errors. However, this approach has some overhead too because we need dynamic downcasting and boxing, as we do not know the size at compile time.

Threads can also directly interact with each other over memory within the program. The last example of this chapter uses channels, but for now we can make do with an Arc, Mutex, and a Condvar to create the system depicted in Figure 1-4.

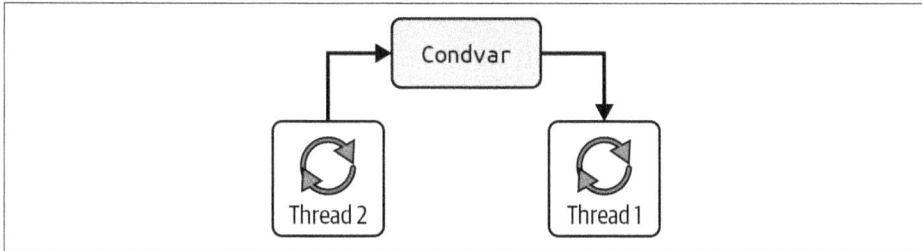

Figure 1-4. A Condvar alerting another thread of a change

Here, we'll have two threads. One thread is going to update the Condvar, and the other thread is going to listen to the Condvar for updates and print out that there was an update to the file the moment the update occurred. Before we write any code, however, we need to establish the following structs:

Arc

This stands for *atomic reference counting*, meaning that Arc keeps count of the references to the variable that is wrapped in an Arc. So, if we were to define an Arc<i32> and then reference it over four threads, the reference count would increase to four. The Arc<i32> would only be dropped when all four threads had finished referencing it, resulting in the reference count being zero.

Mutex

Remember that Rust only allows us to have one mutable reference to a variable at any given time. A Mutex (*mutual exclusion*) is a smart pointer type that provides *interior mutability* by having the value inside the Mutex. This means that we can provide mutable access to a single variable over multiple threads. This is achieved by a thread acquiring the lock. When we acquire the lock, we get the single mutable reference to the value inside the Mutex. We perform a transaction and then give up the lock to allow other threads to perform a transaction. The lock ensures that only one thread will have access to the mutable reference at a time, ensuring that Rust's rule of only one mutable reference at a time is not violated. Acquiring the lock requires some overhead, as we might have to wait until it is released.

Condvar

Short for *conditional variable*, this allows our threads to sleep and be woken when a notification is sent through the Condvar. We cannot send variables through the Condvar, but multiple threads can subscribe to a single Condvar.

Now that we have covered what we are using, we can build our system by initially importing the following:

```
use std::sync::{Arc, Condvar, Mutex};
use std::thread;
use std::time::Duration;
use std::sync::atomic::AtomicBool;
use std::sync::atomic::Ordering::Relaxed;
```

Inside our main function, we can then define the data that we are going to share across our two threads:

```
let shared_data = Arc::new((Mutex::new(false), Condvar::new()));
let shared_data_clone = Arc::clone(&shared_data);
let STOP = Arc::new(AtomicBool::new(false));
let STOP_CLONE = Arc::clone(&STOP);
```

Here we have a tuple that is wrapped in Arc. Our boolean variable that is going to be updated is wrapped in a Mutex. We then clone our data package so both threads have access to the shared data. The shared_data_clone thread is passed to back ground_thread, while the original shared_data remains with the main thread, which later uses it in updater_thread. Without cloning, the ownership of shared_data would be moved to the first thread it's passed to, and the main thread would lose access to it.

Now that our data is available, we can define our first thread:

```
let background_thread = thread::spawn(move || {
    let (lock, cvar) = &*shared_data_clone;
    let mut received_value = lock.lock().unwrap();
    while !STOP.load(Relaxed) {
        received_value = cvar.wait(received_value).unwrap();
        println!("Received value: {}", *received_value);
    }
});
```

Here we can see that we wait on the Condvar notification. At the point of waiting, the thread is said to be *parked*. This means that the thread is blocked and not executing. Once the notification comes in from the Condvar, the thread accesses the variable in the Mutex after being woken by the Condvar. We then print out the variable, and the thread goes back to sleep. We are relying on the AtomicBool being false for the loop to continue indefinitely. This enables us to stop the thread if needed.

> We are using unwrap a lot in the code. This keeps the code concise so we can focus on the main concepts around async, but remember that production code should have error handling. The only time using unwrap() might be acceptable is when locking a mutex because the only reason it would panic is if a thread previously panicked while holding the lock, which is called lock poisoning.

In the next thread, we only execute four iterations before completing the thread:

```
let updater_thread = thread::spawn(move || {
    let (lock, cvar) = &*shared_data;
    let values = [false, true, false, true];

    for i in 0..4 {
        let update_value = values[i as usize];
        println!("Updating value to {}...", update_value);
        *lock.lock().unwrap() = update_value;
        cvar.notify_one();
        thread::sleep(Duration::from_secs(4));
    }
    STOP_CLONE.store(true, Relaxed);
    println!("STOP has been updated");
    cvar.notify_one();
});
updater_thread.join().unwrap();
```

We update the value and then notify the other thread that the value has changed. We then block the main program until `updater_thread` has finished.

Notice that we have used the `Relaxed` term. It is critical to ensure that operations occur in a specific order to avoid data races and strange inconsistencies. This is where memory ordering comes into play. The `Relaxed` ordering, used with `AtomicBool` (*https://oreil.ly/yQIeb*), ensures that the operations on the atomic variable are visible to all threads but does not enforce any particular order on the surrounding operations. This is sufficient for our example because we only need to check the value of STOP and don't care about strict ordering of other operations.

Running the program gives us the following output:

```
Updating value to false...
Received value: false
Updating value to true...
Received value: true
Updating value to false...
Received value: false
Updating value to true...
Received value: true
```

Our updater thread is updating the value of the shared data and notifying our first thread which accesses it.

The values are consistent, which is what we want, although admittedly it's a crude implementation of what we could describe as async behavior. The thread is stopping and waiting for updates. Adding multiple `Condvars` for `updater_thread` to cycle through and check would result in one thread keeping track of multiple tasks and acting on them when changed. While this will certainly spark a debate online on whether this is truly async behavior or not, we can certainly say that this is not an optimum or standard way of implementing async programming. However, we can see that threads are a key building block for async programming. Async runtimes handle tasks in a way that allows multiple asynchronous operations to run concurrently within a single thread. This thread is usually separate from the main thread. Runtimes can also have multiple threads executing tasks. In the next section, we will use standard implementations of async code.

Where Can We Utilize Async?

We have introduced you to asynchronous programming and demonstrated some of its benefits in the examples (such as multiple HTTP requests). These have been toy examples designed to show you the power of async. This section presents real-life uses of async and why you might want to include them in your next project.

Let's first think about what we can use async for. Unsurprisingly, the main use cases involve operations that have a delay or potential delay in doing something or receiving something—for example, I/O calls to the filesystem or network requests. Async allows the program that calls these operations to continue without blocking, which could cause the program to hang and become less responsive.

I/O operations like writing files are considered slow compared to in-memory operations because they usually rely on external devices such as hard drives. Most hard drives still rely on mechanical parts that need to physically move, so they are slower than electronic operations in RAM or the CPU. In addition, the speed at which data can be transferred from the CPU to the device may be limited—for example, by a USB connection.

To put this into perspective, let's compare the time scales involved:

Nanoseconds (ns)
  This is a billionth of a second (1/1,000,000,000 of a second). Operations within the CPU and memory typically happen in nanoseconds. For example, accessing data in RAM might take around 100 ns.

Milliseconds (ms)
  This is a thousandth of a second (1/1,000 of a second). I/O operations, like writing to a hard drive or sending data over a network, usually occur in milliseconds. For example, writing data to a traditional hard drive might take several milliseconds.

These differences might seem trivial, but in the world of computing, they are huge. A CPU can perform millions of operations in the time it takes for a single file to be opened. This is why I/O operations are often the bottleneck in a program's performance.

At the time of this writing, async file reads are not actually sped up by async. This is because file I/O operations are still bound by disk performance, so the bottleneck is in the disk write and read speed rather than CPU. What async can do, however, is make sure that while your file I/O is occurring, your program can continue and is not blocked by these operations.

We will now work through an example using async for a file I/O program. Imagine that we need to keep track of changes to a file and perform an action when a change in the file has been detected.

Using Async for File I/O

To track file changes, we need to have a loop in a thread that checks the metadata of the file and then feeds back to the main loop in the main thread when the file metadata changes, as depicted in Figure 1-5.

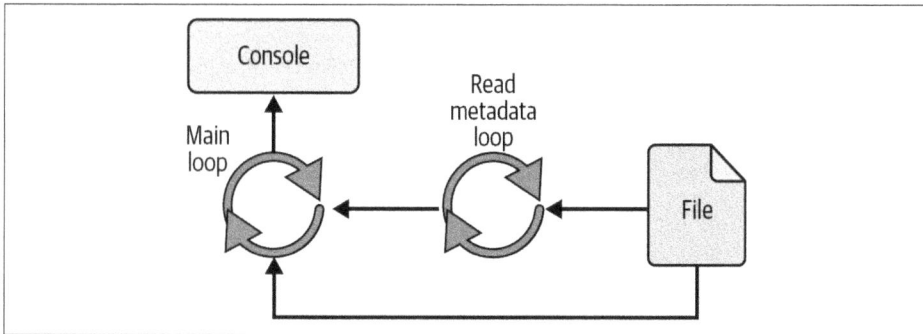

Figure 1-5. A system keeping track of changes in a file

We can do all manner of things after the change is detected, but for the purpose of this exercise, we will print the contents to the console. Before we start tackling the components in Figure 1-5, we need to import the following structs and traits:

```
use std::path::PathBuf;
use tokio::fs::File as AsyncFile;
use tokio::io::AsyncReadExt;
use tokio::sync::watch;
use tokio::time::{sleep, Duration};
```

We will cover how these structs and traits are used as we go along. Referring back to Figure 1-5, it makes sense to tackle the file operations first and the main loop later. Our simplest operation is reading the file with a function:

```
async fn read_file(filename: &str) -> Result<String, std::io::Error> {
    let mut file = AsyncFile::open(filename).await?;
    let mut contents = String::new();
    file.read_to_string(&mut contents).await?;
```

```
        Ok(contents)
    }
```

We open the file and read the contents to a string, returning that string. However, note that at the time of this writing, the standard implementation of async file reading is not async. Instead, it is blocking, so the file open operation is not truly async. The inconsistency of async file reading comes down to the file API that the OS supports. For instance, if you have Linux with a kernel version of 5.10 or higher, you can use the *Tokio-uring* crate that will enable true asynchronous I/O calls to the file API. However, for now, our function does the job we need.

We can now move on to our loop that periodically checks the metadata of our file:

```
async fn watch_file_changes(tx: watch::Sender<bool>) {
    let path = PathBuf::from("data.txt"); ❶

    let mut last_modified = None; ❷
    loop { ❸
        if let Ok(metadata) = path.metadata() {
            let modified = metadata.modified().unwrap(); ❹

            if last_modified != Some(modified) { ❺
                last_modified = Some(modified);
                let _ = tx.send(());
            }
        }
        sleep(Duration::from_millis(100)).await; ❻
    }
}
```

We can see that our function is an async function that carries out the following steps:

❶ We get the path to the file that we are checking.

❷ We set the last modified time to none, as we have not checked the file yet.

❸ We then have an infinite loop.

❹ In that loop, we extract the time that the file was last modified.

❺ If the extracted timestamp is not the same as our cached timestamp, we then update our cached timestamp and send a message through a channel using the sender that we passed into our function. This message then alerts our main loop that the file has been updated.

   We ignore the result of `tx.send(())` because the only error that could occur is if the receiver is no longer listening. In this case, there's nothing more our function needs to do, so it's safe to ignore the result.

❻ For each iteration, we sleep a short time just so that we are not constantly hitting the file that we are checking on.

> If we use a *Tokio* thread to run this function, the *Tokio* runtime will be able to switch context and execute another thread in the same process. If we use the standard library's sleep function, the thread will block. This is because the standard library's sleep will not send the task to the *Tokio* executor. We will go over executors in Chapter 3.

Now that our first loop is defined, we can move on to the loop that is run in main. At this point, if you know how to spin up *Tokio* threads and channels, you could try to write the main function yourself.

If you did attempt to write your own main function, hopefully it looks similar to the following:

```
#[tokio::main]
async fn main() {
    let (tx, mut rx) = watch::channel(false); ❶

    tokio::spawn(watch_file_changes(tx)); ❷

    loop { ❸
        // Wait for a change in the file
        let _ = rx.changed().await; ❹

        // Read the file and print its contents to the console
        if let Ok(contents) = read_file("data.txt").await { ❺
            println!("{}", contents);
        }
    }
}
```

Our main function carries out the following steps:

❶ We create a channel that is a single producer, multi-consumer channel that only retains the last set value. This channel allows one producer to send messages to multiple consumers, enabling concurrent data distribution.

❷ We pass the transmitter of that channel into our file-watching function, which is being run in a *Tokio* thread that we spin off.

❸ Now that our file-watching loop is running, we move onto our loop that holds until the value of the channel is changed.

❹ Because we do not care about the value coming from the channel, we denote the variable assignment as an underscore. Our main loop will stay there until a change occurs in the value inside the channel.

❺ Once the value inside the channel changes due to the metadata of the file changing, the rest of the loop interaction executes, reading the file and printing out the contents.

Before we run this, we need a *data.txt* file in the root of our project, next to our *Cargo.toml*. We can then run the system, open the *data.txt* file in an IDE, and type something into the file. Once you save the file, you will get its contents printed out in the console!

Now that we have used async programming locally, we can go back to implementing async programming with networks.

Improving HTTP Request Performance with Async

I/O operations concern not just reading and writing files but also getting information from an API, executing operations on a database, or receiving information from a mouse or keyboard. What ties them together is that these operations are slower than the in-memory operations that can be performed in RAM. Async allows the program to continue without being blocked by the ongoing operation. Other tasks can be executed while we await the async operation.

In the following example, let's imagine a user has logged into a website, and we want to display some data along with the time since that user's login. To fetch the data, we'll be using an external API that provides a specific delay. We need to process this data once it's received, so we'll define a `Response` struct and annotate it with the `Deserialize` trait to enable deserialization of the API data into a usable object.

To make the API calls, we'll use the *reqwest* package. Since we'll be working with JSON data, we'll enable the JSON feature of *reqwest* by specifying `features=["json"]` in the dependency configuration. This allows us to conveniently handle JSON data when making API requests and processing the responses.

We need to add these dependencies to our *Cargo.toml*:

```
[dependencies]
tokio = { version = "1", features = ["full"] }
reqwest = { version = "0.11", features = ["json"] }
serde = { version = "1.0", features = ["derive"] }
serde_json = "1.0"
```

Next we import the libraries we need and define the `Response` struct:

```
use reqwest::Error;
use serde::Deserialize;
```

```
use tokio::time::sleep;
use std::time::Duration;
use std::time::Instant;
use serde_json;

#[derive(Deserialize, Debug)]
struct Response {
    url: String,
    args: serde_json::Value,
}
```

We now implement the `fetch_data` function. When called, it sends a GET request to *https://httpbin.org/delay/*, which will return a response after a specified number of seconds. In our example, we set the delay to 5 seconds to emphasize the importance of designing a program capable of handling delays effectively in real-world scenarios:

```
async fn fetch_data(seconds: u64) -> Result<Response, Error> {
    let request_url = format!("https://httpbin.org/delay/{}", seconds);
    let response = reqwest::get(&request_url).await?;
    let delayed_response: Response = response.json().await?;
    Ok(delayed_response)
}
```

While the data is being fetched, we create a function that calculates the time since the user logged in. This would usually require a database check, but we will simulate the time it takes to check this by setting a sleep for 1 second. This simplifies the example so we do not need to get into database setups:

```
async fn calculate_last_login() {
    sleep(Duration::from_secs(1)).await;
    println!("Logged in 2 days ago");
}
```

Now we put the code together:

```
#[tokio::main]
async fn main() -> Result<(), Error> {
    let start_time = Instant::now();
    let data = fetch_data(5);
    let time_since = calculate_last_login();
    let (posts, _) = tokio::join!(
        data, time_since
    );
    let duration = start_time.elapsed();
    println!("Fetched {:?}", posts);
    println!("Time taken. [.?]", duration),
    Ok(())
}
```

Let's examine the output:

```
Fetched Ok(Response { url: "https://httpbin.org/delay/5", args: Object {} })
Time taken: 5.494735083s
```

In the main function, we initiate the API call by using the fetch_data function before calling the calculate_last_login function. The API request is designed to take 5 seconds to return a response. Since fetch_data is an asynchronous function, it is executed in a nonblocking manner, allowing the program to continue its execution. As a result, a calculate_last_login is executed, and its output is printed to the terminal first. After the 5-second delay, fetch_data completes, and its result is returned and printed.

Unlike our initial HTTP request example, this demonstrates how asynchronous programming allows concurrent execution of tasks without blocking the program's flow, resulting in network requests completing out of order. Therefore, we can use async for multiple network requests, as long as we await each request in the order that we need the data.

Summary

In this chapter we introduced async programming and how it relates to the computer system in terms of threads and processes. We then covered basic high-level interactions with threads and processes to demonstrate that threads can be useful in async programming. We then explored basic high-level async programming, improving the performance of multiple HTTP calls by sending more requests while waiting for other requests to respond. We also used async principles to keep track of file changes.

We hope that this chapter has demonstrated that async is a powerful tool for juggling multiple tasks simultaneously that do not need constant CPU time. Therefore, async enables us to have one thread handling multiple tasks at the same time. Now that you understand where async programming sits in the context of a computer system, we will explore basic async programming concepts in Chapter 2.

CHAPTER 2

Basic Async Rust

This chapter introduces the important components of using async in Rust and gives an overview of tasks, futures, async, and await. We cover context, pins, polling, and closures—important concepts for fully taking advantage of async programming in Rust. We have chosen the examples in this chapter to demonstrate the learning points; they may not necessarily be optimal for efficiency. The chapter concludes with an example of building an async audit logger for a sensitive program, pulling all the concepts together.

By the end of this chapter, you will be able to define a task and a future. You'll also understand the more technical components of a future, including context and pins.

Understanding Tasks

In asynchronous programming, a *task* represents an asynchronous operation. The task-based asynchronous pattern (TAP) provides an abstraction over asynchronous code. You write code as a sequence of statements. You can read that code as though each statement completes before the next begins. For instance, let's think about making a cup of coffee and toast, which requires the following steps:

1. Put bread in toaster
2. Butter toasted bread
3. Boil water in kettle
4. Pour milk
5. Put in instant coffee granules (not the best, but simplifies the example)
6. Pour boiled water

We can definitely apply async programming to speed this up, but first we need to break down all the steps into two big steps, *make coffee* and *make toast*, as follows:

1. Make coffee
   a. Boil water in kettle
   b. Pour milk
   c. Put in instant coffee
   d. Pour boiled water
2. Make toast
   a. Put bread in toaster
   b. Butter toasted bread

Even though each of us has only one pair of hands, we can run these two steps at the same time. We can boil the water, and while the water is boiling, we can put the bread in the toaster. We have a bit of dead time while we wait for the kettle and toaster, so if we wanted to be more efficient and we were comfortable with the risk that we could end up pouring the boiled water before adding the coffee and milk due to an instant boil, we could break the steps down even more as follows:

1. Prep coffee mug
   a. Pour milk
   b. Put in instant coffee
2. Make coffee
   a. Boil water in kettle
   b. Pour boiled water
3. Make toast
   a. Put bread in toaster
   b. Butter toasted bread

While waiting for the boiling of the water and toasting of the bread, we can execute the pouring of the milk and adding the coffee, reducing the dead time. First of all, we can see that steps are not goal specific. When we walk into the kitchen, we will think *make toast* and *make coffee*, which are two separate goals. But we have defined three steps for those two goals. Steps are about what you can run at the same time out of sync to achieve all your goals.

Note that a trade-off arises when it comes to assumptions and what we are willing to tolerate. For instance, it may be completely unacceptable to pour boiling water before adding milk and coffee. This is a risk if there is no delay in the boiling of the kettle. However, we can make the safe assumption that there will be a delay.

Now that you understand what steps are, we can turn back to our example by using a high-level crate like *Tokio* that enables us to focus on the concepts of steps and how they relate to tasks. Don't worry—we will use other crates in later chapters when we delve into lower-level concepts. First, we need to import the following:

```
use std::time::Duration;
use tokio::time::sleep;
use std::thread;
use std::time::Instant;
```

We use the *Tokio* sleep for steps that we can wait on, such as the boiling of the kettle and the toasting of the bread. Because the *Tokio* sleep function is nonblocking, we can switch to another step when the water is boiling or the bread is toasting. We use thread::sleep to simulate a step that we use both our hands for, as we can't do anything else while pouring milk/water or buttering toast. In general, programming these steps will be CPU intensive. We can then define our prepping of the mug step with the following code:

```
async fn prep_coffee_mug() {
    println!("Pouring milk...");
    thread::sleep(Duration::from_secs(3));
    println!("Milk poured.");
    println!("Putting instant coffee...");
    thread::sleep(Duration::from_secs(3));
    println!("Instant coffee put.");
}
```

We then define the "make coffee" step:

```
async fn make_coffee() {
    println!("boiling kettle...");
    sleep(Duration::from_secs(10)).await;
    println!("kettle boiled.");
    println!("pouring boiled water...");
    thread::sleep(Duration::from_secs(3));
    println!("boiled water poured.");
}
```

And we define our last step:

```
async fn make_toast() {
    println!("putting bread in toaster...");
    sleep(Duration::from_secs(10)).await;
    println!("bread toasted.");
    println!("buttering toasted bread...");
    thread::sleep(Duration::from_secs(5));
    println!("toasted bread buttered.");
}
```

You may have noticed that `await` is used on the *Tokio* `sleep` functions that represent the steps that are not intensive and that we can wait on. We use the `await` keyword to suspend the execution of our step until the result is ready. When the `await` is hit, the async runtime can switch to another async task.

> You can read more about `async` and `await` syntaxes on the Rust RFC book website (*https://oreil.ly/BHVPe*).

Now that we have all our steps defined, we can run them in asynchronously with this code:

```
#[tokio::main]
async fn main() {
    let start_time = Instant::now();
    let coffee_mug_step = prep_coffee_mug();
    let coffee_step = make_coffee();
    let toast_step = make_toast();

    tokio::join!(coffee_mug_step, coffee_step, toast_step);
    let elapsed_time = start_time.elapsed();
    println!("It took: {} seconds", elapsed_time.as_secs());
}
```

Here, we define our steps, which are called *futures*. We will cover futures in the next section. For now, think of futures as placeholders for something that may or may not have completed yet. We then wait for our steps to complete and then print out the time taken. If we run our program, we get the following:

```
Pouring milk...
Milk poured.
Putting instant coffee...
Instant coffee put.
boiling kettle...
putting bread in toaster...
kettle boiled.
pouring boiled water...
boiled water poured.
bread toasted.
buttering toasted bread...
toasted bread buttered.
It took: 24 seconds
```

This printout is a bit lengthy, but it is important. We can see that it looks strange. If we are being efficient, we would not start pouring milk and adding coffee. Instead, we would get the kettle boiling and put the bread in the toaster, and then go to pour milk. We can see that preparing the mug was first passed into the `tokio::join` macro. If we run our program again and again, the preparation of the mug will always be the first future to be executed. Now, if we go back to the mug preparation function, we simply add a nonblocking sleep function before the rest of the processes:

```
async fn prep_coffee_mug() {
    sleep(Duration::from_millis(100)).await;
    . . .
}
```

This gives us the following printout:

```
boiling kettle...
putting bread in toaster...
Pouring milk...
Milk poured.
Putting instant coffee...
Instant coffee put.
bread toasted.
buttering toasted bread...
toasted bread buttered.
kettle boiled.
pouring boiled water...
boiled water poured.
It took: 18 seconds
```

OK, now the order makes sense: we are boiling the water, putting bread in the toaster, and then pouring milk, and as a result, we saved 6 seconds. However, the cause and effect is counterintuitive. Putting in an extra sleep function has reduced our overall time. This is because that extra sleep function allowed the async runtime to switch context to other tasks and execute them until their await line was executed, and so on. This insertion of an artificial delay in the future to get the call rolling on other futures is informally referred to as *cooperative multitasking*.

When we pass our futures into the tokio::join macro, all the async expressions are evaluated concurrently in the same task. The join macro does not create tasks; it merely enables multiple futures to be executed concurrently within the task. For instance, we can spawn a task with the following code:

```
let person_one = tokio::task::spawn(async {
    prep_coffee_mug().await;
    make_coffee().await;
    make_toast().await;
});
```

Each future in the task will block further execution of that task until the future is finished. So, say we use the following annotation to ensure that the runtime has one worker:

```
#[tokio::main(flavor = "multi_thread", worker_threads = 1)]
```

We create two tasks, each representing a person, which will result in a 36-second runtime:

```
let person_one = tokio::task::spawn(async {
    let coffee_mug_step = prep_coffee_mug();
    let coffee_step = make_coffee();
    let toast_step = make_toast();
    tokio::join!(coffee_mug_step, coffee_step, toast_step);
}).await;

let person_two = tokio::task::spawn(async {
    let coffee_mug_step = prep_coffee_mug();
    let coffee_step = make_coffee();
    let toast_step = make_toast();
    tokio::join!(coffee_mug_step, coffee_step, toast_step);
}).await;
```

We can redefine the task with a join as opposed to blocking futures:

```
let person_one = tokio::task::spawn(async {
    let coffee_mug_step = prep_coffee_mug();
    let coffee_step = make_coffee();
    let toast_step = make_toast();
    tokio::join!(coffee_mug_step, coffee_step, toast_step);
});

let person_two = tokio::task::spawn(async {
    let coffee_mug_step = prep_coffee_mug();
    let coffee_step = make_coffee();
    let toast_step = make_toast();
    tokio::join!(coffee_mug_step, coffee_step, toast_step);
});

let _ = tokio::join!(person_one, person_two);
```

Joining on two tasks representing people will result in a 28-second runtime. Join three tasks representing people would result in a 42-second runtime. Seeing as the total blocking time for each task is 14 seconds, the time increase makes sense. We can deduce from the linear increase in time that although three tasks are sent to the async runtime and put on the queue, the executor is setting the task to idle when coming across an await and working on the next task in the queue while polling the idle tasks.

Async runtimes can have multiple workers and queues, and we will explore writing our own runtime in Chapter 3. Considering what we have covered in this section, we can give the following definition of a task:

> A task is an asynchronous computation or operation that is managed and driven by an executor to completion. It represents the execution of a future, and it may involve multiple futures being composed or chained together.

Now let's discuss what a future is.

Futures

One of the key features of async programming is the concept of a *future*. We've mentioned that a future is a placeholder object that represents the result of an asynchronous operation that has not yet completed. Futures allow you to start a task and continue with other operations while the task is being executed in the background.

To truly understand how a future works, we'll cover its lifecycle. When a future is created, it is idle. It has yet to be executed. Once the future is executed, it can either yield a value, resolve, or go to sleep because the future is pending (awaiting on a result). When the future is polled again, the poll can return either a `Pending` or `Ready` result. The future will continue to be polled until it is either resolved or cancelled.

To illustrate how futures work, let's build a basic counter future. It will count up to 5 and then will be ready. First, we need to import the following:

```
use std::future::Future;
use std::pin::Pin;
use std::task::{Context, Poll};
use std::time::Duration;

use tokio::task::JoinHandle;
```

You should be able to understand most of this code. We will cover `Context` and `Pin` after building our basic future. Because our future is a counter, the struct takes the following form:

```
struct CounterFuture {
    count: u32,
}
```

We then implement the future trait:

```
impl Future for CounterFuture {
    type Output = u32;

    fn poll(
            mut self: Pin<&mut Self>,
            cx: &mut Context<'_>
    ) -> Poll<Self::Output> {
        self.count += 1;
        println!("polling with result: {}", self.count);
        std::thread::sleep(Duration::from_secs(1));
        if self.count < 5 {
            cx.waker().wake_by_ref();
            Poll::Pending
        } else {
            Poll::Ready(self.count)
        }
    }
}
```

Let's not focus on Pin or Context just yet, but on the poll function as a whole. Every time the future is polled, the count is increased by one. If the count is at three, we then state that the future is ready. We introduce the std::thread::sleep function to merely exaggerate the time taken so it is easier to follow this example when running the code. To run our future, we simply need the following code:

```
#[tokio::main]
async fn main() {
    let counter_one = CounterFuture { count: 0 };
    let counter_two = CounterFuture { count: 0 };
    let handle_one: JoinHandle<u32> = tokio::task::spawn(async move {
        counter_one.await
    });
    let handle_two: JoinHandle<u32> = tokio::task::spawn(async move {
        counter_two.await
    });
    tokio::join!(handle_one, handle_two);
}
```

Running two of our futures in different tasks gives us the following printout:

```
polling with result: 1
polling with result: 1
polling with result: 2
polling with result: 2
polling with result: 3
polling with result: 3
polling with result: 4
polling with result: 4
polling with result: 5
polling with result: 5
```

One of the futures was taken off the queue, polled, and set to idle, while another future was taken off the task queue to be polled. These futures were polled in alternate fashion. You may have noticed that our poll function is not async. This is because an async poll function would return a circular dependency, as you would be sending a future to be polled in order to resolve a future being polled. With this, we can see that the future is the bedrock of the async computation.

The poll function takes a mutable reference of itself. However, this mutable reference is wrapped in a Pin, which we need to discuss.

Pinning in Futures

In Rust, the compiler often moves values around in memory. For instance, if we move a variable into a function, the memory may be moved.

It's not just moving values that may result in moving memory addresses. Collections can also change memory addresses. For instance, if a vector gets to capacity, the vector will have to be reallocated in memory, changing the memory address.

Most normal primitives such as number, string, bool, structs, and enum implement the Unpin trait, enabling them to be moved around. If you are unsure of whether your data type implements the Unpin trait, run a doc command and check the traits your data type implements. For example, Figure 2-1 shows the auto-trait implementations on an i32 in the standard docs.

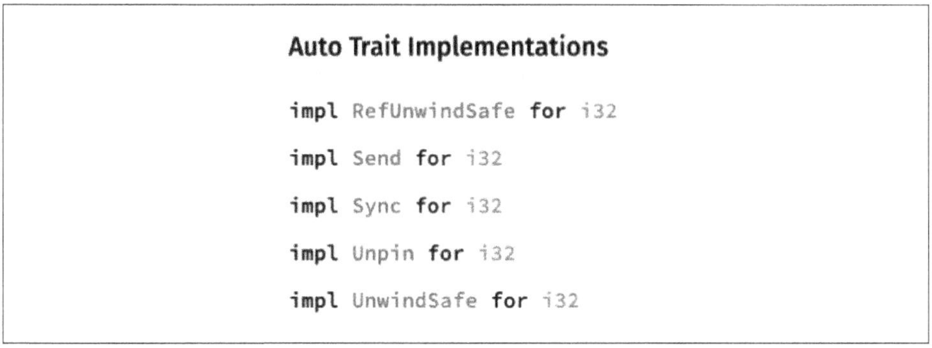

Auto Trait Implementations

impl RefUnwindSafe for i32

impl Send for i32

impl Sync for i32

impl Unpin for i32

impl UnwindSafe for i32

Figure 2-1. Auto-trait implementations in documentation showing thread safety of a struct or primitive

So why do we concern ourselves with pinning (*https://oreil.ly/gS2Gx*) and unpinning (*https://oreil.ly/wRT7_*)? We know that futures get moved, as we use async move in our code when spawning a task. However, moving can be dangerous. To demonstrate the data, we can build a basic struct that references itself:

```
use std::ptr;

struct SelfReferential {
    data: String,
    self_pointer: *const String,
}
```

The *const String is a raw pointer to a string. This pointer directly references the memory address of the data. The pointer offers no safety guarantees. Therefore, the reference does not update if the data being pointed to moves. We are using a raw pointer to demonstrate why pinning is needed. For this demonstration to take place, we need to define the constructor of the struct and printing of the struct's reference, as follows:

```
impl SelfReferential {
    fn new(data: String) -> SelfReferential {
        let mut sr = SelfReferential {
            data,
            self_pointer: ptr::null(),
        };
        sr.self_pointer = &sr.data as *const String;
        sr
    }
```

```
    fn print(&self) {
        unsafe {
            println!("{}", *self.self_pointer);
        }
    }
}
```

To then expose the danger of moving the struct by creating two instances of the `SelfReferential` struct, swap these instances in memory and print what data the raw pointer is pointing to with the following code:

```
fn main() {
    let first = SelfReferential::new("first".to_string());
    let moved_first = first; // Move the struct
    moved_first.print();
}
```

If you try to run the code, you will get an error, which is likely a segmentation fault. A *segmentation fault* is an error caused by accessing memory that does not belong to the program. We can see that moving a struct with a reference to itself can be dangerous. Pinning ensures that the future remains at a fixed memory address. This is important because futures can be paused or resumed, which can change the memory address.

We have covered nearly all the components in the basic future that we have defined. The only remaining component is the context.

Context in Futures

A `Context` only serves to provide access to a waker to wake a task. A *waker* is a handle that notifies the executor when the task is ready to be run.

While this is the primary role of `Context` today, it's important to note that this functionality might evolve in the future. The design of `Context` has allowed space for expansion, such as the introduction of additional responsibilities or capabilities as Rust's asynchronous ecosystem grows.

Let's look at a stripped-down version of our `poll` function so we can focus on the path of waking up the future:

```
fn poll(mut self: Pin<&mut Self>, cx: &mut Context<'_>) -> Poll<Self::Output> {
    . . .
    if self.count < 5 {
        cx.waker().wake_by_ref();
        Poll::Pending
    } else {
        Poll::Ready(self.count)
    }
}
```

The waker is wrapped in the context and is only used when the result of the poll is going to be Pending. The waker is essentially waking up the future so it can be executed. If the future is completed, then no more execution needs to be done. If we were to remove the waker and run our program again, we would get the following printout:

```
polling with result: 1
polling with result: 1
```

Our program does not complete, and the program hangs. This is because our tasks are still idle, but there is no way to wake them up again to be polled and executed to completion. Futures need the Waker::wake() function so it can be called when the future should be polled again. The process takes the following steps:

1. The poll function for a future is called, and the result is that the future needs to wait for an async operation to complete before the future is able to return a value.

2. The future registers its interest in being notified of the operation's completion by calling a method that references the waker.

3. The executor takes note of the interest in the future's operation and stores the waker in a queue.

4. At some later time, the operation completes, and the executor is notified. The executor retrieves the wakers from the queue and calls wake_by_ref on each one, waking up the futures.

5. The wake_by_ref function signals the associated task that should be scheduled for execution. The way this is done can vary depending on the runtime.

6. When the future is executed, the executor will call the poll method of the future again, and the future will determine whether the operation has completed, returning a value if completion is achieved.

We can see that futures are used with an async/await function, but let's think about how else they can be used. We can also use a timeout on a thread of execution: the thread finishes when a certain amount of time has elapsed, so we do not end up with a program that hangs indefinitely. This is useful when we have a function that can be slow to complete and we want to move on or error early. Remember that threads provide the underlying functionality for executing tasks. We import timeout from tokio::time and set up a slow task. In this case, we put this as a sleep for 10 seconds to exaggerate the effect.

```
use std::time::Duration;
use tokio::time::timeout;

async fn slow_task() -> &'static str {
    tokio::time::sleep(Duration::from_secs(10)).await;
```

```
        "Slow Task Completed"
    }
```

Now we set up our timeout—in this case, setting it to 3 seconds. The thread will end if the future is not completed within these 3 seconds. We match the result and print `Task timed out`:

```
#[tokio::main]
async fn main() {
    let duration = Duration::from_secs(3);
    let result = timeout(duration, slow_task()).await;

    match result {
        Ok(value) => println!("Task completed successfully: {}", value),
        Err(_) => println!("Task timed out"),
    }
}
```

Cancel Safety

When we apply a timeout to a future, as shown in the previous example, the future (in this case, `slow_task`) could be cancelled if it doesn't complete within the specified duration. This introduces the concept of *cancel safety*.

Cancel safety ensures that when a future is canceled, any state or resources it was using are handled correctly. If a task is in the middle of an operation when it's canceled, it shouldn't leave the system in a bad state, like holding onto locks, leaving files open, or partially modifying data.

In Rust's async ecosystem, most operations are cancel-safe by default; they can be safely interrupted without causing issues. However, it's still a good practice to be aware of how your tasks interact with external resources or state and ensure that those interactions are cancel-safe.

In our example, if the `slow_task()` is canceled due to the timeout, the task itself is simply stopped, and the timeout returns an error indicating the task didn't complete in time. Since `tokio::time::sleep` is a cancel-safe operation, there's no risk of resource leaks or inconsistent states. However, if the task involves more complex operations, such as network communication or file I/O, additional care might be needed to ensure that the cancellation is handled appropriately.

For CPU-intensive work, we can also offload work to a separate threadpool and the future resolves when the work is finished. We have now covered the context of futures.

Polling directly is not the most efficient way as our executor will be busy polling futures that are not ready. To explain how we can prevent busy polling, we will move onto waking futures remotely.

Waking Futures Remotely

Imagine that we make a network call to another computer using async Rust. The routing of the network call and receiving of the response happens outside of our Rust program. Considering this, it does not make sense to constantly poll our networking future until we get a signal from the OS that data has been received at the port we are listening to. We can hold on the polling of the future by externally referencing the future's waker and waking the future when we need to.

To see this in action, we can simulate an external call with channels. First, we need the following imports:

```
use std::pin::Pin;
use std::task::{Context, Poll, Waker};
use std::sync::{Arc, Mutex};
use std::future::Future;
use tokio::sync::mpsc;
use tokio::task;
```

With these imports, we can now define our future, which takes the following form:

```
struct MyFuture {
    state: Arc<Mutex<MyFutureState>>,
}

struct MyFutureState {
    data: Option<Vec<u8>>,
    waker: Option<Waker>,
}
```

Here, we can see that the state of our `MyFuture` can be accessed from another thread. The state of our `MyFuture` has the waker and data. To make our `main` function more concise, we define a constructor for `MyFuture` with the following code:

```
impl MyFuture {
    fn new() -> (Self, Arc<Mutex<MyFutureState>>) {
        let state = Arc::new(Mutex::new(MyFutureState {
            data: None,
            waker: None,
        }));
        (
            MyFuture {
                state: state.clone(),
            },
            state,
        )
    }
}
```

For our constructor, we can see that we construct the future, but we also return a reference to the state so we can access the waker outside of the future. Finally, we implement the Future trait for our future with the following code:

```
impl Future for MyFuture {
    type Output = String;

    fn poll(self: Pin<&mut Self>, cx: &mut Context<'_>)
        -> Poll<Self::Output> {
        println!("Polling the future");
        let mut state = self.state.lock().unwrap();

        if state.data.is_some() {
            let data = state.data.take().unwrap();
            Poll::Ready(String::from_utf8(data).unwrap())
        } else {
            state.waker = Some(cx.waker().clone());
            Poll::Pending
        }
    }
}
```

Here we can see that we print every time we poll the future to keep track of how many times we poll our future. We then access the state and see if there is any data. If there is no data, we pass the waker into the state so we can wake the future from outside of the future. If there is data in the state, we know that we are ready, and we return a Ready.

Our future is now ready to test. Inside our main function, we create our future, channel for communication, and spawn our future with the following code:

```
let (my_future, state) = MyFuture::new();
let (tx, mut rx) = mpsc::channel::<()>(1);
let task_handle = task::spawn(async {
    my_future.await
});
tokio::time::sleep(tokio::time::Duration::from_secs(3)).await;
println!("spawning trigger task");
```

We can see that we are sleeping for three seconds. This sleep gives us time to check if we are polling multiple times. If our approach works as intended, we should only get one poll during the time of sleeping. We then spawn our trigger task with the following code:

```
let trigger_task = task::spawn(async move {
    rx.recv().await;
    let mut state = state.lock().unwrap();
    state.data = Some(b"Hello from the outside".to_vec());
    loop {
        if let Some(waker) = state.waker.take() {
            waker.wake();
```

```
            break;
        }
    }
});
tx.send(()).await.unwrap();
```

We can see that once our trigger task receives the message in the channel, it gets the state of our future, and populates the data. We then check to see if the waker is present. Once we get hold of the waker, we wake the future.

Finally, we await on both of the async tasks with the following code:

```
let outome = task_handle.await.unwrap();
println!("Task completed with outcome: {}", outome);
trigger_task.await.unwrap();
```

If we run our code, we get this printout:

```
Polling the future
spawning trigger task
Polling the future
Task completed with outcome: Hello from the outside
```

We can see that our polling only happens once on the initial setup and then happens one more time when we wake the future with the data. Async runtimes set up efficient ways to listen to OS events so they do not have to blindly poll futures. For instance, Tokio has an event loop that listens to OS events and then handles them so the event wakes up the right task. However, throughout this book, we want to keep the coding examples simple, so we will be calling the waker directly in the `poll` function. This is because we want to reduce the amount of superfluous code when focusing on other areas of async programming.

Now that we have covered how futures are woken from outside events, we now move onto sharing data between futures.

Sharing Data Between Futures

Although it can complicate things, we can share data between futures. We may want to share data between futures for the following reasons:

- Aggregating results
- Dependent computations
- Caching results
- Synchronization
- Shared state
- Task coordination and supervision
- Resource management

- Error propagation

While sharing data between futures is useful, there are some things that we need to be mindful of when doing so. We can highlight them as we work through a simple example. First, we will be relying on the standard Mutex with the following import:

```
use std::sync::{Arc, Mutex};
use tokio::task::JoinHandle;
use core::task::Poll;
use tokio::time::Duration;
use std::task::Context;
use std::pin::Pin;
use std::future::Future;
```

We are using the standard Mutex rather than the *Tokio* version because we do not want async functionality in our poll function.

For our example, we will be using a basic struct that has a counter. One async task will be for increasing the count, and the other task will be decreasing the count. If both tasks hit the shared data the same number of times, the end result will be zero. Therefore, we need to build a basic enum to define what type of task is being run with the following code:

```
#[derive(Debug)]
enum CounterType {
    Increment,
    Decrement
}
```

We can then define our shared data struct with the following code:

```
struct SharedData {
    counter: i32,
}

impl SharedData {
    fn increment(&mut self) {
        self.counter += 1;
    }
    fn decrement(&mut self) {
        self.counter -= 1;
    }
}
```

Now that our shared data struct is defined, we can define our counter future with the following code:

```
struct CounterFuture {
    counter_type: CounterType,
    data_reference: Arc<Mutex<SharedData>>,
    count: u32
}
```

Here, we have defined the type of operation the future will perform on the shared data. We also have access to the shared data and a count to stop the future once the total number of executions of the shared data has happened for the future.

The signature of our `poll` function takes the following form:

```
impl Future for CounterFuture {
    type Output = u32;

    fn poll(mut self: Pin<&mut Self>, cx: &mut Context<'_>)
    -> Poll<Self::Output> {
        . . .
    }
}
```

Inside our `poll` function, we first cover getting access to the shared data with the following code:

```
std::thread::sleep(Duration::from_secs(1));
let mut guard = match self.data_reference.try_lock() {
    Ok(guard) => guard,
    Err(error) => {
        println!(
            "error for {:?}: {}",
            self.counter_type, error
        );
        cx.waker().wake_by_ref();
        return Poll::Pending
    }
};
```

We sleep to merely exaggerate the difference so it is easier for us to follow the flow of our program when running it. We then use a `try_lock`. This is because we are using the standard library `Mutex`. It would be nice to use the *Tokio* version of the `Mutex`, but remember that our poll function cannot be async. Here lies a problem. If we acquire the `Mutex` using the standard lock function, we can block the thread until the lock is acquired. Remember, we could have one thread handling multiple tasks in our runtime. We would defeat the purpose of the async runtime if we locked the entire thread until the `Mutex` is acquired. Instead, the `try_lock` function attempts to acquire the lock, returning a result immediately in whether the lock was acquired or not. If the lock is not acquired, we print out the error to inform us for educational purposes and then return a poll pending. This means that the future will be polled periodically until the lock is acquired so the future does not hold up the async runtime unnecessarily.

If we do get the lock, we then move forward in our poll function to act on the shared data with the following code:

```
let value = &mut *guard;
```

```
match self.counter_type {
    CounterType::Increment => {
        value.increment();
        println!("after increment: {}", value.counter);
    },
    CounterType::Decrement => {
        value.decrement();
        println!("after decrement: {}", value.counter);
    }
}
```

Now that the shared data has been altered, we can return the right response depending on the count with the following code:

```
std::mem::drop(guard);
self.count += 1;
if self.count < 3 {
    cx.waker().wake_by_ref();
    return Poll::Pending
} else {
    return Poll::Ready(self.count)
}
```

We can see that we drop the guard before bothering to work out the return. This increases the time the guard is free for other futures and enables us to update the self.count.

Running two different variants of our future can be done with the following code:

```
#[tokio::main]
async fn main() {
    let shared_data = Arc::new(Mutex::new(SharedData{counter: 0}));
    let counter_one = CounterFuture {
        counter_type: CounterType::Increment,
        data_reference: shared_data.clone(),
        count: 0
    };
    let counter_two = CounterFuture {
        counter_type: CounterType::Decrement,
        data_reference: shared_data.clone(),
        count: 0
    };
    let handle_one: JoinHandle<u32> = tokio::task::spawn(async move {
        counter_one.await
    });
    let handle_two: JoinHandle<u32> = tokio::task::spawn(async move {
        counter_two.await
    });
    tokio::join!(handle_one, handle_two);
}
```

Now we had to run the program a couple of times before we got an error that was printed out, but when an error acquiring the lock occurred, we got the following printout:

```
after decrement: -1
after increment: 0
error for Increment: try_lock failed because the operation would block
after decrement: -1
after increment: 0
after decrement: -1
after increment: 0
```

The end result is still zero, so the error did not affect the overall outcome. The future just got polled again. While this has been interesting, we can mimic the exact same behavior using a higher level abstraction from a third-party crate such as *Tokio* for an easier implementation.

High-Level Data Sharing Between Futures

The future that we built in the previous section can be replaced with the following async function:

```
async fn count(count: u32, data: Arc<tokio::sync::Mutex<SharedData>>,
                        counter_type: CounterType) -> u32 {
    for _ in 0..count {
        let mut data = data.lock().await;
        match counter_type {
            CounterType::Increment => {
                data.increment();
                println!("after increment: {}", data.counter);
            },
            CounterType::Decrement => {
                data.decrement();
                println!("after decrement: {}", data.counter);
            }
        }
        std::mem::drop(data);
        std::thread::sleep(Duration::from_secs(1));
    }
    return count
}
```

Here we merely loop through the total number acquiring the lock in an async way and sleeping to enable the second future to operate on the shared data. This can simply be run with the following code:

```
let shared_data = Arc::new(tokio::sync::Mutex::new(SharedData{counter: 0}));
let shared_two = shared_data.clone();

let handle_one: JoinHandle<u32> = tokio::task::spawn(async move {
    count(3, shared_data, CounterType::Increment).await
```

```
    });
    let handle_two: JoinHandle<u32> = tokio::task::spawn(async move {
        count(3, shared_two, CounterType::Decrement).await
    });
    tokio::join!(handle_one, handle_two);
```

If we run this, we get the exact same printout and behavior as our futures in the previous section. However, it's clearly simpler and easier to write. There are trade-offs to both approaches. For instance, if we just wanted to write futures that have the behavior we have coded, it would make sense to use just an async function. However, if we needed more control over how a future was polled, or we do not have access to an async implementation but we have a blocking function that tries, then it would make sense to write the poll function ourselves.

How Futures in Rust Are Different

Other languages implement futures for async programming, and some of these languages rely on the callback model. The callback model uses a function that fires when another function completes. This callback function is usually passed in as an argument to this function. This did not work for Rust because the callback model relies on dynamic dispatch, which means at runtime the exact function that was going to be called was determined at runtime as opposed to compile time. This produced additional overhead because the program had to work out what function to call at runtime. This violates the *zero-cost* approach and resulted in reduced performance.

Rust opted for an alternative approach with the aim of optimizing runtime performance by using the Future trait, which uses polls. The runtime is responsible for managing when to call polls. It does not need to schedule callbacks and worry about working out what function to call, instead it can use polls to see if the future is completed. This is more efficient because futures can be represented as a state machine in a single heap allocation, and the state machine captures local variables that are needed to execute the async function. This means there is one memory allocation per task, without any concern that the memory allocation will be the incorrect size. This decision is truly a testament to the Rust programming language, where the developers take the time to get the implementation right.

Oftentimes we are not using async/await in isolation and we want to do something else when a task is complete. We can specify this with specific combinators like and_then or or_else which are provided by *Tokio*.

How Are Futures Processed?

Let's talk through how a future gets processed by walking through the steps at a high level:

Create a future

A future can be created in multiple ways. One common approach is by defining an async function using the async keyword before the function. However, as we've seen earlier, you can also manually create a future by implementing the Future trait yourself. When we call an async function, it returns a future. At this point, the future hasn't performed any computation yet, and the await has not been called on it.

Spawn a task

We spawn a task with the future with await, which means we register with an executor. The executor then takes responsibility for taking the task to completion. To do this, it maintains a queue of tasks.

Polling the task

The executor processes the futures in the task by calling the poll method. This is a feature of the Future trait and will need to be implemented even if you are writing your own future. The future is either ready or it is still pending.

Schedules the next execution

If the future is not pending (i.e., not ready), the executor places the task back into the queue to be executed in the future.

Completion of future

At some point, all the future in the task will complete, and the poll will return a ready. We should note that the result might be a Result or an Error. At this point, the executor can release any resources that it no longer needs and pass the results onwards.

> **Note on Async Runtimes**
>
> It must be noted that there are different variances of how async runtimes are implemented, and *Tokio*'s async runtime is much more complex and will be covered in Chapter 7.

We have now covered why we pin futures to prevent undefined behavior, context in futures, and data sharing between futures. Next, let's put it all together in a quick example.

Putting It All Together

We've discussed tasks and futures and their role in asynchronous programming. Now, we'll implement a system that applies these concepts. Imagine a server or daemon that processes incoming requests or messages. The data received needs to be logged to a file in case we need to inspect what happened. This problem means that we cannot predict when a log will happen. For instance, if we are just writing to a file in a single problem, our write operations can be blocking. However, receiving multiple requests from different programs can result in considerable overhead. It makes sense to send a write task to the async runtime and have the log written to the file when it is possible. It must be noted that this example is for educational purposes. While async writing to a file might be useful for a local application, if you have a server that is designed to take a lot of traffic, then you should explore database options.

In the following example, we are creating an audit trail for an application that logs interactions. This is an important part of many products that use sensitive data, like in the medical field. We want to log the user's actions, but we do not want that logging action to hold up the program because we still want to facilitate a quick user experience. For this exercise to work, you will need the following dependencies:

```
[dependencies]
tokio = { version = "1.39.0", features = ["full"] }
futures-util = "0.3"
```

Using these dependencies, we need to import the following:

```
use std::fs::{File, OpenOptions};
use std::io::prelude::*;
use std::sync::{Arc, Mutex};
use std::future::Future;
use std::pin::Pin;
use std::task::{Context, Poll};
use tokio::task::JoinHandle;
use futures_util::future::join_all;
```

At this stage, pretty much all of this should make sense and you should be able to work out what we are using them for. We will be referring to the handle throughout the program, so we might as well define the type now with the following line:

```
type AsyncFileHandle = Arc<Mutex<File>>;
type FileJoinHandle = JoinHandle<Result<bool, String>>;
```

Seeing as we do not want two tasks trying to write to the file at the same time, it makes sense to ensure that only one task has mutable access to the file at one time.

We may want to write to multiple files. For instance, we might want to write all logins to one file and error messages to another file. If you have medical patients in your system, you want to have a log file per patient (as you would probably inspect log files on a patient-by-patient basis), and you'd want to prevent unauthorized people looking at actions on a patient that they are not allowed to view. Considering there are needs for multiple files when logging, we can create a function that creates a file or obtains the handle of an existing file with the following code:

```
fn get_handle(file_path: &dyn ToString) -> AsyncFileHandle {
    match OpenOptions::new().append(true).open(file_path.to_string()) {
        Ok(opened_file) => {
            Arc::new(Mutex::new(opened_file))
        },
        Err(_) => {
            Arc::new(Mutex::new(File::create(file_path.to_string()).unwrap()))
        }
    }
}
```

Now that we have our file handles, we need to work on our future that will write to the log. The fields of the future take the following form:

```
struct AsyncWriteFuture {
    pub handle: AsyncFileHandle,
    pub entry: String
}
```

We are now at a stage in our worked example where we can implement the Future trait for our AsyncWriteFuture struct and define the poll function. We will be using the same methods that we have covered in this chapter. Because of this, you can attempt to write the Future implementation and poll function yourself. Hopefully your implementation will look similar to this:

```
impl Future for AsyncWriteFuture {

    type Output = Result<bool, String>;

    fn poll(self: Pin<&mut Self>, cx: &mut Context<'_>) -> Poll<Self::Output> {
        let mut guard = match self.handle.try_lock() {
            Ok(guard) => guard,
            Err(error) => {
                println!("error for {} : {}", self.entry, error);
                cx.waker().wake_by_ref();
                return Poll::Pending
            }
        };
        let lined_entry = format!("{}\n", self.entry);
        match guard.write_all(lined_entry.as_bytes()) {
            Ok(_) => println!("written for: {}", self.entry),
            Err(e) => println!("{}", e)
        };
        Poll::Ready(Ok(true))
    }
}
```

The Self::Output type is not super important to get right. We just decided it would be nice to have a true value to say it was written, but an empty bool or anything else works. The main focus of the previous code is that we try to get the lock for the file handle. If we do not manage to get the lock, we return a Pending. If we do get the lock, we write our entry to the file.

When it comes to writing to the log, it is not very intuitive for other developers to construct our future and spawn off a task into the async runtime. They just want to write to the log file. Therefore, we need to write our own write_log function that accepts the handle of the file and the line that is to be written to the log. Inside this function, we then spin off a *Tokio* task and return the handle of the task. This is a good opportunity for you to attempt to write this function yourself.

If you attempted to write the write_log function yourself, it should take a similar approach to the following code:

```
fn write_log(file_handle: AsyncFileHandle, line: String) -> FileJoinHandle {
    let future = AsyncWriteFuture{
        handle: file_handle,
        entry: line
    };
    tokio::task::spawn(async move {
        future.await
    })
}
```

It must be noted that even though the function does not have async in front of the function definition, it still behaves like an async function. We can call it and get the handle, which we can then choose to await on later on in our program like so:

```
let handle = write_log(file_handle, name.to_string());
```

Or we can directly await on it like this:

```
let result = write_log(file_handle, name.to_string()).await;
```

We can now run our async logging functions with the following main function:

```
#[tokio::main]
async fn main() {
    let login_handle = get_handle(&"login.txt");
    let logout_handle = get_handle(&"logout.txt");

    let names = ["one", "two", "three", "four", "five", "six"];
    let mut handles = Vec::new();

    for name in names {
        let file_handle = login_handle.clone();
        let file_handle_two = logout_handle.clone();
        let handle = write_log(file_handle, name.to_string());
        let handle_two = write_log(file_handle_two, name.to_string());
        handles.push(handle);
```

```
            handles.push(handle_two);
        }
        let _ = join_all(handles).await;
    }
```

If you look at the printout, you will see something similar to the following code. We have not included the whole printout for brevity. We can see that six cannot be written to the file because of the try_lock(), but five is written successfully.:

```
. . .
error for six : try_lock failed because the operation would block
written for: five
error for six : try_lock failed because the operation would block
. . .
```

To make sure this has all worked in an async fashion, lets look at the login.txt file. Your file may have a different order, but mine looks like this:

```
one
four
three
five
two
six
```

You can see here that the numbers which were in order prior to entering the loop have been logged out of order in an async way.

Ensuring Order in Asynchronous Operations

This is an important observation to note. Obtaining the lock is not deterministic, so we cannot assume the order in which the log is written. Locks are not just the only cause of this disorder. Delays in the reponse of any async operation can result in a disordered result, because when we are awaiting on one result, we process another. Therefore, when reaching for async solutions, we cannot rely on the results being processed in a certain order.

If the order is essential, then keeping to one future and using data collections like queues will slow down the completion of all steps but will ensure that the steps are processed in the order you need them to be. In this case, if we needed to write to the file in order, we could wrap a queue in a Mutex and give one future the responsibility of checking the queue on every poll. Another future could then add to that queue.

Increasing the number of futures with access to the queue on either side will compromise the assumption of order. While restricting the number of futures accessing the queue to one on each side reduces speed, we will still benefit if there are I/O delays. This is because the waiting of log inputs will not block our thread.

And there we have it! We have built an async logging function that is wrapped up in a single function, making it easy to interface with. Hopefully this worked example has reinforced the concepts that we have covered in this chapter.

Summary

In this chapter, we've embarked on a journey through the landscape of asynchronous programming in Rust, highlighting the pivotal role of tasks. These units of asynchronous work, grounded in futures, are more than just technical constructs; they are the backbone of efficient concurrency in practice. For instance, consider the everyday task of preparing coffee and toast. By breaking it down into async blocks, we have seen firsthand that multitasking in code can be as practical and timesaving as in our daily routines.

However, async is not deterministic, meaning the execution order of async tasks is not set in stone, which, while initially daunting, opens a playground for optimization. Cooperative multitasking isn't just a trick; it's a strategy to get the most out of our resources, something we've applied to accelerate our async operations.

We have also covered the sharing of data between tasks, which can be a double-edged sword. It's tempting to think that access to data is a nice tool for designing our solution, but without careful control, as demonstrated with our `Mutex` examples, it can lead to unforeseen delays and complexity. Here lies a valuable lesson: shared state must be managed, not just for the sake of order but for the sanity of our code's flow.

Finally, our look into the `Future` trait was more than an academic exercise; it offered us a lens to understand and control the intricacies of task execution. It's a reminder that power comes with responsibility—the power to control task polling comes with the responsibility to understand the impact of each await expression. As we move forward, remember that implementing and utilizing async operations is not just about putting tasks into motion. It's about grasping the underlying dynamics of each async expression. We can understand the underlying dynamics further by constructing our own async queues in Chapter 3. There, you will gain the insights needed to define and control asynchronous workflows in Rust.

CHAPTER 3

Building Our Own Async Queues

Although we have explored basic async syntax and solved a problem using high-level async concepts, you still might not be completely sure of what tasks and futures really are and how they flow through the async runtime. Describing futures and tasks can be difficult to do, and they can be hard to understand. This chapter consolidates what you have learned about futures and tasks so far, and how they run through an async runtime, by walking you through building your own async queues with minimal dependencies.

This async runtime will be customizable by choosing the number of queues and the number of consuming threads that will be processing these queues. The implementation does not have to be uniform. For instance, we can have a low-priority queue with two consuming threads and a high-priority queue with five consuming threads. We will then be able to choose which queue a future is going to be processed on. We will also be able to implement task stealing, whereby consuming threads can steal tasks from other queues if their queue is empty. Finally, we will build our own macros to enable high-level use of our async runtime.

By the end of this chapter, you will be able to implement custom async queues and fully understand how futures and tasks travel through the async runtime. You will also have the skills to customize async runtimes to solve problems that are specific to you and that a standard out-of-the-box runtime environment might not be able to handle. Even if you do not want to implement your own async queues ever again, you will have a deeper understanding of async runtimes so you can manipulate high-level async crates more effectively to solve problems. You will also understand the trade-offs of async code even when implementing async code at a high level.

We begin our exploration of building async queues by defining how tasks are spawned, as task spawning serves as the entry point to the runtime. This async runtime will be customizable, allowing you to choose how many queues you have and how many consuming threads will process these queues.

Building Our Own Async Queue

In this section, we will walk through the process of building a custom asynchronous queue. If we break our implementation into steps, we will see firsthand how our futures get converted into tasks and executed.

In this example, we are building a simple asynchronous queue, and we are going to be dealing with three tasks. We will describe each task as we define it.

Before we write any code, we need the following dependencies:

```
[dependencies]
async-task = "4.4.0"
futures-lite = "1.12.0"
flume = "0.10.14"
```

We are using these dependencies:

async-task
> This crate is essential for spawning and managing tasks within an async runtime. It provides the core functionality needed to convert futures into tasks.

futures-lite
> A lightweight implementation of futures.

flume
> A multiproducer, multi-consumer channel that we'll use to implement our async queue, allowing tasks to be safely passed around within the runtime. We could use async-channel here but are opting for flume because we want to be able to clone receivers, as we are going to be distributing tasks among consumers. Additionally, flume provides unbounded channels that can hold an unlimited number of messages and implements lock-free algorithms. This makes flume particularly beneficial for highly concurrent programs, where the queue might need to handle a large number of messages in parallel, unlike the standard library channels that rely on a blocking mutex for synchronization.

Next, we need to import the following into our *main.rs* file:

```
use std::{future::Future, panic::catch_unwind, thread};
use std::pin::Pin;
use std::task::{Context, Poll};
use std::time::Duration;
use std::sync::LazyLock;

use async_task::{Runnable, Task};
use futures_lite::future;
```

We will cover what we have imported when we use the imports in the code through-out the chapter so you understand their context.

Each of our three tasks needs to be able to be passed into the queue. We should start by building the task-spawning function. This is where we pass a future into the function. The function then converts the future into a task and puts the task on the queue to be executed. At this point, it might seem like a complex function, so let's start with this signature:

```
fn spawn_task<F, T>(future: F) -> Task<T>
where
    F: Future<Output = T> + Send + 'static,
    T: Send + 'static,
{
    . . .
}
```

This is a generic function that accepts any type that implements both the Future and Send traits. This makes sense because we do not want to be restricted to sending one type of future through our function. The Future trait denotes that our future is going to result in either an error or the value T. Our future needs the Send trait because we are going to be sending our future into a different thread where the queue is based. The Send trait enforces constraints that ensure that our future can be safely shared among threads.

The static means that our future does not contain any references that have a shorter lifetime than the static lifetime. Therefore, the future can be used for as long as the program is running. Ensuring this lifetime is essential, as we cannot force programmers to wait for a task to finish. If the developer never waits for a task, the task could run for the entire lifetime of the program. Because we cannot guarantee when a task is finished, we must ensure that the lifetime of our task is static. When browsing async code, you may have seen async move utilized. This is where we move the ownership of variables used in the async closure (*https://oreil.ly/JHc27*) to the task so we can ensure that the lifetime is static.

Now that we have defined our spawn_task function signature, we move on to the first block of code in the function, which defines the task queue:

```
static QUEUE: LazyLock<flume::Sender<Runnable>> = LazyLock::new(|| {
    . . .
});
```

With static we are ensuring that our queue is living throughout the lifetime of the program. This makes sense, as we will want to send tasks to our queue throughout the program's lifetime. The LazyLock struct gets initialized on its first access. Once the struct is initialized, it is not initialized again. This is because we will be calling our task-spawning function every time we send a future to the async runtime. If we initialize the queue every time we call `spawn_task`, we would be wiping the queue of previous tasks. We now have the transmitting end of a channel, which sends `Runnable`.

`Runnable` is a handle for a runnable task. Every spawned task has a single `Runnable` handle, which exists only when the task is scheduled for running. The handle has the `run` function that polls the task's future once. Then the runnable is dropped. The runnable appears again only when the waker wakes the task in turn, scheduling the task again. Recall from Chapter 2, if we do not pass the waker into our future, it will not be polled again. This is because the future cannot be woken to be polled again. We can build an async runtime that will poll futures no matter whether a waker is present, and we explore this in Chapter 10.

Now that we have defined our signature of the queue, we can look into the closure that we passed into `LazyLock`. We need to create our channel as well as a mechanism for receiving futures sent to that channel:

```
let (tx, rx) = flume::unbounded::<Runnable>();

thread::spawn(move || {
    while let Ok(runnable) = rx.recv() {
        println!("runnable accepted");
        let _ = catch_unwind(|| runnable.run());
    }
});
tx
```

After we have created the channel, we spawn a thread that waits for incoming traffic. The waiting for the incoming traffic is blocking because we are building the async queues to handle incoming async tasks. As a result, we cannot rely on async in our thread. Once we have received our runnable, we run it in the `catch_unwind` function. We use this because we do not know the quality of the code being passed to our async runtime. Ideally, all Rust developers would handle possible errors properly, but in case they do not, `catch_unwind` runs the code and catches any error that's thrown while the code is running, returning `Ok` or `Err` depending on the outcome. This is to prevent a badly coded future from blowing up our async runtime. We then return the transmitter channel so we can send runnables to our thread.

We now have a thread that is running and waiting for tasks to be sent to that thread to be processed, which we achieve with this code:

```
let schedule = |runnable| QUEUE.send(runnable).unwrap();
let (runnable, task) = async_task::spawn(future, schedule);
```

Here, we have created a closure that accepts a runnable and sends it to our queue. We then create the runnable and task by using the `async_task` spawn function. This function leads to an unsafe function that allocates the future onto the heap. The task and runnable returned from the spawn function have a pointer to the same future.

In this chapter, we will not be building our own executor or code that creates a runnable or schedules the task. We will do this in Chapter 10 as we build an async server completely from the standard library with no external dependencies.

Now that the runnable and task have pointers to the same future, we have to schedule the runnable to be run and return the task:

```
runnable.schedule();
println!("Here is the queue count: {:?}", QUEUE.len());
return task
```

When we schedule the runnable, we essentially put the task on the queue to be processed. If we did not schedule the runnable, the task would not be run, and our program would crash when we try to block the main thread to wait on the task being executed (because there is no runnable on the queue but we still return the task). Remember, the task and the runnable have pointers to the same future.

Now that we have scheduled our runnable to be run on the queue and returned the task, our basic async runtime is complete. All we need to do is build some basic futures. We are going to have two types of tasks.

The first task type is our `CounterFuture`, which we initially explored in Chapter 2. This future increments a counter and prints the result after each poll, simulating a delay by using a `std::thread::sleep` call. Here is the code:

```
struct CounterFuture {
    count: u32,
}
impl Future for CounterFuture {
    type Output = u32;

    fn poll(mut self: Pin<&mut Self>, cx: &mut Context<'_>)
        -> Poll<Self::Output> {
        self.count += 1;
        println!("polling with result: {}", self.count);
        std::thread::sleep(Duration::from_secs(1));
        if self.count < 3 {
            cx.waker().wake_by_ref();
            Poll::Pending
        } else {
            Poll::Ready(self.count)
        }
    }
}
```

The second task (task 3) is an async function created using the `async/await` syntax. This function sleeps for 1 second before printing a message. Here's the code:

```
async fn async_fn() {
    std::thread::sleep(Duration::from_secs(1));
    println!("async fn");
}
```

In this example, we are not manually writing our own polling mechanism as we did with CounterFuture. Instead, we're using the built-in async functionality provided by Rust's async syntax, which automatically handles the polling and scheduling of the task for us. Note that our sleep in async_fn is blocking because we want to see how the tasks are processed in our queue.

Before we progress, we can take a detour to get an appreciation for how nonblocking async sleep functions work. Throughout this chapter, we are using sleep functions that block the executor. We are doing this for educational purposes so we can easily map how our tasks are processed in our runtime. However, if we want to build an efficient async sleep function, we need to lean into getting the executor to poll our sleep future and return Pending if the time has not elapsed. First we need Instant to calculate the time elapsed and two fields to keep track of the sleep:

```
use std::time::Instant;

struct AsyncSleep {
    start_time: Instant,
    duration: Duration,
}
impl AsyncSleep {
    fn new(duration: Duration) -> Self {
        Self {
            start_time: Instant::now(),
            duration,
        }
    }
}
```

We can then check the time elapsed between now and start_time on every poll, returning Pending if the time elapsed it not sufficient:

```
impl Future for AsyncSleep {
    type Output = bool;

    fn poll(self: Pin<&mut Self>, cx: &mut Context<'_>)
    -> Poll<Self::Output> {
        let elapsed_time = self.start_time.elapsed();
        if elapsed_time >= self.duration {
            Poll::Ready(true)
        } else {
            cx.waker().wake_by_ref();
            Poll::Pending
        }
    }
}
```

This will not block the executor with idle sleep time. Because sleep is only one part of a process, we can call the `await` on our future inside async blocks for our async sleep future as follows:

```
let async_sleep = AsyncSleep::new(Duration::from_secs(5));
let async_sleep_handle = spawn_task(async {
    async_sleep.await;
    . . .
});
```

> Like most things in programming, a trade-off always exists. If a lot of tasks are in front of the sleep task, chances increase that the async sleep task might effectively wait longer than the duration required before finishing because it might have to wait for other tasks to complete before it can complete between every poll. If you have an operation requiring x seconds to pass between two steps, a blocking sleep might be a better option, but you are going to quickly clog up your queues if you have a lot of these tasks.

Going back to our blocking example, we can now run some futures in our runtime with the following `main` function:

```
fn main() {
    let one = CounterFuture { count: 0 };
    let two = CounterFuture { count: 0 };
    let t_one = spawn_task(one);
    let t_two = spawn_task(two);
    let t_three = spawn_task(async {
        async_fn().await;
        async_fn().await;
        async_fn().await;
        async_fn().await;
    });
    std::thread::sleep(Duration::from_secs(5));
    println!("before the block");
    future::block_on(t_one);
    future::block_on(t_two);
    future::block_on(t_three);
}
```

This `main` function has some repetition, but it is needed in order for us to get a sense of how the async runtime we just built processes futures. Notice that task 3 consists of multiple calls to `async_fn`. This helps us see how the runtime handles multiple async operations within a single task. We then wait 5 seconds and print so we can get a sense of how our system runs before calling the `block_on` functions.

Running our program gives us the following lengthy but essential printout in the terminal:

```
Here is the queue count: 1
Here is the queue count: 2
Here is the queue count: 3
runnable accepted
polling with result: 1
runnable accepted
polling with result: 1
runnable accepted
async fn
async fn
before the block
async fn
async fn
runnable accepted
polling with result: 2
runnable accepted
polling with result: 2
runnable accepted
polling with result: 3
runnable accepted
polling with result: 3
```

Our printout gives us a timeline of our async runtime. We can see that our queue is being filled up with the three tasks that we have spawned, and our runtime is processing them in order asynchronously before we call our block_on functions. Even after the first block_on function is called, which blocks on the first task we spawned, the two counter tasks are being processed at the same time.

Note that the async function that we built and called four times in our third task was essentially blocking. There was no await within the async function, even though we use the await syntax like so:

```
async {
    async_fn().await;
    async_fn().await;
    async_fn().await;
    async_fn().await;
}
```

The stack of async_fn futures blocks the thread that's processing the task queue until the entire task is completed. When a poll results in Pending, the task is then put back on the queue to be polled again.

Our async runtime can be summarized by the diagram in Figure 3-1.

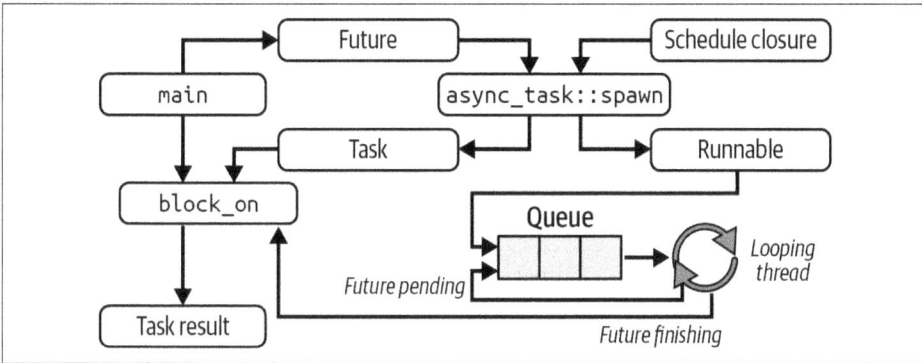

Figure 3-1. Our async runtime

Let's describe what is happening with an analogy. Say that we have a dirty coat that needs cleaning. The label inside the coat that indicates cleaning instructions and material content is the future. We walk into the dry cleaners and hand over the coat with the instructions. The worker at the cleaner makes the coat runnable by putting a plastic cover on it and giving it a number. The worker also gives you a ticket with the number, which is like the task that the `main` function gets.

We then go about our day doing things while the coat is being cleaned. If the coat is not cleaned the first time around, it keeps going through cleaning cycles until it is clean. We then come back with our ticket and hand it over to the worker. This is the same stage as the `block_on` function. If we have really taken our time before coming back, the coat might be clean already and we can take it and go on with our day. If we go to the cleaners too early, the coat will not be clean, and we'll have to wait until the coat is cleaned before taking it home. The clean coat is the result.

Right now, our async runtime has only one thread processing the queue. This would be like us insisting on only one worker at the cleaners. This is not the most efficient use of resources available, as most CPUs have multiple cores. Considering this, it would be useful to explore how to increase the number of workers and queues to increase our capacity to handle more tasks.

Increasing Workers and Queues

To increase our number of threads working on the queue, we can add another thread consuming from the queue with a cloned receiver of our queue channel:

```
let (tx, rx) = flume::unbounded::<Runnable>();

let queue_one = rx.clone();
let queue_two = rx.clone();

thread::spawn(move || {
```

```
        while let Ok(runnable) = queue_one.recv() {
            let _ = catch_unwind(|| runnable.run());
        }
    });
    thread::spawn(move || {
        while let Ok(runnable) = queue_two.recv() {
            let _ = catch_unwind(|| runnable.run());
        }
    });
```

If we send tasks through the channel, the traffic will generally be distributed across both threads. If one thread is blocked with a CPU-intensive task, the other thread will continue to work through tasks. Recall that Chapter 1 proved that CPU-intensive tasks can be run in parallel by using threads with our Fibonacci number example. We can have a more ergonomic approach to building a thread pool with the following code:

```
    for _ in 0..3 {
        let receiver = rx.clone();
        thread::spawn(move || {
            while let Ok(runnable) = receiver.recv() {
                let _ = catch_unwind(|| runnable.run());
            }
        });
    }
```

We could offload CPU-intensive tasks to our thread pool and continue working through the rest of the program, blocking it when we need a result from the task. While this is not really in the spirit of async programming (as we use async programming to optimize the juggling of I/O operations), it is a useful approach to remember that certain problems can be solved by off-loading CPU-intensive tasks early in the program.

> You may have come across warnings along the lines of "async is not for computationally heavy tasks." Async is merely a mechanism, and you can use it for what you want as long as it makes sense. However, the warning is not without merit. For instance, if you are using your async runtime to handle income requests as most web frameworks do, then chucking computationally heavy tasks onto the async runtime queue could potentially block your ability to process incoming requests until those computations are done.

Now that we have explored multiple workers, we should really look into multiple queues.

Passing Tasks to Different Queues

One of the reasons we would want to have multiple queues is that we might have different priorities for tasks. In this section, we are going to build a high-priority queue with two consuming threads and a low-priority queue with one consuming thread. To support multiple queues, we need the following enum to classify the type of queue the task is destined for:

```
#[derive(Debug, Clone, Copy)]
enum FutureType {
    High,
    Low
}
```

We also need our futures to yield the future type when passed into our spawn function by utilizing the trait:

```
trait FutureOrderLabel: Future {
    fn get_order(&self) -> FutureType;
}
```

We then need to add the future type by adding an extra field:

```
struct CounterFuture {
    count: u32,
    order: FutureType
}
```

Our `poll` function stays the same, so we don't need to revisit that. However, we do need to implement the `FutureOrderLabel` trait for our future:

```
impl FutureOrderLabel for CounterFuture {
    fn get_order(&self) -> FutureType {
        self.order
    }
}
```

Our future is now ready to be processed, and we need to reformat our async runtime to use future types. The signature for our `spawn_task` function stays the same, apart from the additional trait:

```
fn spawn_task<F, T>(future: F) -> Task<T>
where
    F: Future<Output = T> + Send + 'static + FutureOrderLabel,
    T: Send + 'static,
{
    . . .
}
```

We can now define our two queues. At this point, you can attempt to code them yourself before moving forward, as we have covered all that we need to build the two queues. If you attempted to build the queues, hopefully they take a form similar to the following:

```
static HIGH_QUEUE: LazyLock<flume::Sender<Runnable>> = LazyLock::new(|| {
    let (tx, rx) = flume::unbounded::<Runnable>();
    for _ in 0..2 {
        let receiver = rx.clone();
        thread::spawn(move || {
            while let Ok(runnable) = receiver.recv() {
                let _ = catch_unwind(|| runnable.run());
            }
        });
    }
    tx
});
static LOW_QUEUE: LazyLock<flume::Sender<Runnable>> = LazyLock::new(|| {
    let (tx, rx) = flume::unbounded::<Runnable>();
    for _ in 0..1 {
        let receiver = rx.clone();
        thread::spawn(move || {
            while let Ok(runnable) = receiver.recv() {
                let _ = catch_unwind(|| runnable.run());
            }
        });
    }
    tx
});
```

The low-priority queue has one consuming thread, and the high-priority queue has two consuming threads. We now need to route futures to the correct queue. This can be done by defining an individual runner closure for each queue and then passing the correct closure based on the future type:

```
let schedule_high = |runnable| HIGH_QUEUE.send(runnable).unwrap();
let schedule_low = |runnable| LOW_QUEUE.send(runnable).unwrap();

let schedule = match future.get_order() {
    FutureType::High => schedule_high,
    FutureType::Low => schedule_low
};
let (runnable, task) = async_task::spawn(future, schedule);
runnable.schedule();
return task
```

We can now create a future that can be inserted into the selected queue:

```
let one = CounterFuture { count: 0 , order: FutureType::High};
```

However, we have a problem. Let's imagine that loads of low-priority tasks get created, and there are no high-priority tasks. We would have one consumer thread working on all the tasks while the other two consumer threads are just sitting idle. We would be working at one-third capacity. This is where task stealing comes in.

> We do not need to write our own async runtime queues to have control over the distribution of tasks. For instance, *Tokio* will allow you to have control over the distribution of tasks by using Local Set. We cover this in Chapter 7.

Task Stealing

In *task stealing*, consuming threads steal tasks from other queues when their own queue is empty. Figure 3-2 shows task stealing in relation to our current async system.

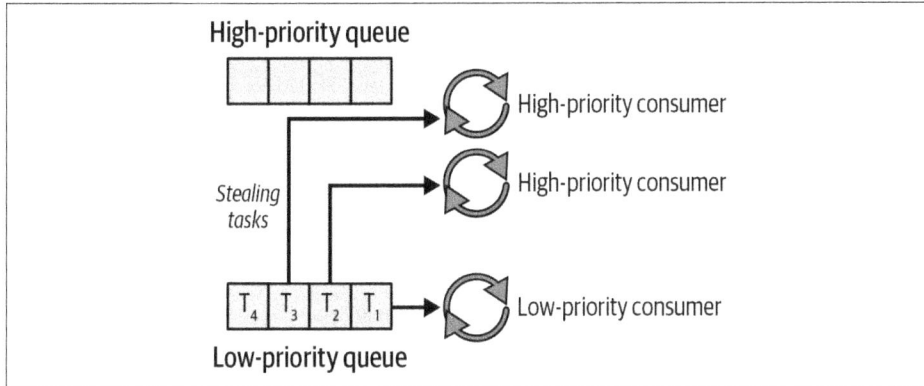

Figure 3-2. Task stealing

We also must appreciate that stealing can go the other way. If the low-priority queue is empty, we would want the low-priority consumer thread to steal tasks from the high-priority queue.

To achieve task stealing, we need to pass in channels for the high- and low-priority queues into both queues. Before we can define our channels, we need this import:

```
use flume::{Sender, Receiver};
```

If we used the standard library for our Sender and Receiver, we would not be able to send the Sender or Receiver over to other threads. With flume, we make both of the channels static that are lazily evaluated inside our spawn_task function:

```
static HIGH_CHANNEL: LazyLock<(Sender<Runnable>, Receiver<Runnable>)> =
        LazyLock::new(|| flume::unbounded::<Runnable>());
static LOW_CHANNEL: LazyLock<(Sender<Runnable>, Receiver<Runnable>)> =
    LazyLock::new(|| flume::unbounded::<Runnable>());
```

Now that we have our two channels, we need to define our high-priority queue consumer threads to carry out the following steps for each iteration in an infinite loop:

1. Check `HIGH_CHANNEL` for a message.

2. If `HIGH_CHANNEL` does not have a message, check `LOW_CHANNEL` for a message.

3. If `LOW_CHANNEL` does not have a message, wait for 100 ms for the next iteration.

> We could park our threads if they are idle and wake them when they need to process incoming tasks. This can save excessive looping and sleeping when there are no tasks to be processed. However, relying on sleeping in your threads can increase response latency, which is undesirable in production code. In production environments, you should aim to avoid sleeping in threads and instead use more responsive mechanisms like thread parking or condition variables. We cover thread parking in relation to async queues in Chapter 10.

Our high-priority queue can carry out these steps with the following code:

```
static HIGH_QUEUE: LazyLock<flume::Sender<Runnable>> = LazyLock::new(|| {
    for _ in 0..2 {
        let high_receiver = HIGH_CHANNEL.1.clone();
        let low_receiver = LOW_CHANNEL.1.clone();
        thread::spawn(move || {
            loop {
                match high_receiver.try_recv() {
                    Ok(runnable) => {
                        let _ = catch_unwind(|| runnable.run());
                    },
                    Err(_) => {
                        match low_receiver.try_recv() {
                            Ok(runnable) => {
                                let _ = catch_unwind(|| runnable.run());
                            },
                            Err(_) => {
                                thread::sleep(Duration::from_millis(100));
                            }
                        }
                    }
                }
            };
        }
    });
    }
    HIGH_CHANNEL.0.clone()
});
```

Our low-priority queue would merely swap steps 1 and 2 around and return `LOW_CHANNEL.0.clone`. We now have both queues pulling tasks from their own queues first and then pulling tasks from other queues when there are no tasks on their own queue. When no tasks are left, we then have our consumer threads slow down.

> Remember that the queues and channels are lazy in their evaluation. A task needs to be sent to the queue in order for the queue to start running. If you send tasks to only the low-priority queue and never to the high-priority queue, the high-priority queue will never start up and therefore will never steal tasks from the low-priority queue.

At this milestone, we can sit back and think about what we have done. We have created our own async runtime queue and defined different queues! We now have fine-grained control over how our async tasks run. Note that we may not want task stealing. For instance, if we put CPU-intensive tasks onto the high-priority queue and lightweight networking tasks on the low-priority queue, we would not want the low-priority queue stealing tasks from the high-priority queue. Otherwise, we run the risk of shutting down our network processing because of the low-priority-queue consumer threads being held up on CPU-intensive tasks.

While it was interesting to have the trait constraint and see how it could be implemented onto our future, we are now disadvantaged. We cannot pass in simple async blocks or async functions because they do not have the `FutureOrderLabel` trait implemented. Other developers will just want a nice interface to run their tasks. Could you imagine how bloated our code would be if we had to implement the `Future` trait for every async task and implement the `FutureOrderLabel` on all of them? We need to refactor our `spawn_task` function for a better developer experience.

Refactoring Our spawn_task Function

When it comes to allowing async blocks and async functions into our `spawn_task` function, we need to remove the `FutureOrderLabel` trait and remove our `order` field in our `CounterFuture` struct. We then must remove the constraint of the `Future OrderLabel` trait in our `spawn_task` function and add another argument for the order, giving the following function signature:

```
fn spawn_task<F, T>(future: F, order: FutureType) -> Task<T>
where
    F: Future<Output = T> + Send + 'static,
    T: Send + 'static,
{
```

We also need to update the selection of the correct scheduling closure in the `spawn_task` function:

```
let schedule = match order {
    FutureType::High => schedule_high,
    FutureType::Low => schedule_low
};
```

Still, we do not want our developers stressing over the order, so we can create a macro for the `spawn_task` function:

```
macro_rules! spawn_task {
    ($future:expr) => {
        spawn_task!($future, FutureType::Low)
    };
    ($future:expr, $order:expr) => {
        spawn_task($future, $order)
    };
}
```

This macro allows us to pass in just the future. If we pass in only the future, we then pass in the low-priority type, meaning that this is the default type. If the order is passed in, it is passed into the `spawn_task` function. From this macro, Rust works out that you need to at least pass in the future expression, and it will not compile unless the future is supplied. We now have a more ergonomic way of spawning tasks, as you can see with the following example:

```
fn main() {
    let one = CounterFuture { count: 0 };
    let two = CounterFuture { count: 0 };

    let t_one = spawn_task!(one, FutureType::High);
    let t_two = spawn_task!(two);
    let t_three = spawn_task!(async_fn());
    let t_four = spawn_task!(async {
        async_fn().await;
        async_fn().await;
    }, FutureType::High);

    future::block_on(t_one);
    future::block_on(t_two);
    future::block_on(t_three);
    future::block_on(t_four);
}
```

This macro is flexible. A developer using it could casually spawn tasks without thinking about it but also has the ability to state that the task is a high priority if needed. We can also pass in async blocks and async functions because these are just syntactic sugar for futures. However, we are repeating ourselves when blocking the `main` function to wait on multiple tasks. We need to create our own join macro to prevent this repetition.

Creating Our Own Join Macro

To create our own join macro, we need to accept a range of tasks and call the block_on function. We can define our own join macro with the following code:

```
macro_rules! join {
    ($($future:expr),*) => {
        {
            let mut results = Vec::new();
            $(
                results.push(future::block_on($future));
            )*
            results
        }
    };
}
```

It is essential that we keep the order of the results the same as the order of the futures passed in. Otherwise, the user will have no way of knowing which result belongs to which task. Also note that our join macro will return only one type, so we use our join macro as follows:

```
let outcome: Vec<u32> = join!(t_one, t_two);
let outcome_two: Vec<()> = join!(t_four, t_three);
```

The outcome is a vector of the outputs of the counters, and outcome_two is a vector of the outputs for the async functions that didn't return anything. As long as we have the same return type, this code will work.

We must remember that our tasks are being directly run. An error could occur in the execution of the task. To return a vector of results, we can create a try_join macro with this code:

```
macro_rules! try_join {
    ($($future:expr),*) => {
        {
            let mut results = Vec::new();
            $(
                let result = catch_unwind(|| future::block_on($future));
                results.push(result);
            )*
            results
        }
    };
}
```

This is similar to our join! macro but will return results of the tasks.

We now have nearly everything we need to run async tasks on our runtime in an ergonomic way with task stealing and different queues. Though spawning our tasks is not ergonomic, we still need a nice interface to configure our runtime environment.

Configuring Our Runtime

You may remember that the queue is lazy: it will not start until it is called. This directly affects our task stealing. The example we gave was that if no tasks were sent to the high-priority queue, that queue would not start and therefore would not steal tasks from the low-priority queue if empty, and vice versa. Configuring a runtime to get things going and refine the number of consuming loops is not an unusual way of solving this problem. For instance, we can look at the following *Tokio* example of starting its runtime:

```
use tokio::runtime::Runtime;

// Create the runtime
let rt = Runtime::new().unwrap();

// Spawn a future onto the runtime
rt.spawn(async {
    println!("now running on a worker thread");
});
```

At the time of this writing, the preceding example is in the *Tokio* documentation of the runtime struct. The *Tokio* library also uses procedural macros to set up the runtime, but they are beyond the scope of this book. You can find more information on procedural macros in the Rust documentation (*https://oreil.ly/SG0bv*). For our runtime, we can build a basic runtime builder to define the number of consuming loops on the high- and low-priority queues.

We first start with our runtime struct:

```
struct Runtime {
    high_num: usize,
    low_num: usize,
}
```

The high number is the number of consuming threads for the high-priority queue, and the low number is the number of consuming threads for the low-priority queue. We implement the following functions for our runtime:

```
impl Runtime {
    pub fn new() -> Self {
        let num_cores = std::thread::available_parallelism().unwrap()
                                                             .get();
        Self {
            high_num: num_cores - 2,
            low_num: 1,
        }
    }
    pub fn with_high_num(mut self, num: usize) -> Self {
        self.high_num = num;
        self
```

```
    }
    pub fn with_low_num(mut self, num: usize) -> Self {
        self.low_num = num;
        self
    }
    pub fn run(&self) {
        . . .
    }
}
```

Here we have a standard way of defining the numbers based on the number of available cores on the computer running our async program. We then have the option to define the low and high numbers ourselves if we want. Our run function defines the environment variables for the numbers and then spawns two tasks to both queues to set up the queues:

```
pub fn run(&self) {
    std::env::set_var("HIGH_NUM", self.high_num.to_string());
    std::env::set_var("LOW_NUM", self.low_num.to_string());

    let high = spawn_task!(async {}, FutureType::High);
    let low = spawn_task!(async {}, FutureType::Low);
    join!(high, low);
}
```

We use our join so that after the run function has been executed, both of our queues are ready to steal tasks.

Before we try our runtime, we need to use these environment variables to establish the number of consumer threads for each queue. In our spawn_task function, we refer to the environment variable inside each queue definition:

```
static HIGH_QUEUE: LazyLock<flume::Sender<Runnable>> = LazyLock::new(|| {
    let high_num = std::env::var("HIGH_NUM").unwrap().parse::<usize>()
                                                        .unwrap();
    for _ in 0..high_num {
        . . .
```

The same goes for the low queue. We can then define our runtime with default numbers in our main function before anything else:

```
Runtime::new().run();
```

Or we can use custom numbers with the following:

```
Runtime::new().with_low_num(2).with_high_num(4).run();
```

We are now capable of running our spawn_task function and join macro whenever we want throughout the rest of the program. We have our own runtime that is configurable with two types of queues and task stealing!

We now have nearly everything tied up. However, we need to cover one last concept before finishing the chapter: background processes.

Running Background Processes

Background processes are tasks that execute in the background periodically for the entire lifetime of the program. These processes can be used for monitoring and for maintenance tasks such as database cleanup, log rotation, and data updates to ensure that the program always has access to the latest information. Implementing a basic background process as a task in the async runtime will illustrate how to handle our long-running tasks.

Before we handle the background task, we need to create a future that will never stop being polled. At this stage in the chapter, you should be able to build this yourself, and you should attempt to do this before moving on.

If you have attempted to build your own future, it should take the following form if the process being carried out is blocking:

```
#[derive(Debug, Clone, Copy)]
struct BackgroundProcess;

impl Future for BackgroundProcess {
    type Output = ();

    fn poll(self: Pin<&mut Self>, cx: &mut Context<'_>)
            -> Poll<Self::Output> {
        println!("background process firing");
        std::thread::sleep(Duration::from_secs(1));
        cx.waker().wake_by_ref();
        Poll::Pending
    }
}
```

Your implementation might be different, but the key takeaway is that we are always returning `Pending`.

We need to acknowledge here that if we drop a task in our `main` function, the task being executed in the async runtime will be cancelled and will not be executed, so our background task must be present throughout the entire lifetime of the program. We need to send the background task at the very beginning of `main`, right after we have defined our runtime:

```
Runtime::new().with_low_num(2).with_high_num(4).run();
let _background = spawn_task!(BackgroundProcess{});
```

And our background process will run periodically throughout the entire lifetime of our program.

However, this is not ergonomic. For instance, let's say that a struct or function could create a background-running task. We do not need to try to juggle the task around the program so it does not get dropped, cancelling the background task. We can remove the need for juggling tasks to keep the background task running by using the `detach` method:

```
Runtime::new().with_low_num(2).with_high_num(4).run();
spawn_task!(BackgroundProcess{}).detach();
```

This method moves the pointer in the task into an unsafe loop that will poll the task and schedule it until it is finished. The pointer associated with the task in the `main` function is then dropped, dropping the need for keeping hold of the tasks in `main`.

Summary

In this chapter, we implemented our own runtime, and you learned a lot in the process. We initially built a basic async runtime environment that accepted futures and created tasks and runnables. The runnables were put on the queue to be processed by consumer threads, and the task was returned back to the `main` function, which we can block to wait for the result of the task. Here we spent some time solidifying the steps that the futures and tasks go through in the async runtime. Finally, we implemented queues with different numbers of consuming threads and used this pattern to implement task stealing for situations when a queue is empty. We then created our own macros for users so they could easily spawn tasks and join them.

The nuance that task stealing introduces highlights the true nature of async programming. An async runtime is merely a tool that you use to solve your problems. Nothing is stopping you from having one thread on a queue for accepting network traffic and five threads processing long, CPU-intensive tasks if you have a program with little traffic but that traffic requests the triggering of long-running tasks. In this case, you would not want your network queue to steal from the CPU-intensive queue. Of course, your solutions should strive to be sensible. However, with deeper understanding of the async runtime you're using comes the ability to solve complex problems in interesting ways.

The async runtime we built certainly is not the best out there. Established async runtimes have teams of very smart people ironing out problems and edge cases. However, now that you are at the end of this chapter, you should understand the need to read around the specifics of your chosen runtime so you can apply its attributes to your own set of problems that you're trying to solve. Also note that the simple implementation of the `async_task` queue with the `flume` channel can be used in production.

In Chapter 4, we cover integrating HTTP with our own async runtime.

Integrating Networking into Our Own Async Runtime

In Chapter 3, we built our own async runtime queue to illustrate how async tasks run through an async runtime. However, we used only basic sleep and print operations. Focusing on simple operations is useful initially, but simple sleep and print functions are limiting. In this chapter, we build on the async runtime we defined previously and integrate networking protocols so they can run on our async runtime.

By the end of this chapter, you will be able to use traits to integrate the *hyper* crate for HTTP requests into our runtime. This means you will be able to take this example and integrate other third-party dependencies into our async runtime via traits after reading the documentation of that crate. Finally, we will go to a lower level by implementing the *mio* crate to directly poll sockets in our futures. This will show you how to utilize fine-grained control over the way the socket is polled, read, and written to in our async runtime. With this exposure and further external reading, you will be able to implement your own custom networking protocols.

This is the hardest chapter to follow, and it is not essential if you are not planning to integrate networking into a custom runtime. If you are not feeling it, feel free to skip this chapter and come back after reading the rest of the book. This content is placed in this chapter because it builds off the code written in Chapter 3.

Before we progress through the chapter, we need the following additional dependencies alongside the dependencies we used in Chapter 3:

```
[dependencies]
hyper = { version = "0.14.26",
features = ["http1", "http2", "client", "runtime"] }
smol = "1.3.0"
anyhow = "1.0.70"
async-native-tls = "0.5.0"
```

```
http = "0.2.9"
tokio = "1.14.0"
```

We are using these dependencies:

hyper
  This crate is a fast and popular HTTP implementation. We are going to use this to make requests. We need the features `client` to allow us to make HTTP requests and `runtime` to allow compatibility with a custom async runtime.

smol
  This crate is a small and fast async runtime. It is particularly good with lightweight tasks with low overhead.

anyhow
  This crate is an error-handling library.

async-native-tls
  This crate provides asynchronous Transport Layer Security (TLS) support.

http
  This crate provides types for working with HTTP requests and their responses.

Tokio
  We used this crate before for demonstrating our async runtime and will use it again in this chapter.

As you can see, we are going to be using *hyper* for this example. This is to give you a different set of tools than those we used in previous examples and to demonstrate that tools like *Tokio* are layered in other commonly used libraries. Before we write any code, however, we must introduce executors and connectors.

Understanding Executors and Connectors

An *executor* is responsible for running futures to completion. It is the part of the runtime that schedules tasks and makes sure they run (or are executed) when they are ready. We need an executor when we introduce networking into our runtime because without it, our futures such as HTTP requests would be created but never actually run.

A *connector* in networking is a component that establishes a connection between our application and the service we want to connect to. It handles activities like opening TCP connections and maintaining them through the lifetime of the request.

Integrating hyper into Our Async Runtime

Now that you understand what executors and connectors are, let's look at how these concepts are essential when integrating a library like *hyper* into our async runtime. Without an appropriate executor and connector, our runtime wouldn't be able to handle the HTTP requests and connections that *hyper* relies on.

If we look at *hyper* official documentation or various online tutorials, we might get the impression that we can perform a simple GET request using the *hyper* crate with the following code:

```
use hyper::{Request, Client};

let url = "http://www.rust-lang.org";
let uri: Uri = url.parse().unwrap();

let request = Request::builder()
    .method("GET")
    .uri(uri)
    .header("User-Agent", "hyper/0.14.2")
    .header("Accept", "text/html")
    .body(hyper::Body::empty()).unwrap();

let future = async {
    let client = Client::new();
    client.request(request).await.unwrap()
};
let test = spawn_task!(future);
let response = future::block_on(test);
println!("Response status: {}", response.status());
```

However, if we run the tutorial code, we would get the following error:

```
thread '<unnamed>' panicked at 'there is no reactor
running, must be called from the context of a Tokio 1.x runtime
```

This is because under the hood, *hyper* by default runs on the *Tokio* runtime and no executor is specified in our code. If you were going to use the *reqwest* or other popular crates, chances are you will get a similar error.

To address the issue, we will create a custom executor that can handle our tasks within the custom async runtime we've built. Then we'll build a custom connector to manage the actual network connections, allowing our runtime to seamlessly integrate with *hyper* and other similar libraries.

The first step is to import the following into our program:

```
use std::net::Shutdown;
use std::net::{TcpStream, ToSocketAddrs};
use std::pin::Pin;
use std::task::{Context, Poll};
```

```
use anyhow::{bail, Context as _, Error, Result};
use async_native_tls::TlsStream;
use http::Uri;
use hyper::{Body, Client, Request, Response};
use smol::{io, prelude::*, Async};
```

We can build our own executor as follows:

```
struct CustomExecutor;

impl<F: Future + Send + 'static> hyper::rt::Executor<F> for CustomExecutor {
    fn execute(&self, fut: F) {
        spawn_task!(async {
            println!("sending request");
            fut.await;
        }).detach();
    }
}
```

This code defines our custom executor and the behavior of the execute function. Inside this function, we call our spawn_task macro. Inside, we create an async block and await for the future that was passed into the execute function. We employ the detach function; otherwise, the channel will be closed, and we will not continue with our request because of the task moving out of scope and simply being dropped. As you may recall from Chapter 3, detach will send the pointer of the task to a loop to be polled until the task has finished, before dropping the task.

We now have a custom executor that we can pass into the *hyper* client. However, our *hyper* client will still fail to make the request because it is expecting the connection to be managed by the *Tokio* runtime. To fully integrate *hyper* with our custom async runtime, we need to build our own async connector that handles network connections independently of *Tokio*.

Building an HTTP Connection

When it comes to networking requests, the protocols are well-defined and standardized. For instance, TCP has a three-step handshake to establish a connection before sending packets of bytes through that connection. Implementing the TCP connection from scratch has zero benefit unless you have very specific needs that the standardized connection protocols cannot provide. In Figure 4-1, we can see that HTTP and HTTPS are application layer protocols running over a transport protocol such as TCP.

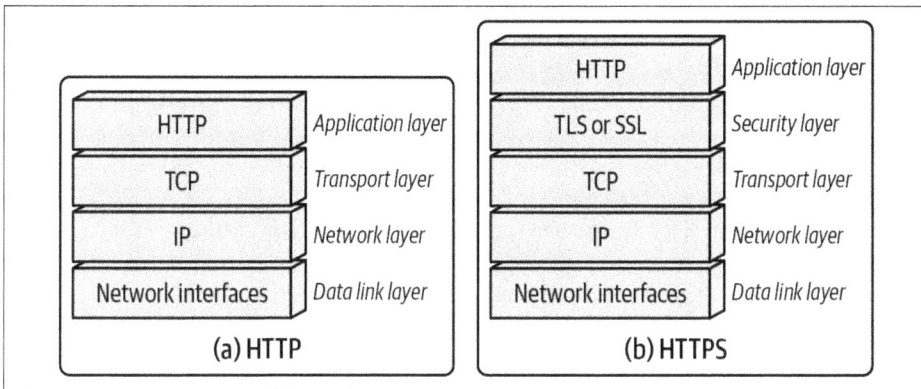

Figure 4-1. Networking protocol layers

With HTTP, we are sending over a body, header, and so forth. HTTPS has even more steps, as a certificate is checked and sent over to the client before the client starts sending over data. This is because the data needs to be encrypted. Considering all the back-and-forth in these protocols and waiting for responses, networking requests are a sensible target for async. We cannot get rid of the steps in networking without losing security and assurance that the connection is made. However, we can release the CPU from networking requests when waiting for responses with async.

For our connector, we are going to support HTTP and HTTPS, so we need the following enum:

```
enum CustomStream {
    Plain(Async<TcpStream>),
    Tls(TlsStream<Async<TcpStream>>),
}
```

The `Plain` variant is an async TCP stream. Considering Figure 4-1, we can deduce that the `Plain` variant supports HTTP requests. With the `Tls` variant, we remember that HTTPS is merely a TLS layer between the TCP and the HTTP, which means that our `Tls` variant supports HTTPS.

We can now use this custom stream enum to implement the *hyper* `Service` trait for a custom connector struct:

```
#[derive(Clone)]
struct CustomConnector;

impl hyper::service::Service<Uri> for CustomConnector {
    type Response = CustomStream;
    type Error = Error;
    type Future = Pin<Box<dyn Future<Output = Result<
                        Self::Response, Self::Error>> + Send
                    >>;
    fn poll_ready(&mut self, _: &mut Context<'_>)
```

```
        -> Poll<Result<(), Self::Error>> {
        . . .
    }
    fn call(&mut self, uri: Uri) -> Self::Future {
        . . .
    }
}
```

The Service trait defines the future for the connection. Our connection is a thread-safe future that returns our stream enum. This enum is either an async TCP connection or an async TCP connection that is wrapped in a TLS stream.

We can also see that our poll_ready function just returns Ready. This function is used by *hyper* to check whether a service is ready to process requests. If we return Pending, the task will be polled until the service becomes ready. We return an error when the service can no longer process requests. Because we are using the Service trait for a client call, we will always return Ready for the poll_ready. If we were implementing the Service trait for a server, we could have the following poll_ready function:

```
fn poll_ready(&mut self, cx: &mut Context<'_>)
    -> Poll<Result<(), Error>> {
    Poll::Ready(Ok(()))
}
```

We can see that our poll_ready function returns that the future is ready. We could, ideally, not bother defining poll_ready, as our implementation makes calling it redundant. However, this function is a requirement for the Service trait.

We can now move on to the response function, which is call. The poll_ready function needs to return Ok before we can use call. Our call function has the following outline:

```
fn call(&mut self, uri: Uri) -> Self::Future {
    Box::pin(async move {
        let host = uri.host().context("cannot parse host")?;

        match uri.scheme_str() {
            Some("http") => {
                . . .
            }
            Some("https") => {
                . . .
            }
            scheme => bail!("unsupported scheme: {:?}", scheme),
        }
    })
}
```

We remember that the `pin` and `async` block returns a future. So, our pinned future will be the `async` block's return statement. For our HTTPS block, we build a future with the following code:

```
let socket_addr = {
    let host = host.to_string();
    let port = uri.port_u16().unwrap_or(443);
    smol::unblock(move || (host.as_str(), port).to_socket_addrs())
        .await?
        .next()
        .context("cannot resolve address")?
};
let stream = Async::<TcpStream>::connect(socket_addr).await?;
let stream = async_native_tls::connect(host, stream).await?;
Ok(CustomStream::Tls(stream))
```

The port is 443 because this is the standard port for HTTPS. We then pass a closure into the unblock function. The closure returns the socket address. The unblock function runs blocking code on a thread pool so we can have the async interface on blocking code. While we are resolving the socket address, we can free up the thread to do something else. We connect our TCP stream and then connect it to our native TLS. Once our connection is achieved, we finally return the `CustomStream` enum.

When it comes to building our HTTP code, it is nearly the same. The port is 80 instead of 443, and the TLS connection is not required, resulting in returning `Ok(CustomStream::Plain(stream))`.

Our `call` function is now defined. However, if we try to make an HTTPS call to a website with our stream enum or connection struct at this point, we will get an error message stating that we have not implemented the `AsyncRead` and `AsyncWrite` *Tokio* traits for our stream trait. This is because *hyper* requires these traits to be implemented in order for our connection enum to be used.

Implementing the Tokio AsyncRead Trait

The `AsyncRead` trait (*https://oreil.ly/Y2oLi*) is similar to the `std::io::Read` trait but integrates with asynchronous task systems. When implementing our `AsyncRead` trait, we have to define only the `poll_read` function, which returns a `Poll` enum as a result. If we return `Poll::Ready`, we are saying that the data was immediately read and placed into the output buffer. If we return `Poll::Pending`, we are saying that no data was read into the buffer that we provided. We are also saying that the I/O object is not currently readable but may become readable in the future. The return of `Pending` results in the current future's task being scheduled to be unparked when the object is readable. The final `Poll` enum variant that we can return is `Ready` but with an error that would usually be a standard I/O error.

Our implementation of the `AsyncRead` trait is defined in the code here:

```
impl tokio::io::AsyncRead for CustomStream {
    fn poll_read(
        mut self: Pin<&mut Self>,
        cx: &mut Context<'_>,
        buf: &mut tokio::io::ReadBuf<'_>,
    ) -> Poll<io::Result<()>> {
        match &mut *self {
            CustomStream::Plain(s) => {
                Pin::new(s)
                    .poll_read(cx, buf.initialize_unfilled())
                    .map_ok(|size| {
                        buf.advance(size);
                    })
            }
            CustomStream::Tls(s) => {
                Pin::new(s)
                    .poll_read(cx, buf.initialize_unfilled())
                    .map_ok(|size| {
                        buf.advance(size);
                    })
            }
        }
    }
}
```

Our other streams have essentially the same treatment; we pass in either the async TCP stream or an async TCP stream with TLS. We then pin this stream and execute the stream's `poll_read` function, which performs a read and returns a `Poll` enum indicating how much the buffer grew because of the read. Once the `poll_read` is done, we execute `map_ok`, which takes in `FnOnce(T)`, which is either a function or a closure that can be called only once.

> In the context of `map_ok`, the closure's purpose is to advance the buffer by the size returned from `poll_read`. This is a one-time operation for each read, and hence `FnOnce` is sufficient and preferred. If the closure needed to be called multiple times, `Fn` or `FnMut` would be required. By using `FnOnce`, we ensure that the closure can take ownership of the environment it captures, providing flexibility for what the closure can do. This is particularly useful in async programming, where ownership and lifetimes must be carefully managed.

The `map_ok` also references itself, which is the result from `poll_read`. If the `Poll` result is `Ready` but with an error, `Ready` with the error is returned. If the `Poll` result is `Pending`, `Pending` is returned. We pass the context into `poll_read` so a waker is used if we have a `Pending` result. If we have a `Ready` with an `Ok` result, the closure is called with the result from the `poll_read`, and Ready Ok is returned from the `map_ok` function. Our closure passed into our `map_ok` function advances the buffer.

A lot is going on under the hood, but essentially, our stream is pinned, a read is performed on the pinned stream, and if the read is successful, we advance the size of the buffer's filled region because the read data is now in the buffer. The polling in `poll_read`, and the matching of the `Poll` enum in `map_ok`, enable this read process to be compatible with an async runtime.

So we can now read into our buffer asynchronously, but we also need to write asynchronously for our HTTP request to be complete.

Implementing the Tokio AsyncWrite Trait

The `AsyncWrite` trait is similar to `std::io::Write` but interacts with asynchronous task systems. It write bytes asynchronously, and like the `AsyncRead` we just implemented, comes from *Tokio*.

When implementing the `AsyncWrite` trait, we need the following outline:

```
impl tokio::io::AsyncWrite for CustomStream {
    fn poll_write(
        mut self: Pin<&mut Self>,
        cx: &mut Context<'_>,
        buf: &[u8],
    ) -> Poll<io::Result<usize>> {
        . . .
    }
    fn poll_flush(mut self: Pin<&mut Self>, cx: &mut Context<'_>)
    -> Poll<io::Result<()>> {
        . . .
    }
    fn poll_shutdown(mut self: Pin<&mut Self>, cx: &mut Context<'_>)
    -> Poll<io::Result<()>> {
        . . .
    }
}
```

The `poll_write` function should not be a surprise, but note that we also have `poll_flush` and `poll_shutdown` functions. All the functions return a variant of the `Poll` enum and accept the context. Therefore, we can deduce that all functions are able to put the task to sleep to be woken again and to check whether the future is ready for shutting down, flushing, and writing to the connection.

We should start with our `poll_write` function:

```
match &mut *self {
    CustomStream::Plain(s) => Pin::new(s).poll_write(cx, buf),
    CustomStream::Tls(s) => Pin::new(s).poll_write(cx, buf),
}
```

We are matching the stream, pinning the stream, and executing the `poll_write` function of the stream. At this point in the chapter, it should not come as a surprise that `poll_write` tries to write bytes from the buffer into an object. Like the read, if the write is successful, the number of bytes written is returned. If the object is not ready for writing, we will get `Pending`; if we get 0, this usually means that the object is no longer able to accept bytes.

Inside the `poll_write` function of the stream, a loop is executed and the mutable reference of the I/O handler is obtained. The loop then repeatedly tries to write to the underlying I/O until all the bytes from the buffer are written. Each write attempt has a result that is handled. If the error of the write is `io::ErrorKind::WouldBlock`, this means that the write could not complete immediately, and the loop repeats until the write is complete. If the result is any other error, the loop waits for the resource to be available again by returning `Pending` for the future to be polled again later.

Now that we have written `poll_write`, we can define the body of the `poll_flush` function:

```
match &mut *self {
    CustomStream::Plain(s) => Pin::new(s).poll_flush(cx),
    CustomStream::Tls(s) => Pin::new(s).poll_flush(cx),
}
```

This has the same outline as our `poll_write` function. However, in this case, we call `poll_flush` on our stream. A flush is like a write except we ensure that all the contents of the buffer immediately reach the destination. The underlying mechanism of the flush is exactly the same as the write with the loop, but the flush function will be called in the loop as opposed to the write function.

We can now move on to our final function, which is `shutdown`:

```
match &mut *self {
    CustomStream::Plain(s) => {
        s.get_ref().shutdown(Shutdown::Write)?;
        Poll::Ready(Ok(()))
    }
    CustomStream::Tls(s) => Pin::new(s).poll_close(cx),
}
```

The way we implement the different types of our custom stream varies slightly. The `Plain` stream is shut down directly. Once it is shut down, we return a `Poll` that is ready. However, the `Tls` stream is an async implementation by itself. Therefore, we need to pin it to avoid having it moved in memory, because it could be put on the task queue multiple times until the poll is complete. We call the `poll_close` function, which will return a poll result by itself.

We have now implemented our async read and write traits for our *hyper* client. All we need to do now is connect and run HTTP requests to test our implementation.

Connecting and Running Our Client

In this section, we are wrapping up what we have done and testing it. We can create our connection request-sending function as follows:

```
impl hyper::client::connect::Connection for CustomStream {
    fn connected(&self) -> hyper::client::connect::Connected {
        hyper::client::connect::Connected::new()
    }
}

async fn fetch(req: Request<Body>) -> Result<Response<Body>> {
    Ok(Client::builder()
        .executor(CustomExecutor)
        .build::<_, Body>(CustomConnector)
        .request(req)
        .await?)
}
```

Now all we need to do is run our HTTP client on our async runtime in the `main` function:

```
fn main() {
    Runtime::new().with_low_num(2).with_high_num(4).run();

    let future  = async {
        let req = Request::get("https://www.rust-lang.org")
                                    .body(Body::empty())
                                    .unwrap();
        let response = fetch(req).await.unwrap();


        let body_bytes = hyper::body::to_bytes(response.into_body())
                            .await.unwrap();
        let html = String::from_utf8(body_bytes.to_vec()).unwrap();
        println!("{}", html);
    };
    let test = spawn_task!(future);
    let _outcome = future::block_on(test);
}
```

And here we have it: we can run our code to get the HTML code from the Rust website. We can now say that our async runtime can communicate with the internet asynchronously, but what about accepting requests? We already covered implementing traits from other crates to get an async implementation. So let's go one step lower and directly listen to events in sockets with the *mio* crate.

Introducing mio

When it comes to implementing async functionality with sockets, we cannot really get any lower than *mio* (*metal I/O*) without directly calling the OS. This low-level, nonblocking I/O library in Rust provides the building blocks for creating high-performance async applications. It acts as a thin abstraction over the OS's asynchronous I/O capabilities.

The *mio* crate is so crucial because it serves as a foundation for other higher-level async runtimes, including *Tokio*. These higher-level libraries abstract the complexity away to make them easier to work with. The *mio* crate is useful for developers who need fine-grained control over their I/O operations and want to optimize for performance. Figure 4-2 shows how *Tokio* is built on *mio*.

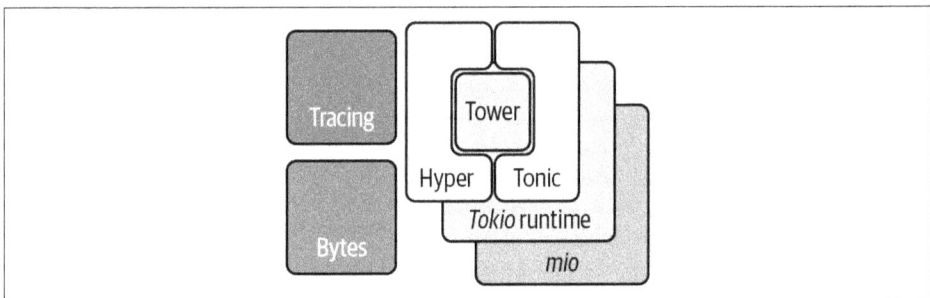

Figure 4-2. How Tokio builds on mio

Previously in this chapter, we connected *hyper* to our runtime. To get the full picture, we are now going to explore *mio* and integrate it in our runtime. Before we proceed, we need the following dependency in *Cargo.toml*:

```
mio = {version = "1.0.2", features = ["net", "os-poll"]}
```

We also need these imports:

```
use mio::net::{TcpListener, TcpStream};
use mio::{Events, Interest, Poll as MioPoll, Token};
use std::io::{Read, Write};
use std::time::Duration;
use std::error::Error;

use std::future::Future;
use std::pin::Pin;
use std::task::{Context, Poll};
```

mio Versus hyper

Our exploration of *mio* in this chapter is not an optimal approach to creating a TCP server. If you want to create a production server, you should take an approach similar to this *hyper* example:

```
#[tokio::main]
async fn main() -> Result<(), Box<dyn std::error::Error + Send + Sync>> {
    let addr = SocketAddr::from(([127, 0, 0, 1], 3000));
    let listener = TcpListener::bind(addr).await?;
    loop {
        let (stream, _) = listener.accept().await?;
        let io = TokioIo::new(stream);
        tokio::task::spawn(async move {
            if let Err(err) = http1::Builder::new()
                .serve_connection(io, service_fn(hello))
                .await
            {
                println!("Error serving connection: {:?}", err);
            }
        });
    }
}
```

The main thread is waiting for incoming data, and when incoming data arrives, a new task is spawned to handle that data. This keeps the listener ready to accept more incoming data. While our *mio* examples will help you understand how polling TCP connections work, it is most sensible to use the listener that the framework or library gives you when building a web application. We will discuss some web concepts to give context to our example, but a comprehensive overview of web development is beyond the scope of this book.

Now that we have laid all the groundwork, we can move on to polling TCP sockets in futures.

Polling Sockets in Futures

The *mio* crate is built for handling many sockets (thousands). Therefore, we need to identify which socket triggered the notification. Tokens enable us to do this. When we register a socket with the event loop, we pass it a token, and that token is returned in the handler. The token is a struct tuple around `usize`. This is because every OS allows a pointer amount of data to be associated with a socket. So in the handler we can have a mapping function where the token is the key, and we map it with a socket.

mio is not using callbacks here because we want a zero cost abstraction, and tokens are the only way of doing that. We can build callbacks, streams, and futures on top of *mio*.

With tokens, we now have the following steps:

1. Register the sockets with the event loop.

2. Wait for socket readiness.

3. Look up the socket state by using the token.

4. Operate on the socket.

5. Repeat.

Our simple example negates the need for mapping, so we are going to define our tokens with the following code:

```
const SERVER: Token = Token(0);
const CLIENT: Token = Token(1);
```

Here, we just have to ensure that our tokens are unique. The integer passed into Token is used to differentiate it from other tokens. Now that we have our tokens, we define the future that is going to poll the socket:

```
struct ServerFuture {
    server: TcpListener,
    poll: MioPoll,
}
impl Future for ServerFuture {

    type Output = String;

    fn poll(mut self: Pin<&mut Self>, cx: &mut Context<'_>)
        -> Poll<Self::Output> {
        . . .
    }
}
```

We are using TcpListener to accept incoming data and MioPoll to poll the socket and tell the future when the socket is readable. Inside our future poll function, we can define the events and poll the socket:

```
let mut events = Events::with_capacity(1);

let _ = self.poll.poll(
    &mut events,
    Some(Duration::from_millis(200))
).unwrap();


for event in events.iter() {
    . . .
}
cx.waker().wake_by_ref();
return Poll::Pending
```

The poll will extract the events from the socket into the events iterator. We also set the socket poll to time out after 200 ms. If there are no events in the socket, we proceed without any events and return Pending. We will continue polling until we get an event.

When we do get events, we loop through them. In the preceding code, we set the capacity to 1, but we can increase the capacity to handle multiple events if needed. When processing an event, we need to clarify the event type. For our future, we need to ensure that the socket is readable and that the token is the SERVER token:

```
if event.token() == SERVER && event.is_readable() {
    let (mut stream, _) = self.server.accept().unwrap();
    let mut buffer = [0u8; 1024];
    let mut received_data = Vec::new();

    loop {
        . . .
    }
    if !received_data.is_empty() {
        let received_str = String::from_utf8_lossy(&received_data);
        return Poll::Ready(received_str.to_string())
    }
    cx.waker().wake_by_ref();
    return Poll::Pending
}
```

The event is readable if the socket contains data. If our event is the correct one, we extract TcpStream and define a data_received collection on the heap with Vec, using the buffer slice to perform the reads. If the data is empty, we return Pending so we can poll the socket again if the data is not there. We then convert the data to a string and return it with Ready. This means that our socket listener is finished after we have the data.

> If we wanted our socket to be continually polled throughout the lifetime of our program, we would spawn a detached task to pass the data into an async function to handle the data, as shown here:
>
> ```
> if !received_data.is_empty() {
>     spawn_task!(some_async_handle_function(&received_data))
>         .detach();
>     return Poll::Pending;
> }
> ```

In our loop, we read the data from the socket:

```
loop {
    match stream.read(&mut buffer) {
        Ok(n) if n > 0 => {
            received_data.extend_from_slice(&buffer[..n]);
```

```
        }
        Ok(_) => {
            break;
        }
        Err(e) => {
            eprintln!("Error reading from stream: {}", e);
            break;
        }
    }
}
}
```

It does not matter if the received message is bigger than the buffer; our loop will continue to extract all the bytes to be processed, adding them onto our Vec. If there are no more bytes, we can stop our loop to process the data.

We now have a future that will continue to be polled until it accepts data from a socket. After receiving the data, the future will terminate. We can also make this future continually poll the socket. We could argue that we could use this continual polling future to keep track of thousands of sockets if needed. We would have one socket per future and spawn thousands of futures into our runtime. Now that we have defined our TcpListener logic, we can move on to our client logic to send data over the socket to our future.

Sending Data over the Socket

For our client, we are going to run everything in the main function:

```
fn main() -> Result<(), Box<dyn Error>> {
    Runtime::new().with_low_num(2).with_high_num(4).run();
    . . .
    Ok(())
}
```

In our main, we initially create our listener and our stream for the client:

```
let addr = "127.0.0.1:13265".parse()?;
let mut server = TcpListener::bind(addr)?;
let mut stream = TcpStream::connect(server.local_addr()?)?;
```

Our example requires just one stream, but we can create multiple streams if needed. We register our server with a mio poll and use the server and poll to spawn the listener task:

```
let poll: MioPoll = MioPoll::new()?;
poll.registry()
.register(&mut server, SERVER, Interest::READABLE)?;

let server_worker = ServerFuture{
    server,
    poll,
```

```
};
let test = spawn_task!(server_worker);
```

Now our task is continually polling the TCP port for incoming events. We then create another poll with the CLIENT token for writable events. If the socket is not full, we can write to it. If the socket is full, it is no longer writable and needs to be flushed. Our client poll takes the following form:

```
let mut client_poll: MioPoll = MioPoll::new()?;
client_poll.registry()
.register(&mut stream, CLIENT, Interest::WRITABLE)?;
```

> With *mio*, we can also create polls that can trigger if the socket is readable or writable:
>
> ```
> .register(
>         &mut server,
>         SERVER,
>         Interest::READABLE | Interest::WRITABLE
> )?;
> ```

Now that we have created our poll, we can wait for the socket to become writable before writing to it. We use this poll call:

```
let mut events = Events::with_capacity(128);

let _ = client_poll.poll(
    &mut events,
    None
).unwrap();
```

Note that there is a None for the timeout. This means that our current thread will be blocked until an event is yielded by the poll call. Once we have the event, we send a simple message to the socket:

```
for event in events.iter() {
    if event.token() == CLIENT && event.is_writable() {
        let message = "that's so dingo!\n";
        let _ = stream.write_all(message.as_bytes());
    }
}
```

The message is sent, so we can block our thread and then print out the message:

```
let outcome = future::block_on(test);
println!("outcome: {}", outcome);
```

When running the code, you might get the following printout:

```
Error reading from stream: Resource temporarily unavailable (os error 35)
outcome: that's so dingo!
```

It works, but we get the initial error. This can be a result of nonblocking TCP listeners; *mio* is nonblocking. The `Resource temporarily unavailable` error is usually caused by no data being available in the socket. This can happen when the TCP stream is created, but it is not a problem because we handle these errors in our loop and are returning `Pending` so the socket continues to be polled, as shown here:

```
use std::io::ErrorKind;
. . .
Err(ref e) if e.kind() == ErrorKind::WouldBlock => {
    waker.cx.waker().wake_by_ref();
    return Poll::Pending;
}
```

> With the *mio* polling feature, we have implemented async communication through a TCP socket. We can also use *mio* to send data between processes via a `UnixDatagram`. `UnixDatagrams` are sockets that are restricted to sending data on the same machine. Because of this, `UnixDatagrams` are faster, require less context switching, and do not have to go through the network stack.

Summary

We finally managed to get our async runtime to do something apart from sleep and print. In this chapter, we explored how traits can help us integrate third-party crates into our runtime, and we have gone lower to poll TCP sockets via *mio*. When it comes to getting a custom async runtime running, nothing else is standing in your way as long as you have access to trait documentation. If you want to get a better grip on the async knowledge you've gained so far, you are in the position to create a basic web server that handles various endpoints. Implementing all your communication in *mio* would be difficult, but using it just for async programming is much easier. The *hyper* `HttpListener` will cover the protocol complexity so you can focus on passing the requests as async tasks and on the response to the client.

For our journey in this book, we are exploring async programming as opposed to web programming. Therefore, we are going to move on to how we implement async programming to solve specific problems. We start in Chapter 5 with coroutines.

CHAPTER 5

Coroutines

At this stage in the book, you should be comfortable with async programming. When you see await syntax in code now, you know what is happening under the hood with futures, tasks, threads, and queues. However, what about the building blocks of async programming? What if we can get our code to pause and resume without having to use an async runtime? Furthermore, what if we can use this pause-and-resume mechanism to test our code by using normal tests? These tests can explore how code behaves under various polling orders and configurations. Our pause-and-resume mechanism can also be the interface between synchronous code and async. This is where coroutines come in.

By the end of this chapter, you should be able to define a coroutine and explain how they can be used. You should be able to integrate coroutines into your own programs to keep memory consumption low for tasks that would require large amounts of memory. You will also be able to mimic async functionality without an async runtime by using coroutines and implement a basic executor. This results in getting async functionality in your main thread without the need for an async runtime. You will also be able to gain fine-grained control over when and in what order your coroutines get polled.

At the time of this writing, we are using the coroutine syntax in nightly Rust. The syntax might have changed, or the coroutine syntax might have made its way to stable Rust. Although changing syntax is annoying, it is the fundamentals of coroutines that we are covering in this chapter. Syntax changes will not affect the overall implementation of coroutines and how we can use them.

Introducing Coroutines

Before we can fully explore coroutines, you need to understand what a coroutine is and why you'd want to use it.

What Are Coroutines?

A *coroutine* is a special type of program that can pause its execution and then at a later point in time resume from where it left off. This is different from regular subroutines (like functions), which run to completion and typically return a value or throw an error. Figure 5-1 illustrates the comparison.

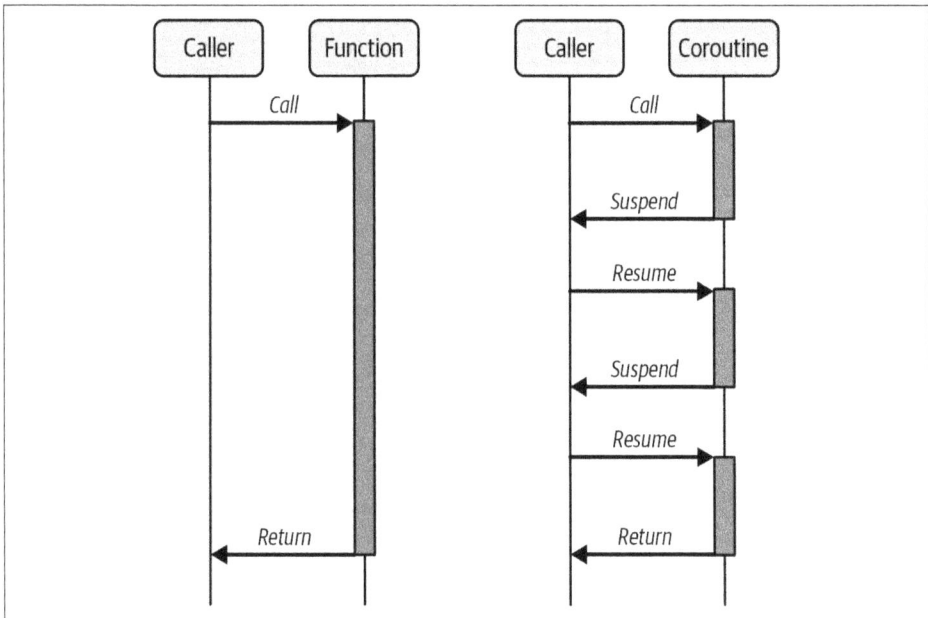

Figure 5-1. A regular subroutine (left) versus a coroutine (right)

Let's compare a coroutine to a subroutine. After a subroutine starts, it executes from the start to the end, and any particular instance of a subroutine returns just one time. A coroutine is different, as it can exit in multiple ways. It can finish like a subroutine, but it can also exit by calling another coroutine (called *yielding*) and then returning later to the same point. Therefore, a coroutine keeps track of the state by storing it during the pause.

A coroutine is not unique to Rust, and many implementations of coroutines exist in different languages. They all share the same basic features to allow for pausing and resuming execution:

Nonblocking

When coroutines get paused, they do not block the thread of execution.

Stateful

Coroutines can store their state when they are paused and then continue from that state when they are resumed. There is no need to start from the beginning.

Cooperative

Coroutines can pause and be resumed at a later stage in a controlled manner.

Now let's think about how coroutines are similar to threads. On the face of it, they seem quite similar—executing tasks and later pausing/resuming. The difference is in the scheduling. A thread is scheduled *preemptively*: the task is interrupted by an external scheduler with the aim that the task will be resumed later. In contrast, a coroutine is cooperative: it can pause or yield to another coroutine without a scheduler or the OS getting involved.

Using coroutines sounds great, so why bother with async/await at all? As with anything in programming, trade-offs exist here. Let's run through some pros to start with. Coroutines remove the need for syncing primitives like mutexes, as the coroutines are running in the same thread. This can make it easier to understand and write the code, not an insignificant consideration. Switching back and forth between coroutines in one thread is much cheaper than switching between threads. It is particularly useful for tasks where you might spend a lot of time waiting. Imagine that you need to keep track of changes in 100 files. Having the OS schedule 100 threads that loop through and check each file would be a pain. Context switching is computationally expensive. It would be more efficient and easier instead to have 100 coroutines checking whether the file they are monitoring has changed and then sending that file into a thread pool to be processed when it has.

The major downside to using coroutines in just one thread is that you are not taking advantage of the power of your computer. Running a program in one thread means you are not splitting tasks across multiple cores. Now that you know what coroutines are, let's explore why we should use them.

Why Use Coroutines?

At a high level, coroutines enable us to suspend an operation, yield control back to the thread that executed the coroutine, and then resume the operation when needed. This sounds a lot like async. An async task can yield control for another task to be executed through polling. With multithreading, we can send data to the thread and check in on the thread as needed through channels and data structures wrapped in Sync primitives. Coroutines, on the other hand, enable us to suspend an operation and resume with the waker without needing an async runtime or thread.

This may seem a little abstract, but we should illustrate the advantages of using a coroutine with a simple file-writing example. Let's imagine that we are getting a lot of integers and we need to write them to a file. Perhaps we are getting numbers from another program, and we can't wait for all the numbers to be received before we start writing, as this would take up too much memory.

For our exercise, we need the following dependency:

```
[dependencies]
rand = "0.8.5"
```

Before we write the code for our demonstration, we need the following imports:

```
#![feature(coroutines)]
#![feature(coroutine_trait)]
use std::fs::{OpenOptions, File};
use std::io::{Write, self};
use std::time::Instant;
use rand::Rng;

use std::ops::{Coroutine, CoroutineState};
use std::pin::Pin;
```

We also need the *rand* crate in our *Cargo.toml*. These imports might seem a little excessive for a simple write exercise, but you will see how they are utilized when we move through this example. The macros are there to allow the experimental features. For our simple file-writing example, we have the following function:

```
fn append_number_to_file(n: i32) -> io::Result<()> {
    let mut file = OpenOptions::new()
        .create(true)
        .append(true)
        .open("numbers.txt")?;
    writeln!(file, "{}", n)?;
    Ok(())
}
```

This function opens the file and writes to it. We now want to test it and measure our performance, so we generate 200 thousand random integers and loop through them, writing to the file. We also time this operation with the following code:

```
fn main() -> io::Result<()> {
    let mut rng = rand::thread_rng();
    let numbers: Vec<i32> = (0..200000).map(|_| rng.gen()).collect();

    let start = Instant::now();
    for &number in &numbers {
        if let Err(e) = append_number_to_file(number) {
            eprintln!("Failed to write to file: {}", e);
        }
    }
    let duration = start.elapsed();
```

Implementing a Simple Generator in Rust

Let's imagine we want to pull in information from a large data structure contained in a datafile. The datafile is very large, and ideally, we do not want to load it into memory all at once. For our example, we will use a very small datafile of just five rows to demonstrate streaming. Remember, this is an educational example; in the real world, using a generator to read a five-line datafile would be considered overkill! You can make this yourself. We have saved a datafile with five rows, with a number on each row in our project called *data.txt*.

We need the coroutine features in the previous example, and we import those components:

```
#![feature(coroutines)]
#![feature(coroutine_trait)]
use std::fs::File;
use std::io::{self, BufRead, BufReader};
use std::ops::{Coroutine, CoroutineState};
use std::pin::Pin;
```

Now let's create our `ReadCoroutine` struct:

```
struct ReadCoroutine {
    lines: io::Lines<BufReader<File>>,
}

impl ReadCoroutine {
    fn new(path: &str) -> io::Result<Self> {
        let file = File::open(path)?;
        let reader = BufReader::new(file);
        let lines = reader.lines();

        Ok(Self { lines })
    }
}
```

Then we implement the `Coroutine` trait for this struct. Our input file contains the numbers 1 to 5, so we are going to be yielding an `i32`:

```
impl Coroutine<()> for ReadCoroutine {
    type Yield = i32;
    type Return = ();

    fn resume(mut self: Pin<&mut Self>, _arg: ())
    -> CoroutineState<Self::Yield, Self::Return> {
        match self.lines.next() {
            Some(Ok(line)) => {
                if let Ok(number) = line.parse::<i32>() {
                    CoroutineState::Yielded(number)
                } else {
                    CoroutineState::Complete(())
                }
```

```
        }
            Some(Err(_)) | None => CoroutineState::Complete(()),
        }
    }
}
```

The coroutine contains a `Yield` statement that allows us to yield a value out of the generator. The coroutine trait has only one required method, which is `resume`. This allows us to resume execution, picking up at the previous execution point. In our case, the `resume` method reads lines from the file, parses them into integers, and yields them until no more lines are left to yield, at which point it completes.

Now we will call our function on our test file:

```
fn main() -> io::Result<()> {
    let mut coroutine = ReadCoroutine::new("./data.txt")?;

    loop {
        match Pin::new(&mut coroutine).resume(()) {
            CoroutineState::Yielded(number) => println!("{:?}", number),
            CoroutineState::Complete(()) => break,
        }
    }

    Ok(())
}
```

You should get this printout:

```
1
2
3
4
5
```

> The `Coroutine` trait was previously known as the `Generator` trait and `GeneratorState`, with the name changes taking place in late 2023. If you have an older version of nightly Rust already installed, you will need to update it for the following code to work.

Now we are going to move on to how we can use two coroutines together, with them yielding to each other. This is where you will start to see some of the power of using coroutines.

Stacking Our Coroutines

In this section, we'll use a file transfer to demonstrate how two coroutines can be used sequentially. This is useful because we might want to transfer a file that is so big, we would not be able to fit all the data into memory. But transferring data bit by bit will enable us to transfer all the data without running out of memory. To enable this solution, one coroutine reads a file and yields values while another coroutine receives values and writes them to a file.

We will reuse our ReadCoroutine and add in our WriteCoroutine from the first section of this chapter. In that example, we wrote 200 thousand random numbers to a file called *numbers.txt*. Let's reuse this as the file that we wish to transfer. We will read in *numbers.txt* and write to a file called *output.txt*.

We rewrite the WriteCoroutine slightly so it is expecting a path rather than hardcoding it in:

```
struct WriteCoroutine {
    pub file_handle: File,
}

impl WriteCoroutine {
    fn new(path: &str) -> io::Result<Self> {
        let file_handle = OpenOptions::new()
            .create(true)
            .append(true)
            .open(path)?;
        Ok(Self { file_handle })
    }
}
```

Now we create a manager that has a reader and writer coroutine:

```
struct CoroutineManager{
    reader: ReadCoroutine,
    writer: WriteCoroutine
}
```

We need to create a function that sets off our file transfer. First, we will create the new function that instantiates the coroutine manager. This sets read and write filepaths. Second, we will create a new function called run. We need to pin the reader and write in memory so that they can be used throughout the lifetime of the program.

We'll then create a loop that incorporates both the reader and write functionality. The reader is matched to either Yielded or Complete. If it is Yielded (i.e., there is an output), the writer coroutine takes this in and writes it to the file.

If there are no more numbers left to read, we break the loop. Here is the code:

```
impl CoroutineManager {
    fn new(read_path: &str, write_path: &str) -> io::Result<Self> {
        let reader = ReadCoroutine::new(read_path)?;
        let writer = WriteCoroutine::new(write_path)?;

        Ok(Self {
            reader,
            writer,
```

```
        })
    }
    fn run(&mut self) {
        let mut read_pin = Pin::new(&mut self.reader);
        let mut write_pin = Pin::new(&mut self.writer);

        loop {
            match read_pin.as_mut().resume(()) {
                CoroutineState::Yielded(number) => {
                    write_pin.as_mut().resume(number);
                }
                CoroutineState::Complete(()) => break,
            }
        }
    }
}
```

We can use this in `main`:

```
fn main() {
    let mut manager = CoroutineManager::new(
        "numbers.txt", "output.txt"
    ).unwrap();
    manager.run();
}
```

Once you have run this, you can open your new *output.txt* file to double-check that you have the correct contents.

Let's recap what we have done here. In essence, we have created a file transfer. One coroutine reads a file line by line and yields its values to another coroutine. This coroutine receives values and writes to the file. In both, the file handles are kept open for the whole execution, which means we don't have to keep contending with slow I/O. With this type of lazy loading and writing, we can queue up a program to work on processing multiple file transfers, one at a time. Zooming out, you can see the benefit of this approach. We could use this to move 100 large files of multiple gigabytes each from one location to another or even over a network.

Calling a Coroutine from a Coroutine

In the previous example, we used a coroutine to yield a value that was then taken in by the writer coroutine. This process is handled by a manager. In an ideal situation, we would like to remove the need for a manager at all and to allow the coroutines to call each other directly and pass back and forth. These are called *symmetric coroutines* and are used in other languages. This feature does not come as standard (yet) in Rust, and in order to implement something similar to this, we need to move away from using the Yielded and Complete syntax.

We will create our own trait called SymmetricCoroutine. This has one function, resume_with_input. This takes in an input and provides an output:

```
trait SymmetricCoroutine {
    type Input;
    type Output;

    fn resume_with_input(
        self: Pin<&mut Self>, input: Self::Input
    ) -> Self::Output;
}
```

We can now implement this trait for our ReadCoroutine. This outputs values of the type i32. Note we are not using Yielded here anymore but are still using the line parser. This will output the values we need:

```
impl SymmetricCoroutine for ReadCoroutine {
    type Input = ();
    type Output = Option<i32>;

    fn resume_with_input(
        mut self: Pin<&mut Self>, _input: ()
    ) -> Self::Output {
        if let Some(Ok(line)) = self.lines.next() {
            line.parse::<i32>().ok()
        } else {
            None
        }
    }
}
```

For the WriteCoroutine, we implement this trait as well:

```
impl SymmetricCoroutine for WriteCoroutine {
    type Input = i32;
    type Output = ();

    fn resume_with_input(
        mut self: Pin<&mut Self>, input: i32
    ) -> Self::Output {
        writeln!(self.file_handle, "{}", input).unwrap();
    }
}
```

Finally, we put this together in main:

```
fn main() -> io::Result<()> {
    let mut reader = ReadCoroutine::new("numbers.txt")?;
    let mut writer = WriteCoroutine::new("output.txt")?;

    loop {
        let number = Pin::new(&mut reader).resume_with_input(());
        if let Some(num) = number {
```

```
            Pin::new(&mut writer).resume_with_input(num);
        } else {
            break;
        }
    }
    }
    Ok(())
}
```

The `main` function is explicitly instructing how the coroutines should work together. This involves manually scheduling, so technically it does not meet the criteria for truly symmetrical coroutines. We are mimicking some of the functionality of symmetrical coroutines as an educational exercise. A true symmetrical coroutine would pass control from the reader to the writer without having to return to the `main` function; this is restricted by Rust's borrowing rules, as both coroutines will need to reference each other. Despite this, it is still a useful example to demonstrate how writing your own coroutines can provide more functionality.

We are now going to move on to looking at async behavior and how we can mimic some of this functionality with simple coroutines.

Mimicking Async Behavior with Coroutines

For this exercise, we need the following imports:

```
#![feature(coroutines, coroutine_trait)]
use std::{
    collections::VecDeque,
    future::Future,
    ops::{Coroutine, CoroutineState},
    pin::Pin,
    task::{Context, Poll},
    time::Instant,
};
```

In the introduction to this chapter, we discussed how similar coroutines are to async programming, because execution is suspended and later resumed when certain conditions are met. A strong argument could be made that all async programming is a subset of coroutines. Async runtimes are essentially coroutines across threads.

We can demonstrate the pausing of executions with this simple example. First, we set up a coroutine that sleeps for 1 second:

```
struct SleepCoroutine {
    pub start: Instant,
    pub duration: std::time::Duration,
}
impl SleepCoroutine {
    fn new(duration: std::time::Duration) -> Self {
        Self {
            start: Instant::now(),
```

```
                duration,
            }
        }
    }
    impl Coroutine<()> for SleepCoroutine {
        type Yield = ();
        type Return = ();

        fn resume(
            self: Pin<&mut Self>, _: ())
        -> CoroutineState<Self::Yield, Self::Return> {
            if self.start.elapsed() >= self.duration {
                CoroutineState::Complete(())
            } else {
                CoroutineState::Yielded(())
            }
        }
    }
}
```

We will set up three instances of SleepCoroutine that will run at the same time. Each instance sleeps for 1 second.

We create a counter and use this to loop through the queue of coroutines—yielding or completing. Finally, we time the whole operation:

```
fn main() {
    let mut sleep_coroutines = VecDeque::new();
    sleep_coroutines.push_back(
        SleepCoroutine::new(std::time::Duration::from_secs(1))
    );
    sleep_coroutines.push_back(
        SleepCoroutine::new(std::time::Duration::from_secs(1))
    );
    sleep_coroutines.push_back(
        SleepCoroutine::new(std::time::Duration::from_secs(1))
    );

    let mut counter = 0;
    let start = Instant::now();

    while counter < sleep_coroutines.len() {
        let mut coroutine = sleep_coroutines.pop_front().unwrap();
        match Pin::new(&mut coroutine).resume(()) {
            CoroutineState::Yielded(_) => {
                sleep_coroutines.push_back(coroutine);
            },
            CoroutineState::Complete(_) => {
                counter += 1;
            },
        }
    }
    println!("Took {:?}", start.elapsed());
}
```

This takes 1 second to complete, yet we are carrying out 3 coroutines that each take 1 second to complete. We might therefore expect it to therefore take 3 seconds in total. The shortened amount of time occurs precisely because they are coroutines: they are able to pause their execution and resume at a later time. We are not using *Tokio* or any other asynchronous runtime. All operations are running in a single thread. They are simply pausing and resuming.

In a way, we have written our own specific executor for this use case. We can even use the executor syntax to make this even clearer. Let's create an `Executor` struct that uses `VecDeque`:

```
struct Executor {
    coroutines: VecDeque<Pin<Box<
        dyn Coroutine<(), Yield = (), Return = ()>
    >>>,
}
```

Now we add the basic functionality of `Executor`:

```
impl Executor {
    fn new() -> Self {
        Self {
            coroutines: VecDeque::new(),
        }
    }
}
```

We define an `add` function that reuses the same code we had before, where coroutines can be returned to the queue:

```
fn add(&mut self, coroutine: Pin<Box<
    dyn Coroutine<(), Yield = (), Return = ()>>>)
{
    self.coroutines.push_back(coroutine);
}
```

Finally, we wrap our coroutine state code into a function called `poll`:

```
fn poll(&mut self) {
    println!("Polling {} coroutines", self.coroutines.len());
    let mut coroutine = self.coroutines.pop_front().unwrap();
    match coroutine.as_mut().resume(()) {
        CoroutineState::Yielded(_) => {
            self.coroutines.push_back(coroutine);
        },
        CoroutineState::Complete(_) => {},
    }
}
```

Our main function can now create the executor, add the coroutines, and then poll them until they are all complete:

```
fn main() {
    let mut executor = Executor::new();

    for _ in 0..3 {
        let coroutine = SleepCoroutine::new(
            std::time::Duration::from_secs(1)
        );
        executor.add(Box::pin(coroutine));
    }
    let start = Instant::now();
    while !executor.coroutines.is_empty() {
        executor.poll();
    }
    println!("Took {:?}", start.elapsed());
}
```

That's it! We have created our first Executor. We will build on this in Chapter 11. Now that we have essentially achieved async functionality from our coroutines and executor, let's really drive home the relationship between async and coroutines by implementing the Future trait for our SleepCoroutine with the following code:

```
impl Future for SleepCoroutine {
    type Output = ();

    fn poll(mut self: Pin<&mut Self>, cx: &mut Context<'_>)
        -> Poll<Self::Output> {
        match Pin::new(&mut self).resume(()) {
            CoroutineState::Complete(_) => Poll::Ready(()),
            CoroutineState::Yielded(_) => {
                cx.waker().wake_by_ref();
                Poll::Pending
            },
        }
    }
}
```

To recap, this example demonstrates that coroutines pause and resume, similarly to the way async/await works. The difference is that we are using coroutines in a single thread. The major drawback here is that you have to write the coroutine and, if you want, your own executor. This means that they can be highly coupled to the problem you are trying to solve.

In addition to this major drawback, we also lose the benefit of having a pool of threads. Defining your own coroutine may be justified when having the async runtime might be overkill. We also could use coroutines when we want extra control. For instance, we do not really have much control over when an async task is polled in relation to other async tasks when the async task is sent to the runtime. This brings us to our next topic, controlling coroutines.

Controlling Coroutines

Throughout this book, we have controlled the flow of the async task internally. For instance, when we implement the `Future` trait, we get to choose when to return `Pending` or `Ready`, depending on the internal logic of the `poll` function. The same goes for our async functions; we choose when the async task might yield control back to the executor with the `await` syntax and choose when the async task returns `Ready` with return statements.

We can control these async tasks with external `Sync` primitives such as atomic values and mutexes by getting the async task to react to changes and values in these atomic values and mutexes. However, the logic reacting to external signals has to be coded into the async task before sending the async task to the runtime. For simple cases, this can be fine, but it does expose the async tasks to being brittle if the system around the async task is evolving. This also makes the async task harder to use in other contexts. The async task might also need to know the state of other async tasks before reacting, and this can lead to potential problems such as deadlocks.

> A deadlock can happen if task A requires something from task B to progress, and task B requires something from task A to progress, resulting in an impasse. We cover deadlocking, livelocking, and other potential pitfalls with ways to test for them in Chapter 11.

This is where the ease of external control in coroutines can come in handy. To demonstrate how external control can simplify our program, we are going to write a simple program that loops through a vector of coroutines that have a value as well as a status of being alive or dead. When the coroutine gets called, a random number gets generated for the value, and this value is then yielded. We can accumulate all these values and come up with a simple rule of when to kill the coroutine. For the random-number generation, we need this dependency:

```
[dependencies]
rand = "0.8.5"
```

And we need the following imports:

```
#![feature(coroutines, coroutine_trait)]
use std::{
    ops::{Coroutine, CoroutineState},
    pin::Pin,
    time::Duration,
};
use rand::Rng;
```

Now we can build a random-number coroutine:

```
struct RandCoRoutine {
    pub value: u8,
    pub live: bool,
}
impl RandCoRoutine {
    fn new() -> Self {
        let mut coroutine = Self {
            value: 0,
            live: true,
        };
        coroutine.generate();
        coroutine
    }
    fn generate(&mut self) {
        let mut rng = rand::thread_rng();
        self.value = rng.gen_range(0..=10);
    }
}
```

Considering that external code is going to be controlling our coroutine, we use a simple generator implementation:

```
impl Coroutine<()> for RandCoRoutine {
    type Yield = u8;
    type Return = ();

    fn resume(mut self: Pin<&mut Self>, _: ())
        -> CoroutineState<Self::Yield, Self::Return> {
        self.generate();
        CoroutineState::Yielded(self.value)
    }
}
```

We can use this generator all over the codebase, as it does what is said on the tin. External dependencies are not needed to run our coroutine, and our testing is also simple. In our main function, we create a vector of these coroutines, calling them until all the coroutines in the vector are dead:

```
let mut coroutines = Vec::new();
for _ in 0..10 {
    coroutines.push(RandCoRoutine::new());
}
let mut total: u32 = 0;

loop {
    let mut all_dead = true;
    for mut coroutine in coroutines.iter_mut() {
        if coroutine.live {
            . . .
        }
    }
```

```
        if all_dead {
            break
        }
    }
    println!("Total: {}", total);
```

If our coroutine in the loop is alive, we can assume that all the coroutines are not dead, setting the all_dead flag to false. We then call the resume function on the coroutine, extract the result, and come up with a simple rule on whether to kill the coroutine:

```
all_dead = false;
match Pin::new(&mut coroutine).resume(()) {
    CoroutineState::Yielded(result) => {
        total += result as u32;
    },
    CoroutineState::Complete(_) => {
        panic!("Coroutine should not complete");
    },
}
if coroutine.value < 9 {
    coroutine.live = false;
}
```

If we reduce the cutoff for killing the coroutine in the loop, the end total will be higher, as the cutoff is harder to achieve. We are in our main thread, so we have access to everything in that thread. For instance, we could keep track of all dead coroutines and start reanimating coroutines if that number gets too high. We could also use the death number to change the rules of when to kill a coroutine. Now, we could still achieve this toy example in an async task. For instance, a future can hold and poll another future inside it with the following simple example:

```
struct NestingFuture {
    inner: Pin<Box<dyn Future<Output = ()> + Send>>,
}
impl Future for NestingFuture {
    type Output = ();

    fn poll(mut self: Pin<&mut Self>, cx: &mut Context<'_>)
        -> Poll<Self::Output> {
        match self.inner.as_mut().poll(cx) {
            Poll::Ready(_) => Poll::Ready(()),
            Poll::Pending => Poll::Pending,
        }
    }
}
```

Nothing is stopping NestingFuture from having a vector of other futures that update their own value field every time they are polled and perpetually return Pending as a result. NestingFuture can then extract that value field and come up with rules on whether the recently polled future should be killed. However, NestingFuture would be operating in a thread in the async runtime, resulting in having limited access to data in the main thread.

Considering the ease of control over coroutines, we need to remember that it is not all or nothing. It's not coroutines versus async. With the following code, we can prove that we can send coroutines over threads:

```
let (sender, receiver) = std::sync::mpsc::channel::<RandCoRoutine>();
let _thread = std::thread::spawn(move || {
    loop {
        let mut coroutine = match receiver.recv() {
            Ok(coroutine) => coroutine,
            Err(_) => break,
        };
        match Pin::new(&mut coroutine).resume(()) {
            CoroutineState::Yielded(result) => {
                println!("Coroutine yielded: {}", result);
            },
            CoroutineState::Complete(_) => {
                panic!("Coroutine should not complete");
            },
        }
    }
});
std::thread::sleep(Duration::from_secs(1));
sender.send(RandCoRoutine::new()).unwrap();
sender.send(RandCoRoutine::new()).unwrap();
std::thread::sleep(Duration::from_secs(1));
```

Because coroutines are thread-safe and easily map the results of coroutines, we can finish our journey of understanding coroutines. We can conclude that coroutines are a computational unit that can be paused and resumed. Furthermore, these coroutines also implement Future traits, which can call the resume function and map the results of that function to the results of the poll function, as shown in Figure 5-2.

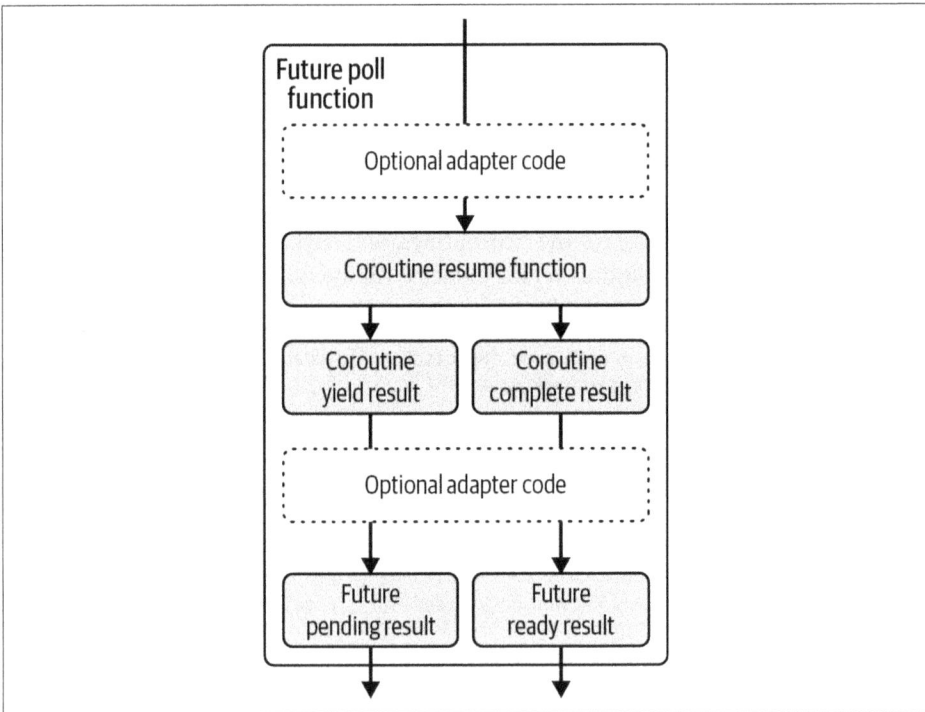

Figure 5-2. How coroutines can be async adapters

Figure 5-2 also shows that we can slot in optional adapter code between the coroutine functions and the future functions. We can then see coroutines as fundamental computational building blocks. These coroutines can be suspended and resumed in synchronous code and therefore are easy to test in standard testing environments because you do not need an async runtime to test these coroutines. You can also choose when to call the resume function of a coroutine, so testing different orders in which coroutines interact with one another is also simple.

Once you are happy with your coroutine and how it works, you can wrap one or multiple coroutines in a struct that implements the Future trait. This struct is essentially an adapter that enables coroutines to interact with the async runtime. This gives us ultimate flexibility and control over the testing and implementation of our computational processes, and a clear boundary between these computational steps and the async runtime, as the async runtime is basically a thread pool with queues. Anyone who is familiar with unit testing knows that we should not have to communicate with a thread pool to test the computational logic of a function or struct. With this in mind, let's wrap up our exploration of how coroutines fit in the world of async with testing.

Testing Coroutines

For our testing example, we do not want to excessively bloat the chapter with complex logic, so we will be testing two coroutines that acquire the same mutex and increase the value in the mutex by one. With this, we can test what happens when the lock is acquired and the end result of the lock after the interaction.

> While testing using coroutines is simple and powerful, you are not completely on the rocks with regards to testing if you are not using coroutines. Chapter 11 is dedicated to testing, and you will not see a single coroutine in that chapter.

We start with our struct that has a handle to the mutex and a threshold where the coroutine will be complete after the threshold is reached:

```
use std::ops::{Coroutine, CoroutineState};
use std::pin::Pin;
use std::sync::{Arc, Mutex};

pub struct MutexCoRoutine {
    pub handle: Arc<Mutex<u8>>,
    pub threshold: u8,
}
```

We then implement the logic behind acquiring the lock and increasing the value by one:

```
impl Coroutine<()> for MutexCoRoutine {
    type Yield = ();
    type Return = ();

    fn resume(mut self: Pin<&mut Self>, _: ())
        -> CoroutineState<Self::Yield, Self::Return> {
        match self.handle.try_lock() {
            Ok(mut handle) => {
                *handle += 1;
            },
            Err(_) => {
                return CoroutineState::Yielded(());
            },
        }
        self.threshold -=1;
        if self.threshold == 0 {
            return CoroutineState::Complete(())
        }
        return CoroutineState::Yielded(())
    }
}
```

We are trying to get the lock, but if we cannot, we do not want to block, so we will return a yield. If we get the lock, we increase the value by one, decrease our threshold by one, and then return a Yielded or Complete depending on whether our threshold is reached.

> Blocking code in an async function can cause the entire async runtime to stall because it prevents other tasks from making progress. In Rust, this concept is often referred to as *function colors*, where functions are either synchronous (blocking) or asynchronous (nonblocking). Mixing these improperly can lead to issues.
>
> For example, if the try_lock method from Mutex were to block, this would be problematic in an async context. While try_lock itself is nonblocking, you should be aware that other locking mechanisms (like lock) would block and thus should be avoided or handled carefully in async functions.

And that's it; we can test our coroutine in the same file with the following template:

```
#[cfg(test)]
mod tests {
    use super::*;
    use std::future::Future;
    use std::task::{Context, Poll};
    use std::time::Duration;

    // sync testing interface
    fn check_yield(coroutine: &mut MutexCoRoutine) -> bool {
        . . .
    }
    // async runtime interface
    impl Future for MutexCoRoutine {
        . . .
    }
    #[test]
    fn basic_test() {
        . . .
    }
    #[tokio::test]
    async fn async_test() {
        . . .
    }
}
```

Here we are going to check how our code works directly and then how our code runs in an async runtime. We have two interfaces. We do not want to have to alter our code to satisfy tests. Instead, we have a simple interface that returns a bool based on the type returned by our coroutine; here's the function definition:

```
fn check_yield(coroutine: &mut MutexCoRoutine) -> bool {
    match Pin::new(coroutine).resume(()) {
        CoroutineState::Yielded(_) => {
            true
        },
        CoroutineState::Complete(_) => {
            false
        },
    }
}
```

With our async interface, we simply map the coroutine outputs to the equivalent async outputs:

```
impl Future for MutexCoRoutine {
    type Output = ();
    fn poll(mut self: Pin<&mut Self>, cx: &mut Context<'_>)
        -> Poll<Self::Output> {
        match Pin::new(&mut self).resume(()) {
            CoroutineState::Complete(_) => Poll::Ready(()),
            CoroutineState::Yielded(_) => {
                cx.waker().wake_by_ref();
                Poll::Pending
            },
        }
    }
}
```

We are now ready to build our first basic test in the basic_test function. We initially define the mutex and coroutines:

```
let handle = Arc::new(Mutex::new(0));
let mut first_coroutine = MutexCoRoutine {
    handle: handle.clone(),
    threshold: 2,
};
let mut second_coroutine = MutexCoRoutine {
    handle: handle.clone(),
    threshold: 2,
};
```

We first want to acquire the lock ourselves and then call both coroutines, checking that they return a yield and that the value of the mutex is still zero because we have lock:

```
let lock = handle.lock().unwrap();
for _ in 0..3 {
    assert_eq!(check_yield(&mut first_coroutine), true);
    assert_eq!(check_yield(&mut second_coroutine), true);
}
assert_eq!(*lock, 0);
std::mem::drop(lock);
```

You may have noticed that we drop the lock after the initial testing of the first two yields. If we do not do this, the rest of the tests will fail, as our coroutines will never be able to acquire the lock.

We execute the loop to prove that the threshold is also not being altered when the coroutine fails to get the lock. If the threshold had been altered, after two iterations the coroutine would have returned a complete, and the next call to the coroutine would have resulted in an error. While the test would have picked this up without the loop, having the loop at the start removes any confusion as to what is causing the break in the test.

After we drop the lock, we call the coroutines twice each to ensure that they return what we expect and check on the mutex between all the calls to ensure that the state is changing in the exact way we want it:

```
assert_eq!(check_yield(&mut first_coroutine), true);
assert_eq!(*handle.lock().unwrap(), 1);
assert_eq!(check_yield(&mut second_coroutine), true);
assert_eq!(*handle.lock().unwrap(), 2);
assert_eq!(check_yield(&mut first_coroutine), false);
assert_eq!(*handle.lock().unwrap(), 3);
assert_eq!(check_yield(&mut second_coroutine), false);
assert_eq!(*handle.lock().unwrap(), 4);
```

And our first test is complete.

In our async test, we create the mutex and coroutines in the exact same way. However, we are now testing that our behavior end result is the same in an async runtime and that our async interface is working the way we expect. Because we are using the *Tokio* testing feature, we can just spawn our tasks, wait on them, and inspect the lock:

```
let handle_one = tokio::spawn(async move {
    first_coroutine.await;
});
let handle_two = tokio::spawn(async move {
    second_coroutine.await;
});
handle_one.await.unwrap();
handle_two.await.unwrap();
assert_eq!(*handle.lock().unwrap(), 4);
```

If we run the command `cargo test`, we will see that both of our tests work. And there we have it! We have inspected the interaction between two coroutines and a mutex step by step, inspecting the state between each iteration. Our coroutines work in synchronous code. But, with a simple adapter, we can also see that our coroutines work in an async runtime exactly the way we expect them to! We can see that we do not have the ability to inspect the mutex at each interaction of a coroutine with the async test. The async executor is doing its own thing.

Summary

In this chapter, we built our own coroutines by implementing the `Coroutine` trait and used `Yield` and `Complete` to pause and resume our coroutine. We implemented a pipeline in which a file can be read by one coroutine that yields values and those values can be used by a second coroutine and written to a file. Finally, we built our own executor and saw how coroutines are truly pausing and resuming.

As you worked through the chapter, you were likely struck by the similarities between `Yield`/`Complete` in coroutines and `Pending`/`Ready` in async. In our opinion, the best way to view this is that `async`/`await` is a subtype of a coroutine. It is a coroutine that operates across threads and uses queues. You can suspend an activity and come back to it in both coroutines and async programming.

Coroutines enable us to structure our code, because they can act as the seam between async and synchronous code. With coroutines, we can build synchronous code modules and then evaluate them by using standard tests. We can build adapters that are coroutines so that our synchronous code can connect with code that needs async functionality, but that async functionality is represented as coroutines. Then, we can unit-test our coroutines to see how they behave when they are polled in various orders and combinations. We can inject those coroutines into `Future` trait implementations to integrate our code into an async runtime, because we can call our coroutines in the future's `poll` function. Here, we just need to keep this async code isolated with interfaces. One async function can call your code and then pass outputs into the third-party async code, and vice versa.

A good way of isolating code is with reactive programming, where our units of code can consume data though subscriptions to broadcast channels. We explore this in Chapter 6.

CHAPTER 6

Reactive Programming

Reactive programming is a programming paradigm where code reacts to changes in data values or events. Reactive programming enables us to build systems that respond dynamically to changes in real time. It is essential to underline that this chapter is written in the context of asynchronous programming. We cannot cover every aspect of reactive programming, as entire books have been written on the topic. Instead, we are going to focus on async approaches to polling and reacting to changes in data by building a basic heater system, where futures react to changes in temperature. We will then build an event bus by using atomics (*https://oreil.ly/am-Pg*), mutexes, and queues to enable us to publish events to multiple subscribers.

By the end of this chapter, you will be familiar with enough async data-sharing concepts to construct thread-safe, mutable data structures. These data structures can be manipulated safely by multiple concurrent async tasks. You will also be able to implement the observer pattern. By the end of this chapter, you'll be equipped with the skills to build async Rust solutions to reactive design patterns that you'll find in further reading.

We start our reactive programming journey with building a basic reactive system.

Building a Basic Reactive System

In building our basic reactive system, we are going to implement the observer pattern (*https://oreil.ly/WhPxe*). With this pattern (*https://oreil.ly/FEV1o*), we have subjects and then observers that subscribe to updates of that subject. When the subject releases an update, the observers generally react to this update depending on the specific requirements of the observer. For our basic reactive system, we will build a simple heating system. The system turns on the heater when the temperature goes below the desired setting, as shown in Figure 6-1.

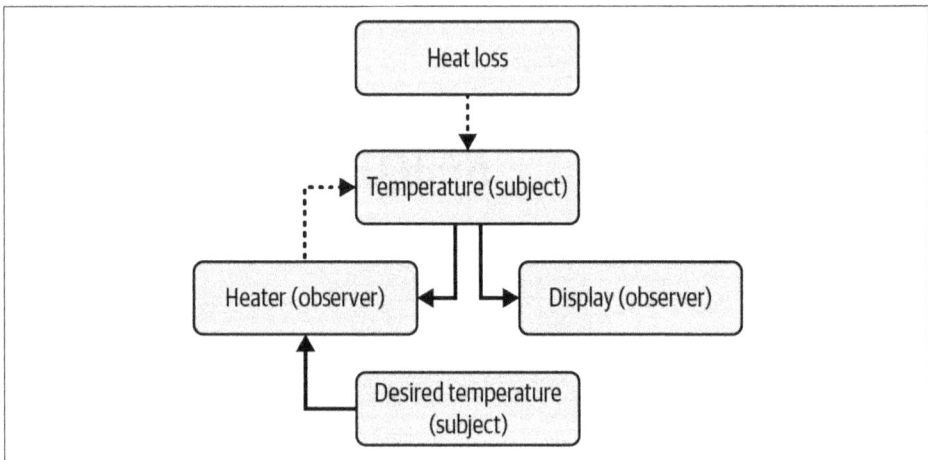

Figure 6-1. Our basic reactive heating system

In this system, the temperature and desired temperature are subjects. The heater and display are observers. Our heater will turn on if the temperature drops below the desired temperature setting. Our display will print out the temperature to the terminal if the temperature changes. In a real-life system, we would just connect our system to a temperature sensor. However, because we are using this example to explore reactive programming, we are skipping the detour into hardware engineering and making do with directly coding the effect of the heater and the heat loss on the temperature. Now that we have our system laid out, we can move onto defining our subjects.

Defining Our Subjects

Our observers in the system are going to be futures with nonstop polling since they are going to be polling the subjects continually throughout the program to see whether the subject has changed. Before we can start building our temperature system, we need the following dependencies:

```
[dependencies]
tokio = { version = "1.26.0", features = ["full"] }
clearscreen = "2.0.1"
```

We are using clearscreen to update the display of our system and the *Tokio* crate for an easy interface of async runtimes. LazyLock (which is now part of the standard library) allows for the lazy initialization of our variables, meaning they are created only when first accessed. With these dependencies, we need these imports to build our system:

```
use std::sync::Arc;
use std::sync::atomic::{AtomicI16, AtomicBool};
```

```
use core::sync::atomic::Ordering;
use std::sync::LazyLock;
use std::future::Future;
use std::task::Poll;
use std::pin::Pin;
use std::task::Context;
use std::time::{Instant, Duration};
```

We now have everything needed, so we can define our subjects:

```
static TEMP: LazyLock<Arc<AtomicI16>> = LazyLock::new(|| {
    Arc::new(AtomicI16::new(2090)) ❶
});
static DESIRED_TEMP: LazyLock<Arc<AtomicI16>> = LazyLock::new(|| {
    Arc::new(AtomicI16::new(2100)) ❷
});
static HEAT_ON: LazyLock<Arc<AtomicBool>> = LazyLock::new(|| {
    Arc::new(AtomicBool::new(false)) ❸
});
```

The subjects have the following responsibilities:

❶ The current temperature of the system.

❷ The desired temperature that we would like the room to be.

❸ Whether the heater should be on or off. If the bool is true, we instruct the heater to turn on. The heater will turn off if the bool is false.

> If you have Googled *reactive programming* or *reactive systems* before, you may have read about passing messages and events. Messages and events are certainly part of reactive programming, but we need to remember that an important part of software development is not to overengineer our system. The more complex our system is, the harder it is to maintain and change. Our system has basic feedback needs; the heater gets turned on or off based on a number. If we look into locks and channels that send messages between threads, they boil down to atomics for the locks and other data collections to handle the data. For now, just using atomics is enough because of the system's simple requirements.

Subscribing to subjects with observers decouples our code. For instance, we can easily increase the number of observers by getting the new observers to observe the subject. We do not have to alter any code in existing subjects.

We now have everything needed for our subjects, so the next step is to build an observer to display our subjects and control our HEAT_ON subject.

Building Our Display Observer

Now that our subjects are defined, we can define our display future:

```rust
pub struct DisplayFuture {
    pub temp_snapshot: i16,
}


impl DisplayFuture {
    pub fn new() -> Self {
        DisplayFuture {
            temp_snapshot: TEMP.load(Ordering::SeqCst)
        }
    }
}
```

When we create the future, we load the value of the temperature subject and store it. We are using `Ordering::SeqCst` here to ensure that the temperature value is consistent across all threads. This strict ordering guarantees that no other thread has modified the temperature in a way that we wouldn't see.

We can then use this stored temperature to compare against the temperature at the time of polling:

```rust
impl Future for DisplayFuture {
    type Output = ();

    fn poll(mut self: Pin<&mut Self>, cx: &mut Context<'_>)
        -> Poll<Self::Output> {
        let current_snapshot = TEMP.load(Ordering::SeqCst); ❶
        let desired_temp = DESIRED_TEMP.load(Ordering::SeqCst);
        let heat_on = HEAT_ON.load(Ordering::SeqCst);

        if current_snapshot == self.temp_snapshot { ❷
            cx.waker().wake_by_ref();
            return Poll::Pending
        }
        if current_snapshot < desired_temp && heat_on == false { ❸
            HEAT_ON.store(true, Ordering::SeqCst);
        }
        else if current_snapshot > desired_temp && heat_on == true { ❹
            HEAT_ON.store(false, Ordering::SeqCst);
        }
        clearscreen::clear().unwrap(); ❺
        println!("Temperature: {}\nDesired Temp: {}\nHeater On: {}", ❻
        current_snapshot as f32 / 100.0,
        desired_temp as f32 / 100.0,
        heat_on);
        self.temp_snapshot = current_snapshot; ❼
        cx.waker().wake_by_ref();
        return Poll::Pending
```

```
        }
    }
```

This code does the following:

❶ We get a snapshot of the system as a whole.

❷ We check for any difference between the snapshot of the temperature that the future holds and the current temperature. If there is no difference, there is no point re-rendering the display or making any heating decisions, so we merely return Pending, ending the poll.

❸ We check whether the current temperature is below the desired temperature. If it is, we turn the HEAT_ON flag to true.

❹ If the temperature is higher than the desired temperature, we turn the HEAT_ON flag to false.

❺ We wipe the terminal for the update.

❻ We print the current state of the snapshot.

❼ We update the snapshot that the future references.

Initially, we get a snapshot of the entire system. This approach can be up for debate. Some people argue that we should be loading the atomic values at every step. This would get the true nature of the state every time we make a decision on altering the state of the subject or displaying it. This is a reasonable argument, but trade-offs always occur when it comes to these sorts of decisions.

For our system, the display is the only observer that is going to alter the state of the HEAT_ON flag, and the logic in our future is making the decision based on the temperature. However, two other factors affect the temperature, and these could affect the temperature between the snapshot and print, as shown in Figure 6-2.

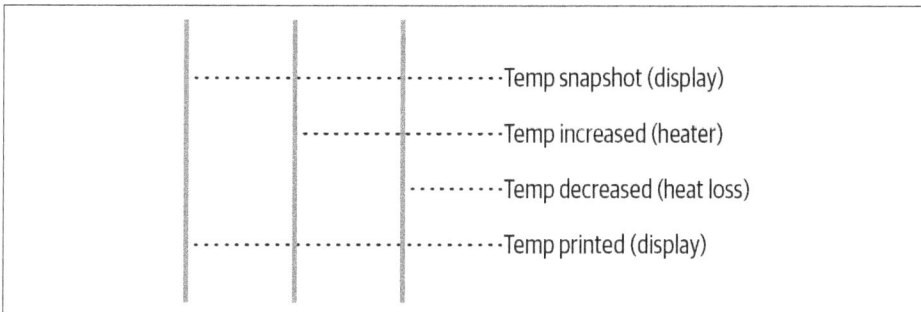

Figure 6-2. Futures affecting the temperature before the temperature snapshot is printed

In our system, it's not the end of the world if the temperature display is slightly off for a split second. It could be argued that it is more important to take a snapshot, make decisions from that snapshot, and print that snapshot in order to see the exact data used to make a decision. This would also give us clear debugging information. We could also make the snapshot, alter the state of the HEAT_ON flag based on that snapshot, and then load every atomic variable for the print to the console so the display is always accurate the split second it is printed. Logging the snapshot for the decision and loading the atomics the moment we print is also an option.

For our simple system, we are getting to the point of splitting hairs, and we will stick to printing the snapshot so we can see how our system adapts and makes decisions. However, it is important to consider these trade-offs when building a reactive system. The data your observer is acting on could already be out of date.

For our simulation, we could remove the risk of operating on out-of-date data by restricting the runtime to just one thread. This would ensure that our snapshot would not be out of date, as another future could not alter the temperature while our display future is being processed. Instead of restricting the runtime to one thread, we could wrap our temperature in a mutex, which would also ensure that our temperature would not change between the snapshot and the print.

However, our system is reacting to temperature. Temperature isn't a construct that our system just made up. Heat loss and the heater can be affecting our temperature in real time, and we would only be lying to ourselves if we came up with tricks to avoid the changing of the temperature in our system while we had another process altering the state of our subjects.

While our system is simple enough that we do not worry about out-of-date data, we can use the compare-and-exchange functionality, as shown in this code example from the standard library documentation:

```
use std::sync::atomic::{AtomicI64, Ordering};

let some_var = AtomicI64::new(5);

assert_eq!(
    some_var.compare_exchange(
        5,
        10,
        Ordering::Acquire,
        Ordering::Relaxed
    ),
    Ok(5)
);
assert_eq!(some_var.load(Ordering::Relaxed), 10);

assert_eq!(
    some_var.compare_exchange(
```

```
        6,
        12,
        Ordering::SeqCst,
        Ordering::Acquire
    ),
    Err(10)
);
assert_eq!(some_var.load(Ordering::Relaxed), 10);
```

This is where we can appreciate why atomics are called *atomics* because their transactions are atomic. This means that no other transaction will happen on the atomic value while a transaction is being performed on the value. In the `compare_exchange` function, we are asserting that the atomic value is a certain value before we update it to the new value. If the value is not what we expect, we return an error with the atomic's actual value. We can use the `compare_exchange` function to prompt observers to make another decision based on the value returned and attempt to make another update on the atomic value based on the updated information. We have now covered enough to highlight the data concurrency issues with reactive programming and areas that provide solutions. We can continue on with building our reactive system with the heater and heat-loss observers.

Building Our Heater and Heat-Loss Observer

For our heater observer to function, we need to read the `HEAT_ON` bool and not worry about the temperature. However, heaters have a time element. Sadly, at the time of this writing, we live in a world where heaters are not instant; they take time to heat up a room. So, instead of a temperature snapshot, our heater future has a time snapshot, giving our heater future the following form:

```
pub struct HeaterFuture {
    pub time_snapshot: Instant,
}

impl HeaterFuture {
    pub fn new() -> Self {
        HeaterFuture {
            time_snapshot: Instant::now()
        }
    }
}
```

Now that we have a time snapshot, we can reference it and increase the temperature after a certain duration with the `poll` function:

```
impl Future for HeaterFuture {
    type Output = ();


    fn poll(
```

```
        mut self: Pin<&mut Self>,
        cx: &mut Context<'_>
    ``) -> Poll<Self::Output> {
    if HEAT_ON.load(Ordering::SeqCst) == false { ❶
        self.time_snapshot = Instant::now();
        cx.waker().wake_by_ref();
        return Poll::Pending
    }
    let current_snapshot = Instant::now();
    if current_snapshot.duration_since(self.time_snapshot) <
                              Duration::from_secs(3) { ❷
        cx.waker().wake_by_ref();
        return Poll::Pending
    }
    TEMP.fetch_add(3, Ordering::SeqCst); ❸
    self.time_snapshot = Instant::now();
    cx.waker().wake_by_ref();
    return Poll::Pending
    }
}
```

In our heater future, we carry out the following steps:

❶ Exit as quickly as possible if the HEAT_ON flag is off because nothing is going to happen. We want to release the future from the executor as quickly as possible to avoid blocking other futures.

❷ If the duration is not over 3 seconds, we also exit because time has not elapsed for the heater to take effect.

❸ Finally, both time has elapsed and the HEAT_ON flag is on, so we increase the temperature by three.

We update self.time_snapshot at every exit opportunity the HEAT_ON flag is false but not enough time has elapsed. If we did not update time_snapshot, our heater future could be polled with the HEAT_ON flag as false until 3 seconds have elapsed. But as soon as the HEAT_ON flag is switched to true, the effect on the temperature would be instant. For our heater future, we need to reset the state between each poll.

For our heat-loss future, we have the following:

```
pub struct HeatLossFuture {
    pub time_snapshot: Instant,
}
impl HeatLossFuture {
    pub fn new() -> Self {
        HeatLossFuture {
            time_snapshot: Instant::now()
        }
```

```
        }
    }
```

For our heat-loss future, the constructor method will be the same as the heater future, because we are referencing time elapsed between each poll. However, with this poll, we reset the snapshot only after the effect has taken place because heat loss is just a constant in this simulation. We recommend that you attempt to build this future yourself. If you did attempt to build the future yourself, it hopefully takes this form:

```
impl Future for HeatLossFuture {
    type Output = ();

    fn poll(mut self: Pin<&mut Self>, cx: &mut Context<'_>) ->
                                        Poll<Self::Output> {
        let current_snapshot = Instant::now();
        if current_snapshot.duration_since(self.time_snapshot) >
                                        Duration::from_secs(3) {
            TEMP.fetch_sub(1, Ordering::SeqCst);
            self.time_snapshot = Instant::now();
        }
        cx.waker().wake_by_ref();
        return Poll::Pending
    }
}
```

We now have all our futures that will poll continually as long as the program is running. Running all our futures with the following code will result in a display that continually updates the temperature and notes whether the heater is on:

```
#[tokio::main]
async fn main() {
    let display = tokio::spawn(async {
        DisplayFuture::new().await;
    });
    let heat_loss = tokio::spawn(async {
        HeatLossFuture::new().await;
    });
    let heater = tokio::spawn(async {
        HeaterFuture::new().await;
    });
    display.await.unwrap();
    heat_loss.await.unwrap();
    heater.await.unwrap();
}
```

After the desired temperature is reached, you should see it mildly oscillate above and below the desired temperature.

Oscillations are standard in classic systems theory. If we add a time snapshot to the display and delay the switching of the HEAT_ON flag, the oscillations will get bigger. Oscillations need to be noted. If you get a delay in an observer acting, and then another observer is also delayed acting on the outcome of the initial observer, you can get a chaotic system that is very hard to understand or predict. This was a big part of supply-chain disruption during and after the COVID-19 pandemic. *Thinking in Systems* by Donella H. Meadows (Chelsea Green Publishing, 2008) shows that a delayed reaction in demand can create oscillations in a supply chain. Long supply chains have multiple parts oscillating. If the oscillations become too out of pace, you get a chaotic system that is complex to resolve. This is partly why it took a long time post pandemic to recover supply chains. Luckily, computer systems are fairly instantaneous. But it is worth keeping in mind the dangers of chaining delays and reacting to them.

Now that our system is working, we can move on to getting input from users using callbacks.

Getting User Input via Callbacks

To get user input from the terminal, we are going to use the *device_query* crate with the following version:

```
device_query = "1.1.3"
```

With this, we use these traits and structs:

```
use device_query::{DeviceEvents, DeviceState};
use std::io::{self, Write};
use std::sync::Mutex;
```

The *device_query* crate uses callbacks, which are a form of asynchronous programming. Callbacks are used to pass a function into another function. The function that is passed in is then called. We can code our own basic callback function with the following:

```
fn perform_operation_with_callback<F>(callback: F)
where
    F: Fn(i32),
{
    let result = 42;
    callback(result);
}

fn main() {
    let my_callback = |result: i32| {
        println!("The result is: {}", result);
```

```
    };
    perform_operation_with_callback(my_callback);
}
```

What we have just done is still blocking. We can make our callbacks nonblocking to the main thread by using an event loop thread that is a constant loop. This loop then accepts incoming events that are callbacks (Figure 6-3).

Figure 6-3. An event loop

For example, Node.js servers usually have a thread pool that the event loop passes events to. If our callback has a channel back to the source of where the event was emitted, data can be sent back to the source of the event when convenient.

For our input, we must keep track of the device state and input with the following:

```
static INPUT: LazyLock<Arc<Mutex<String>>> = LazyLock::new(|| {
    Arc::new(Mutex::new(String::new()))
});
static DEVICE_STATE: LazyLock<Arc<DeviceState>> = LazyLock::new(|| {
    Arc::new(DeviceState::new())
});
```

We have to think about how our code is structured. Right now, our display is being updated when the display future checks the temperature, updating the display if the temperature has changed. However, this is no longer suitable when we have user input. If we think about it, it would not be a good application if the update of the user input is displayed only if the temperature changes. This would lead to users frustratingly pressing the same key multiple times, only to be dismayed to see their multiple presses executed when the temperature updates. Our system needs to update the display the moment the user presses the key. Considering this, we need our own render function that can be called in multiple places. This function takes the following form:

```
pub fn render(temp: i16, desired_temp: i16, heat_on: bool, input: String) {
    clearscreen::clear().unwrap();
    let stdout = io::stdout();
    let mut handle = stdout.lock();
    println!("Temperature: {}\nDesired Temp: {}\nHeater On: {}",
    temp as f32 / 100.0,
    desired_temp as f32 / 100.0,
    heat_on);
    print!("Input: {}", input);
```

```
        handle.flush().unwrap();
    }
```

This function is similar to our display, but we also print out the input. This means that the poll function for our DisplayFuture calls the render function as follows:

```
#[tokio::main]
async fn main() {
    let _guard = DEVICE_STATE.on_key_down(|key| {
        let mut input = INPUT.lock().unwrap();
        input.push_str(&key.to_string());
        std::mem::drop(input);
        render(
            TEMP.load(Ordering::SeqCst),
            DESIRED_TEMP.load(Ordering::SeqCst),
            HEAT_ON.load(Ordering::SeqCst),
            INPUT.lock().unwrap().clone()
        );
    });
    let display = tokio::spawn(async {
        DisplayFuture::new().await;
    });
    let heat_loss = tokio::spawn(async {
        HeatLossFuture::new().await;
    });
    let heater = tokio::spawn(async {
        HeaterFuture::new().await;
    });
    display.await.unwrap();
    heat_loss.await.unwrap();
    heater.await.unwrap();
}
```

Notice the _guard, which is the callback guard. The callback guard in the *device_query* crate is returned when adding a callback. If we drop the guard, the event listener is removed. Luckily for us, our main thread is blocked until we exit the program because our display, heat loss, and heater tasks will continually poll until we force the program to exit.

The on_key_down function creates a thread and runs an event loop. This event loop has callbacks for mouse and keyboard movements. Once we get an event back from a keyboard press, we add it to our input state and re-render the display. We are not going to expend too much effort on mapping keys to various effects of the display, because that's a bit too in the weeds for the goal of this chapter. Running the program now, you should be able to see the input get updated with a trace of the keys that you press.

Callbacks are simple and easy to implement. The callback's execution also has a predictable flow. However, you can fall into the trap of having nested callbacks, which can evolve into a situation called *callback hell*. This results in the code being hard to maintain and follow.

You now have a basic system that takes input from users. If you want to explore this system even further, alter the input code to handle a change in desired temperature. Note that our system reacts only to basic data types. What if our system requires complex data types to represent events? Also, our system might need to know the order of events and react to all events to function correctly.

Not every reactive system is merely reacting to an integer value at the current time. For instance, if we were building a stock-trading system, we would want to know the historical data of a stock, not just the current price after we got around to polling it. We also cannot guarantee when the polling happens in async, so when we do get around to polling stock-price events, we would want access to all that had happened since the last poll in order to decide which events are important. To do this, we need an event bus that we can subscribe to.

Enabling Broadcasting with an Event Bus

An *event bus* is a system that enables parts of a wider system to send messages containing specific information. Unlike broadcast channels that have a simple pub/sub relationship, the event bus can stop at multiple stops where only a select few people get off. This means that we can have multiple subscribers for updates from a single source, but those subscribers can request that they receive only messages of a particular type, not every broadcasted message. We can have a subject that publishes an event to an event bus. Multiple observers can then consume that event in the order it was published. In this section, we are going to build our own event bus in order to explore the underlying mechanisms. However, broadcast channels are readily available in crates like *Tokio*.

> Broadcast channels are comparable to radio broadcasters. When a radio station emits a message, multiple listeners can listen to the same message as long as they all tune into the same channel. For a broadcast channel in programming, multiple listeners can subscribe to and receive the same messages. Broadcast channels are different from regular channels. In regular channels, a message is sent by one part of the program and is received by another part. In broadcast channels, a message is sent by one part of the program, and that same message is received by multiple parts of the program.

Using broadcast channels out of the box is preferable to building your own unless you have specific needs.

Before we build our event bus, we need the following dependencies:

```
tokio = { version = "1.26.0", features = ["full"] }
futures = "0.3.28"
```

And we need these imports:

```
use std::sync::{Arc, Mutex, atomic::{AtomicU32, Ordering}};
use tokio::sync::Mutex as AsyncMutex;
use std::collections::{VecDeque, HashMap};
use std::marker::Send;
```

We now have everything we need to build our event bus struct.

Building Our Event Bus Struct

Because async programming requires sending structs over threads for an async task to be polled, we are going to have to clone each event published and distribute those cloned events to every subscriber to consume. The consumers also need to be able to access a backlog of events if, for some reason, the consumer has been delayed. Consumers also need to be able to unsubscribe to events. Considering all these factors, our event bus struct takes the following form:

```
pub struct EventBus<T: Clone + Send> {
    chamber: AsyncMutex<HashMap<u32, VecDeque<T>>>,
    count: AtomicU32,
    dead_ids: Mutex<Vec<u32>>,
}
```

Our events denoted by T need to implement the Clone trait so they can be cloned and distributed to each subscriber and the Send trait to be sent across threads. Our chamber field is where subscribers with a certain ID can access their queue of events. The count field will be used to allocate IDs, and dead_ids will be used to keep track of consumers that have unsubscribed.

Note that the chamber mutex is async, and the dead_ids mutex is not async. The chamber mutex is async because we could have loads of subscribers looping and polling the chamber to access their individual queue. We do not want an executor to be blocked by an async task waiting for the mutex. This would slow the performance of the system considerably. However, when it comes to our dead_ids, we will not be looping and polling this field. It will be accessed only when a consumer wants to unsubscribe. Having a blocking mutex also enables us to easily implement an unsubscribe process if a handle is dropped. We will cover the details for this when building our handle.

For our event bus struct, we can now implement the following functions:

```
impl<T: Clone + Send> EventBus<T> {

    pub fn new() -> Self {
```

```
        Self {
            chamber: AsyncMutex::new(HashMap::new()),
            count: AtomicU32::new(0),
            dead_ids: Mutex::new(Vec::new()),
        }
    }
    pub async fn subscribe(&self) -> EventHandle<T> {
        . . .
    }
    pub fn unsubscribe(&self, id: u32) {
        self.dead_ids.lock().unwrap().push(id);
    }
    pub async fn poll(&self, id: u32) -> Option<T> {
        . . .
    }
    pub async fn send(&self, event: T) {
        . . .
    }
}
```

All of our functions have a &self reference and no mutable references. This is because we are exploiting interior mutability with the atomics and mutexes, as the mutable reference is inside the mutexes, getting around Rust's rule that we can have only one mutable reference at a time. The atomic also does not need a mutable reference, because we can perform atomic operations. This means that our event bus struct can be wrapped in an Arc and cloned multiple times to be sent across multiple threads, enabling those threads to all safely perform multiple mutable operations on the event bus. For our unsubscribe function, we merely push the ID to the dead_ids field. We cover the reasoning behind this in "Interacting with Our Event Bus via Async Tasks" on page 132.

The first operation that a consumer needs to do is to call the subscribe function of the bus, which is defined as follows:

```
pub async fn subscribe(&self) -> EventHandle<T> {
    let mut chamber = self.chamber.lock().await;
    let id = self.count.fetch_add(1, Ordering::SeqCst);
    chamber.insert(id, VecDeque::new());
    EventHandle {
        id,
        event_bus: Arc::new(self),
    }
}
```

In this code, we return an EventHandle struct, and we will define the handle in the next subsection. We are increasing the count by one, using the new count for the ID, and inserting a new queue under that ID. We then return a reference to self, which is the event bus wrapped in an Arc, coupled with the ID in a handle struct to allow the consumer to interact with the event bus.

Although increasing the count by one and using that as the new ID is an easy way of allocating IDs, high-throughput long-running systems could run out of numbers eventually. If this risk is a serious consideration, you can add another field for IDs to be reclaimed after they have been cleared from the dead_ids field. You can pull from the reclaimed IDs when allocating a new ID. Then the increase of the count happens only if there are no IDs in the reclaimed IDs.

Now that the consumer has subscribed to the bus, it can poll with the following bus function:

```
pub async fn poll(&self, id: u32) -> Option<T> {
    let mut chamber = self.chamber.lock().await;
    let queue = chamber.get_mut(&id).unwrap();
    queue.pop_front()
}
```

We unwrap directly when getting the queue in relation to the ID because we will be interacting through a handle, and we can get that handle only when we subscribe to the bus. Thus, we know that the ID is certainly in the chamber. As each ID has its own queue, each subscriber can consume all the events published in their own time. This simple implementation can be altered so the poll function returns the entire queue, replacing the existing queue with an empty queue. This new approach reduces poll calls to the bus as the consumer loops through the queue it just extracted from a poll function call on the bus. Because we are putting our own structs as the events, we could also create a timestamp trait and state that this is required for events being put on the bus. The timestamp would enable us to discard events that have expired when polling is returning only recent events.

Now that we have a basic poll function defined, we can build our send function for the bus:

```
pub async fn send(&self, event: T) {
    let mut chamber = self.chamber.lock().await;
    for (_, value) in chamber.iter_mut() {
        value.push_back(event.clone());
    }
}
```

We have everything needed for our bus to function on its internal data structures. We now need to build our own handle.

Building Our Event Bus Handle

Our handle needs to have an ID and a reference to the bus so the handle can poll the bus. Our handle is defined with the following code:

```
pub struct EventHandle<'a, T: Clone + Send> {
    pub id: u32,
    event_bus: Arc<&'a EventBus<T>>,
}
impl <'a, T: Clone + Send> EventHandle<'a, T> {

    pub async fn poll(&self) -> Option<T> {
        self.event_bus.poll(self.id).await
    }
}
```

With the lifetime notation, we can see that the handle lifetime cannot outlive the bus lifetime. We must note that Arc counts the references and drops the bus only if there are no Arcs in our async system pointing to the bus. Therefore, we can guarantee that the bus will live as long as the last handle in our system, making our handle thread-safe.

We also need to take care of dropping the handle. If the handle is removed from memory, there is no way to access the queue relating to the ID of that handle, because the handle stores the ID. However, events will keep getting sent to the queue of that ID. If a developer uses our queue and the handle is dropped in their code without explicitly calling the unsubscribe function, they will have an event bus that will fill up with multiple queues that don't have any subscribers. This situation would waste memory and even grow to the point where the computer runs out of memory, depending on certain parameters. This is called a *memory leak*, which is a real risk. Figure 6-4 is a photograph of a coffee machine that is suffering not from a coffee leak but from a memory leak.

To prevent memory leaks, we must implement the Drop trait for our handle, which will unsubscribe from the event bus when the handle is dropped:

```
impl<'a, T: Clone + Send> Drop for EventHandle<'a, T> {
    fn drop(&mut self) {
        self.event_bus.unsubscribe(self.id);
    }
}
```

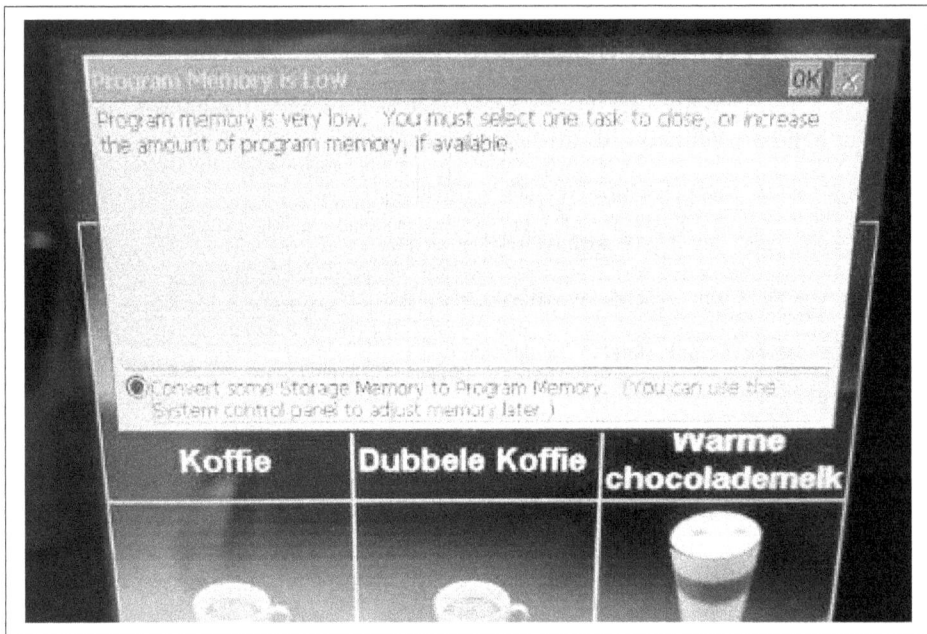

Figure 6-4. A coffee machine displaying a memory leak indicating the machine has run out of memory

Our handle is now complete, and we can use it to safely consume events from the bus without the risk of memory leaks. We are going to use our handle to build tasks that interact with our event bus.

Interacting with Our Event Bus via Async Tasks

Throughout this chapter, our observers have been implementing the Future trait and comparing the state of the subject to the state of the observer. Now that we are having events directly streamed to our ID, we can easily implement a consumer async task by using an async function:

```
async fn consume_event_bus(event_bus: Arc<EventBus<f32>>) {
    let handle = event_bus.subscribe().await;
    loop {
        let event = handle.poll().await;
        match event {
            Some(event) => {
                println!("id: {} value: {}", handle.id, event);
                if event == 3.0 {
                    break;
                }
            },
            None => {}
        }
```

```
        }
    }
```

For our example, we are streaming a float that breaks the loop if 3.0 is sent. This is just for educational purposes, but implementing logic to affect the HEAT_ON atomic bool would be trivial. We could also implement a *Tokio* async sleep function on the None branch if we did not want to loop to aggressively poll the event bus.

> The rate of creation of events can sometimes be bigger than the rate at which events can be processed. This results in a buildup of events, which is called *backpressure*. Backpressure can be solved by a range of approaches beyond the scope of this book. Concepts such as buffering, flow control, rate limiting, batch processing, and load balancing can help reduce backpressure when it builds up. We cover how to test for backpressure of channels in Chapter 11.

We also need a background task to clean up the dead IDs as a batch after a certain amount of time has elapsed. This garbage collection task can also be defined via an async function:

```
async fn garbage_collector(event_bus: Arc<EventBus<f32>>) {
    loop {
        let mut chamber = event_bus.chamber.lock().await;
        let dead_ids = event_bus.dead_ids.lock().unwrap().clone();
        event_bus.dead_ids.lock().unwrap().clear();
        for id in dead_ids.iter() {
            chamber.remove(id);
        }
        std::mem::drop(chamber);
        tokio::time::sleep(std::time::Duration::from_secs(1)).await;
    }
}
```

We drop the chamber straight after the batch removal. We do not want to block other tasks trying to access the chamber when we are not using it.

> In database systems, not deleting the record the moment the delete request is made is a common practice. This is called *tombstoning*. Instead, the database marks a record to indicate GET requests to treat the record as if it has been deleted. Then, garbage collection processes periodically clean up the tombstoned records. Cleaning and reallocating storage on every delete request is an expensive choice because you want to keep handling async requests to the database.

We have everything needed to interact with our event bus. Now, we create our event bus and the references to it:

```
let event_bus = Arc::new(EventBus::<f32>::new());
let bus_one = event_bus.clone();
let bus_two = event_bus.clone();
let gb_bus_ref = event_bus.clone();
```

Now, even if the event_bus is directly dropped, the other references will keep
the EventBus<f32> alive because of the Arc. All four references would have to be
dropped. We then start our consumers and garbage collection process tasks:

```
let _gb = tokio::task::spawn(async {
    garbage_collector(gb_bus_ref).await
});
let one = tokio::task::spawn(async {
    consume_event_bus(bus_one).await
});
let two = tokio::task::spawn(async {
    consume_event_bus(bus_two).await
});
```

In this example, we run the risk of sending events before the two tasks have subscribed, so we wait for one second and then broadcast three events:

```
std::thread::sleep(std::time::Duration::from_secs(1));
event_bus.send(1.0).await;
event_bus.send(2.0).await;
event_bus.send(3.0).await;
```

The third event is a 3.0, meaning that the consuming tasks will unsubscribe from the
bus. We can print the state of the chamber, wait for the garbage collector to wipe the
dead IDs, and then print the state again:

```
let _ = one.await;
let _ = two.await;
println!("{:?}", event_bus.chamber.lock().await);
std::thread::sleep(std::time::Duration::from_secs(3));
println!("{:?}", event_bus.chamber.lock().await);
```

Running this gives us the following printout:

```
id: 0 value: 1
id: 1 value: 1
id: 0 value: 2
id: 1 value: 2
id: 0 value: 3
id: 1 value: 3
{1: [], 0: []}
{}
```

Both subscribers receive the events, and the garbage collection works when they unsubscribe.

The event bus is the backbone of reactive programming. We can continue to add and remove subscribers in a dynamic fashion. We can have control over how the events are distributed and consumed, and implementing code that just hooks into an event bus is simple.

Summary

While it is beyond the scope of this book to give a comprehensive view of reactive programming, we covered its fundamental async properties such as polling subjects and distributing data asynchronously through an event bus we wrote ourselves. You should now be able to come up with async implementations of reactive programming.

Reactive programming is not constrained to just one program with different threads and channels. Reactive programming concepts can be applied to multiple computers and processes under the title *reactive systems*. For instance, our message bus could be sending messages to various servers in a cluster. Event-driven systems are also useful when scaling architecture. We have to remember that with reactive programming, a solution has more moving parts. We moved to event-driven systems only when the live system started to fail in performance. Reaching for reactive programming straightaway can result in convoluted solutions that are hard to maintain, so be careful.

You may have noticed that we relied on *Tokio* for implementing our async code. In Chapter 7, we cover how to customize *Tokio* to solve more problems that have constraints and nuances. Dedicating an entire chapter to *Tokio* could be considered controversial, but it is actually the most widely used async runtime in the Rust ecosystem.

Customizing Tokio

Throughout this book, we have been using *Tokio* for examples because not only is it well established, but it also has a clean syntax and you can get async examples running with just a single macro. Chances are, if you have worked on an async Rust codebase, you will have come across *Tokio*. However, so far we have used this crate only to build a standard *Tokio* runtime and then send async tasks to that runtime. In this chapter, we will customize our *Tokio* runtimes in order to have fine-grained control over how our tasks are processed in various threads of a set. We will also test whether our unsafe access to thread state is actually safe in an async runtime. Finally, we will cover how to enable graceful shutdowns when our async runtime finishes.

By the end of this chapter, you will be able to configure a *Tokio* runtime to solve your specific problem. You will also be able to specify which thread the async task is exclusively processed on so your task can rely on the thread-specific state, potentially reducing the need for locks to access data. Finally, you will be able to specify how the program is shut down when Ctrl-C or kill signals are sent to the program. So, let's get started with building the *Tokio* runtime.

Skipping this chapter will not affect your understanding of the rest of the book, as this content covers how to use *Tokio* to your liking. This chapter does not introduce new async theory.

Building a Runtime

In Chapter 3, we showed how tasks are handled in an async runtime by implementing our own task-spawning function. This gave us a lot of control over the way the tasks were processed. Our previous *Tokio* examples have merely used the #[tokio::main] macro. While this macro was useful for implementing async examples with minimal code, just implementing #[tokio::main] does not give us much control over how the async runtime is implemented. For us to explore *Tokio*, we can start with setting up a *Tokio* runtime that we can choose to call. For our configured runtime, we need the following dependencies:

```
tokio = { version = "1.33.0", features = ["full"] }
```

We also need the following structs and traits:

```
use std::future::Future;
use std::time::Duration;
use tokio::runtime::{Builder, Runtime};
use tokio::task::JoinHandle;
use std::sync::LazyLock;
```

To build our runtime, we can lean on `LazyLock` for a lazy evaluation so our runtime is defined once, just as we did when building our runtime in Chapter 3:

```
static RUNTIME: LazyLock<Runtime> = LazyLock::new(|| {
    Builder::new_multi_thread()
        .worker_threads(4)
        .max_blocking_threads(1)
        .on_thread_start(|| {
            println!("thread starting for runtime A");
        })
        .on_thread_stop(|| {
            println!("thread stopping for runtime A");
        })
        .thread_keep_alive(Duration::from_secs(60))
        .global_queue_interval(61)
        .on_thread_park(|| {
            println!("thread parking for runtime A");
        })
        .thread_name("our custom runtime A")
        .thread_stack_size(3 * 1024 * 1024)
        .enable_time()
        .build()
        .unwrap()
});
```

We get a lot of configuration out of the box, along the following properties:

`worker_threads`
    The number of threads processing async tasks.

`max_blocking_threads`
    The number of threads that can be allocated to blocking tasks. A blocking task does not allow switching because it has no `await` or requires long periods of CPU computation between `await` statements. Therefore, the thread is blocked for a fair amount of time processing the task. CPU-intensive tasks or synchronous tasks are usually referred to as blocking tasks. If we block all our threads, no other tasks can be started. As mentioned throughout the book, this can be OK,

depending on the problem your program is solving. However, if we are using async to process incoming network requests for instance, we want to still process more incoming network requests. Therefore, with `max_blocking_threads`, we can limit the number of additional threads that can be spawned to process blocking tasks. We can spawn blocking tasks with the runtime's `spawn_blocking` function.

`on_thread_start/stop`

Functions that fire when the worker thread starts or stops. This can become useful if you want to build your own monitoring.

`thread_keep_alive`

Timeout for blocking threads. Once the time has elapsed for a blocking thread, the task that has overrun that timeout limit will be cancelled.

`global_queue_interval`

The number of ticks before a new task gets attention from the scheduler. A *tick* represents one instance when the scheduler polls a task to see whether it can be run or needs to wait. In our configuration, after 61 ticks have elapsed, the scheduler will take on a new task that has been sent to the runtime. If there are no tasks to poll, the scheduler will take on a new task sent to the runtime without waiting 61 ticks. A trade-off exists between fairness and overhead. The lower the number of ticks, the quicker new tasks sent to the runtime receive attention. However, we will also be checking the queue for incoming new tasks more frequently, which comes with overhead. Our system might become less efficient if we are constantly checking for new tasks instead of making progress with existing ones. We also must acknowledge the number of `await` statements per task. If our tasks generally contain many `await` statements, the scheduler needs to work through a lot of steps, polling on each `await` statement to complete the task. However, if the task has just one `await` statement, the scheduler will require less polling to progress the task. The *Tokio* team has decided that the default tick number should be 31 for single-threaded runtimes and 61 for multithreaded runtimes. The multithreaded suggestion is a higher tick count as multiple threads are consuming tasks, resulting in these tasks getting attention at a quicker rate.

`on_thread_park`

A function that fires when the worker thread is parked. Worker threads are usually parked when the worker thread has no tasks to consume. The `on_thread_park` function is useful if you want to implement your own monitoring.

`thread_name`

This names the threads that are made by the runtime. The default name is `tokio-runtime-worker`.

thread_stack_size

This allows us to determine the amount of memory in bytes that are allocated for the stack of each worker thread. The *stack* is a section of memory that stores local variables, function return addresses, and the management of function calls. If you know that your computations are simple and you want to conserve memory, reaching for a lower stack size makes sense. The default value for this stack size at the time of this writing is 2 mebibytes (MiB).

enable_time

This enables the time driver for *Tokio*.

Now that we have built and configured our runtime, we can define how we call it:

```
pub fn spawn_task<F, T>(future: F) -> JoinHandle<T>
where
    F: Future<Output = T> + Send + 'static,
    T: Send + 'static,
{
    RUNTIME.spawn(future)
}
```

We do not really need this function, as we can directly call our runtime. However, it is worth noting that the function signature is essentially the same as our spawn_task function in Chapter 3. The only difference is that we return a *Tokio* JoinHandle as opposed to a Task.

Now that we know how to call our runtime, we can define a basic future:

```
async fn sleep_example() -> i32 {
    println!("sleeping for 2 seconds");
    tokio::time::sleep(Duration::from_secs(2)).await;
    println!("done sleeping");
    20
}
```

And then we run our program:

```
fn main() {
    let handle = spawn_task(sleep_example());
    println!("spawned task");
    println!("task status: {}", handle.is_finished());
    std::thread::sleep(Duration::from_secs(3));
    println!("task status: {}", handle.is_finished());
    let result = RUNTIME.block_on(handle).unwrap();
    println!("task result: {}", result);
}
```

We spawn our task and then wait for the task to finish, using the block_on function from our runtime. We also periodically check whether our task has finished. Running the code gives us the following printout:

```
thread starting for runtime A
thread starting for runtime A
sleeping for 2 seconds
thread starting for runtime A
thread parking for runtime A
thread parking for runtime A
spawned task
thread parking for runtime A
task status: false
thread starting for runtime A
thread parking for runtime A
done sleeping
thread parking for runtime A
task status: true
task result: 20
```

Although this printout is lengthy, we can see that our runtime starts creating worker threads, and also starts our async task before all the worker threads are created. Because we have sent only one async task, we can also see that the idle worker threads are being parked. By the time that we get the result of our task, all our worker threads have been parked. We can see that *Tokio* is fairly aggressive at parking its threads. This is useful because if we create multiple runtimes but are not using one all the time, that unused runtime will quickly park its threads, reducing the amount of resources being used.

Now that we have covered how to build and customize *Tokio* runtimes, we can re-create the runtime that we built in Chapter 3:

```
static HIGH_PRIORITY: LazyLock<Runtime> = LazyLock::new(|| {
    Builder::new_multi_thread()
        .worker_threads(2)
        .thread_name("High Priority Runtime")
        .enable_time()
        .build()
        .unwrap()
});
static LOW_PRIORITY: LazyLock<Runtime> = LazyLock::new(|| {
    Builder::new_multi_thread()
        .worker_threads(1)
        .thread_name("Low Priority Runtime")
        .enable_time()
        .build()
        .unwrap()
});
```

This gives us the layout shown in Figure 7-1.

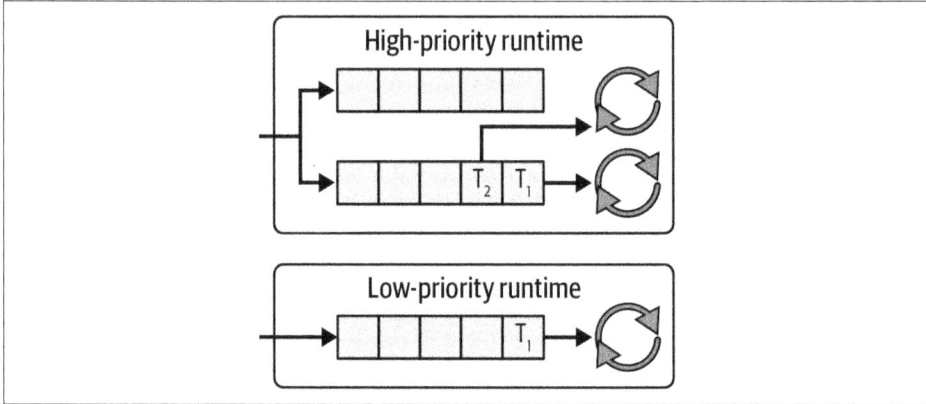

Figure 7-1. Layout of our Tokio runtimes

The only difference between our two *Tokio* runtimes and our runtime that had two queues with task stealing in Chapter 3, is that the threads from the high-priority runtime will not steal tasks from the low-priority runtime. Also, the high-priority runtime has two queues. The differences are not too pronounced because the threads steal tasks in the same runtime, so it is effectively one queue as long as we do not mind the exact order in which tasks are processed.

We also must acknowledge that the threads get parked when no async tasks remain to be processed. If we have more threads than cores, the OS will manage the resource allocation and context switching among these threads. Simply adding more threads past the number of cores will not result in a linear increase in speed. However, if we have three threads for the high-priority runtime and two threads for the low-priority runtime, we can still distribute the resources effectively. If no tasks were to be processed in the low-priority runtime, those two threads would be parked and the three threads in the high-priority runtime would have more CPU allocation.

Now that we have defined our threads and runtimes, we need to interact with these threads in different ways. We can gain more control over the flow of the task by using local pools.

Processing Tasks with Local Pools

With local pools, we can have more control over the threads that are processing our async tasks. Before we explore local pools, we need to include the following dependency:

```
tokio-util = { version = "0.7.10", features = ["full"] }
```

We also need these imports:

```
use tokio_util::task::LocalPoolHandle;
use std::cell::RefCell;
```

When using local pools, we tie the spawned async task to the specific pool. This means we can use structs that do not have the Send trait implemented because we are ensuring that the task stays on a specific thread. However, because we are ensuring that the async task runs on a particular thread, we will not be able to exploit task stealing; we will not get the performance of a standard *Tokio* runtime out of the box.

To see how our async tasks map through our local pool, we first need to define some local thread data:

```
thread_local! {
    pub static COUNTER: RefCell<u32> = RefCell::new(1);
}
```

Every thread will have access to its COUNTER variable. We then need a simple async task that blocks the thread for a second, increases the COUNTER of the thread that the async task is operating in, and then prints out the COUNTER and number:

```
async fn something(number: u32) -> u32 {
    std::thread::sleep(std::time::Duration::from_secs(3));
    COUNTER.with(|counter| {
        *counter.borrow_mut() += 1;
        println!("Counter: {} for: {}", *counter.borrow(), number);
    });
    number
}
```

With this task, we will see how configurations of the local pool will process multiple tasks.

In our main function, we still need a *Tokio* runtime because we still need to await on the spawned tasks:

```
#[tokio::main(flavor = "current_thread")]
async fn main() {
    let pool = LocalPoolHandle::new(1);
    . . .
}
```

Our *Tokio* runtime has a flavor of current_thread. The flavor at the time of this writing is either CurrentThread or MultiThread. The MultiThread option executes tasks across multiple threads. CurrentThread executes all tasks on the current thread. Another flavor, MultiThreadAlt, also claims to execute tasks across multiple threads but is unstable. So the runtime that we have implemented will execute all tasks on the current thread, and the local pool has one thread in the pool.

Now that we have defined our pool, we can use it to spawn our tasks:

```
let one = pool.spawn_pinned(|| async {
    println!("one");
    something(1).await
});
let two = pool.spawn_pinned(|| async {
    println!("two");
    something(2).await
});
let three = pool.spawn_pinned(|| async {
    println!("three");
    something(3).await
});
```

We now have three handles, so we can await on these handles and return the sum of these tasks:

```
let result = async {
    let one = one.await.unwrap();
    let two = two.await.unwrap();
    let three = three.await.unwrap();
    one + two + three
};
println!("result: {}", result.await);
```

When running our code, we get the following printout:

```
one
Counter: 2 for: 1
two
Counter: 3 for: 2
three
Counter: 4 for: 3
result: 6
```

Our tasks are processed sequentially, and the highest COUNTER value is 4, meaning that all the tasks were processed in one thread. Now, if we increase the local pool size to 3, we get the following printout:

```
one
three
two
Counter: 2 for: 1
Counter: 2 for: 3
Counter: 2 for: 2
result: 6
```

All three tasks started processing as soon as they were spawned. We can also see that the COUNTER has a value of 2 for each task. This means that our three tasks were distributed across all three threads.

We can also focus on particular threads. For example, we can spawn a task to a thread that has the index of zero:

```
let one = pool.spawn_pinned_by_idx(|| async {
    println!("one");
    something(1).await
}, 0);
```

If we spawn all our tasks on the thread with the index of zero, we get this printout:

```
one
Counter: 2 for: 1
two
Counter: 3 for: 2
three
Counter: 4 for: 3
result: 6
```

Our printout is the same as the single-threaded pool, even though we have three threads in the pool. If we were to swap the standard sleep for a *Tokio* sleep, we would get the following printout:

```
one
two
three
Counter: 2 for: 1
Counter: 3 for: 2
Counter: 4 for: 3
result: 6
```

Because the *Tokio* sleep is async, our single thread can juggle multiple async tasks, but the COUNTER access is after the sleep. We can see the COUNTER value is 4, meaning that although our thread juggled multiple async tasks at the same time, our async tasks never traversed over another thread.

With local pools, we can have fine-grained control of where we send our tasks to be processed. Although we are sacrificing task stealing, we may want to use the local pool for the following advantages:

*Handling non-*send *futures*
> If the future cannot be sent between threads, we can process them with a local thread pool.

Thread affinity
> Because we can ensure that a task is being executed on a specific thread, we can take advantage of its state. A simple example of this is caching. If we need to compute or fetch a value from another resource such as a server, we can cache this in a specific thread. All tasks in that thread then have access to the value, so all tasks you send to that specific thread will not need to fetch or calculate the value.

Performance for thread-local operations

You can share data across threads with mutexes and atomic reference counters. However, the synchronization of threads carries some overhead. For instance, acquiring a lock that other threads are also acquiring is not free. As we can see in Figure 7-2, if we have a standard *Tokio* async runtime with four worker threads and our counter is Arc<Mutex<T>>, only one thread can access the counter at a time.

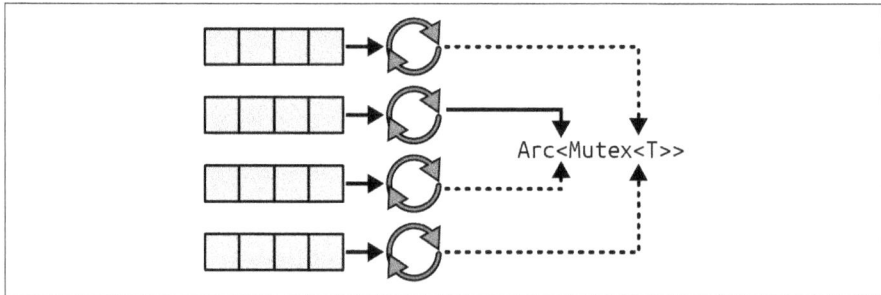

Figure 7-2. A mutex will allow only one Tokio thread to access it at a time

The other three threads will have to wait to get access to Arc<Mutex<T>>. Keeping the state of the counter local to each thread will remove the need for that thread to wait for access to a mutex, speeding up the process. However, the local counters in each thread would not contain the complete picture. These counters do not know the state of the other counters in other threads. One approach for getting the entire state of the count can be sending an async task that gets the counter to each thread, combining the results of each thread at the end. We cover this approach in "Graceful Shutdowns" on page 149. The local access to data within the thread can also aid in the optimizations of CPU-bound tasks when it comes to the CPU caching data.

Safe access to non-send resources

Sometimes the data resource will not be thread-safe. Keeping that resource in one thread and sending tasks into that thread to be processed is a way of getting around this.

> We have highlighted the potential for blocking a thread with a blocking task throughout the book. However, it must be stressed that the damage blocking can do on our local pool can be more pronounced, as we do not have any task stealing. Using the *Tokio* spawn_blocking function will prevent this.

So far, we have been able to access the state of the thread in our async task by using RefCell. It enables us to access data via Rust checking the borrow rules at runtime. However, this checking carries some overhead when borrowing the data in RefCell. We can remove these checks and still safely access the data with unsafe code, which we will explore in the next section.

Getting Unsafe with Thread Data

To remove the runtime checks for mutable borrows of our thread data, we need to wrap our data in UnsafeCell. This means that we access our thread data directly, without any checks. However, I know what you are thinking. If we are using Unsafe Cell, is that dangerous? Potentially yes, so we must be careful to ensure that we are safe.

If we think about our system, we have a single thread processing async tasks that will not transfer to other threads. We must remember that although this single thread can juggle multiple async tasks at the same time through polling, it can actively process only one async task at a time. Therefore, we can assume that while one of our async tasks is accessing the data in UnsafeCell and processing it, no other async task is accessing the data because UnsafeCell is not async. However, we need to make sure that we do not have an await when the reference to the data is in scope. If we do, our thread could context-switch to another task while the existing task still has a reference to the data.

We can test this by exposing a hashmap in unsafe code to thousands of async tasks and increasing the value of a key in each of those tasks. To run this test, we need the following imports:

```
use tokio_util::task::LocalPoolHandle;
use std::time::Instant;
use std::cell::UnsafeCell;
use std::collections::HashMap;
```

We then define our thread state:

```
use std::cell::UnsafeCell;
use std::collections::HashMap;
thread_local! {
    pub static COUNTER: UnsafeCell<HashMap<u32, u32>> = UnsafeCell::new
    (HashMap::new());
}
```

Next, we can define our async task that is going to access and update the thread data by using unsafe code:

```
async fn something(number: u32) {
    tokio::time::sleep(std::time::Duration::from_secs(number as u64)).await;
    COUNTER.with(|counter| {
```

```
        let counter = unsafe { &mut *counter.get() };
        match counter.get_mut(&number) {
            Some(count) => {
                let placeholder = *count + 1;
                *count = placeholder;
            },
            None => {
                counter.insert(number, 1);
            }
        }
    });
}
```

We add in a *Tokio* sleep with the duration of the number put in to shuffle the async tasks around, in the order that the tasks are going to access the thread data. We then obtain a mutable reference to the data and perform an operation. Notice the COUNTER.with block where we access the data. This is not an async block, meaning that we cannot use await operations while accessing the data. We cannot context-switch to another async task while accessing the unsafe data. Inside the COUNTER.with block, we use unsafe code to directly access the data and increase the count.

Once our test is done, we need to print out the thread state. Therefore, we need to pass an async task into the thread to perform the print operation, which takes this form:

```
async fn print_statement() {
    COUNTER.with(|counter| {
        let counter = unsafe { &mut *counter.get() };
        println!("Counter: {:?}", counter);
    });
}
```

We now have everything, so all we need to do is run our code in our main async function. First, we set up our local thread pool, which is just a single thread, and 100 thousand sequences of 1 to 5:

```
let pool = LocalPoolHandle::new(1);
let sequence = [1, 2, 3, 4, 5];
let repeated_sequence: Vec<_> = sequence.iter()
                                        .cycle()
                                        .take(5000)
                                        .cloned()
                                        .collect();
```

This gives us half a million async tasks with varying *Tokio* sleep durations that we are going to chuck into this single thread. We then loop through these numbers, spinning off tasks that call our async function twice so the task sent to the thread makes the thread context-switch between each function and inside each function:

```
let mut futures = Vec::new();
for number in repeated_sequence {
```

```
        futures.push(pool.spawn_pinned(move || async move {
            something(number).await;
            something(number).await
        }));
    }
```

We are really encouraging the thread to context-switch multiple times when process-ing a task. This context switching, combined with the varying sleep durations and high number of tasks in total, will lead to inconsistent outcomes in the counts if we have clashes when accessing the data. Finally, we loop through the handles, joining them all to ensure that all the async tasks have executed, and we print out the count with the following code:

```
for i in futures {
    let _ = i.await.unwrap();
}
let _ = pool.spawn_pinned(|| async {
    print_statement().await
}).await.unwrap();
```

The end result should be as follows:

```
Counter: {2: 200000, 4: 200000, 1: 200000, 3: 200000, 5: 200000}
```

No matter how many times we run them, the counts will always be the same. Here we did not have to perform atomic operations such as compare and swap, with multiple tries if an inconsistency occurs. We also did not need to `await` on a lock. We didn't even need to check whether there were any mutable references before making a mutable reference to our data. Our unsafe code in this context is safe.

We can now use the state of a thread to affect our async tasks. However, what happens if our system is shut down? We might want to have a cleanup process so we can re-create our state when we spin up our runtime again. This is where graceful shutdowns come in.

Graceful Shutdowns

In a *graceful shutdown*, we catch when the program is shutting down in order to per-form a series of processes before the program exits. These processes can be sending signals to other programs, storing state, clearing up transactions, and anything else you would want to do before the program exits.

Our first exploration of this topic can be the Ctrl-C signal. Usually when we run a Rust program through the terminal, we can stop our program by pressing Ctrl-C, prompting the program to exit. However, we can overwrite this preemptive exit with the `tokio::signal` module. To really prove that we have overwritten the Ctrl-C signal, we can build a simple program that has to accept the Ctrl-C signal three times before we exit our program. We can achieve this by building the background async task as follows:

```
async fn cleanup() {
    println!("cleanup background task started");
    let mut count = 0;
    loop {
        tokio::signal::ctrl_c().await.unwrap();
        println!("ctrl-c received!");
        count += 1;
        if count > 2 {
            std::process::exit(0);
        }
    }
}
```

Next, we can run our background task and loop indefinitely with the following main function:

```
#[tokio::main]
async fn main() {
    tokio::spawn(cleanup());
    loop {
    }
}
```

When running our program, if we press Ctrl-C three times, we will get this printout:

```
cleanup background task started
^Cctrl-c received!
^Cctrl-c received!
^Cctrl-c received!
```

Our program did not exit until the signal was sent three times. Now we can exit our program on our own terms. However, before we move on, let's add a blocking sleep to our loop in our background task before we await for the Ctrl-C signal, giving the following loop:

```
loop {
    std::thread::sleep(std::time::Duration::from_secs(5));
    tokio::signal::ctrl_c().await.unwrap();
    . . .
}
```

If we were to run our program again, pressing Ctrl-C before the 5 seconds is up, the program would exit. With this, we can deduce that our program will handle the Ctrl-C signal as we want only when our program is directly awaiting the signal. We can get around this by spawning a thread that will manage an async runtime. We then use the rest of the main thread to listen for our signal:

```
#[tokio::main(flavor = "current_thread")]
async fn main() {
    std::thread::spawn(|| {
```

```
let runtime = tokio::runtime::Builder::new_multi_thread()
    .enable_all()
    .build()
    .unwrap();

runtime.block_on(async {
    println!("Hello, world!");
});
    });
    let mut count = 0;
    loop {
        tokio::signal::ctrl_c().await.unwrap();
        println!("ctrl-c received!");
        count += 1;
        if count > 2 {
            std::process::exit(0);
        }
    }
}
```

Now, no matter what our async runtime is processing, our main thread is ready to act on our Ctrl-C signal, but what about our state? In our cleanup process, we can extract the current state and then write it to a file so we can load the state when the program is started again. Writing and reading files is trivial, so we will focus on the extraction of the state from all the isolated threads we built in the previous section. The main difference from the previous section is that we are going to distribute the tasks over four isolated threads. First, we can wrap our local thread pool in a lazy evaluation:

```
static RUNTIME: LazyLock<LocalPoolHandle> = LazyLock::new(|| {
    LocalPoolHandle::new(4)
});
```

We need to define our async task that extracts the state of a thread:

```
fn extract_data_from_thread() -> HashMap<u32, u32> {
    let mut extracted_counter: HashMap<u32, u32> = HashMap::new();
    COUNTER.with(|counter| {
        let counter = unsafe { &mut *counter.get() };
        extracted_counter = counter.clone();
    });
    return extracted_counter
}
```

We can send this task through each thread, which gives us a nonblocking way to sum the total number of counts for the entire system (Figure 7-3).

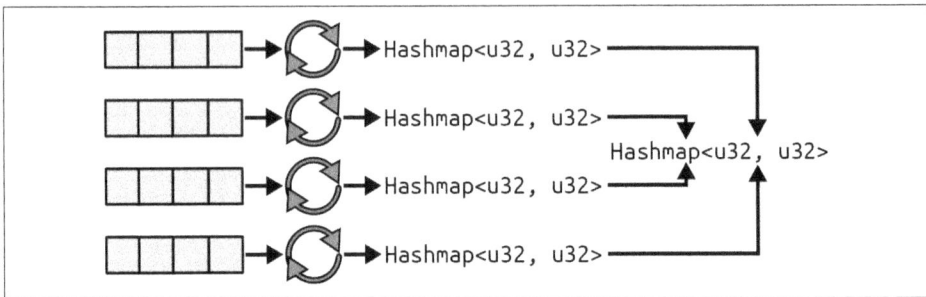

Figure 7-3. Flow of extracting state from all threads

We can implement the process mapped out in Figure 7-3 with the following code:

```
async fn get_complete_count() -> HashMap<u32, u32> {
    let mut complete_counter = HashMap::new();
    let mut extracted_counters = Vec::new();
    for i in 0..4 {
        extracted_counters.push(RUNTIME.spawn_pinned_by_idx(||
            async move {
                extract_data_from_thread()
            }, i));
    }
    for counter_future in extracted_counters {
        let extracted_counter = counter_future.await
                                .unwrap_or_default();
        for (key, count) in extracted_counter {
            *complete_counter.entry(key).or_insert(0) += count;
        }
    }
    return complete_counter
}
```

We call `spawn_pinned_by_idx` to ensure that we send only one `extract_data_from_thread` task to every thread.

We are now ready to run our system with the following `main` function:

```
#[tokio::main(flavor = "current_thread")]
async fn main() {
    let _handle = tokio::spawn( async {
        . . .
    });
    tokio::signal::ctrl_c().await.unwrap();
    println!("ctrl-c received!");
    let complete_counter = get_complete_count().await;
    println!("Complete counter: {:?}", complete_counter);
}
```

We spawn tasks to increase the counts inside `tokio::spawn`:

```
let sequence = [1, 2, 3, 4, 5];
let repeated_sequence: Vec<_> = sequence.iter().cycle()
                                    .take(500000)
                                    .cloned()
                                    .collect();
let mut futures = Vec::new();
for number in repeated_sequence {
    futures.push(RUNTIME.spawn_pinned(move || async move {
        something(number).await;
        something(number).await
    }));
}
for i in futures {
    let _ = i.await.unwrap();
}
println!("All futures completed");
```

Our system is now ready to run. If we run the program until you get the printout that all futures are completed before pressing Ctrl-C, we get the following printout:

```
Complete counter: {1: 200000, 4: 200000, 2: 200000, 5: 200000, 3: 200000}
```

Because we know that we sent only one extract task to each thread using the `spawn_pinned_by_idx` function, and that our total count is the same as it was when we were running all our tasks through one thread, we can conclude that our data extraction is accurate. If we press Ctrl-C before the futures have finished, we should get something similar to this printout:

```
Complete counter: {2: 100000, 3: 32290, 1: 200000}
```

We have exited the program before the program finishes, and we get the current state. Our state is now ready to be written before we exit if we want.

While our code facilitates a cleanup when we press Ctrl-C, this signal is not always the most practical method of shutting down our system. For instance, we might have our async system running in the background so our terminal is not tethered to the program. We can shut down our program by sending a SIGHUP signal to our system. To listen for the SIGHUP signal, we need the following import:

```
use tokio::signal::unix::{signal, SignalKind};
```

We can then replace the Ctrl-C code at bottom of our main function as follows:

```
let pid = std::process::id();
println!("The PID of this process is: {}", pid);
let mut stream = signal(SignalKind::hangup()).unwrap();
stream.recv().await;
let complete_counter = get_complete_count().await;
println!("Complete counter: {:?}", complete_counter);
```

We print out our PID so that we know which PID to send the signal to with the following command:

```
kill -SIGHUP <pid>
```

When running the `kill` command, you should have similar results to when you were pressing Ctrl-C. We can now say that you know how to customize *Tokio* in the way the runtime is configured, the tasks are run, and the runtime is shut down.

Summary

In this chapter, we went into the specifics of setting up a *Tokio* runtime and how its settings affect the way it operates. With these specifics, we really got to take control of the runtime's number of workers and blocking threads and the number of ticks performed before accepting a new task to be polled. We also explored defining different runtimes in the same program so we can choose which runtime to send the task on. Remember, the threads in the *Tokio* runtime get parked when they are not being used, so we will not be wasting resources if a *Tokio* runtime is not being constantly used.

We then controlled how our tasks were handled by threads with local pools. We even tested our unsafe access to our thread state in the *Tokio* runtime to show that accessing the thread state in a task is safe. Finally, we covered graceful shutdowns. Although we do not have to write our own boilerplate code, *Tokio* still gives us the ability to configure our runtime with a lot of flexibility. We have no doubt that in your async Rust career, you will come across a codebase that is using *Tokio*. You should now be comfortable customizing the *Tokio* runtime in the codebase and managing the way your async tasks are being processed. In Chapter 8, we will implement the actor model to solve problems in an async way that is modular.

CHAPTER 8

The Actor Model

Actors (*https://oreil.ly/RyPdG*) are isolated pieces of code that communicate exclusively through message passing. Actors can also have state that they can reference and manipulate. Because we have async-compatible nonblocking channels, our async runtime can juggle multiple actors, progressing these actors only when they receive a message in their channel.

The isolation of actors enables easy async testing and simple implementation of async systems. By the end of this chapter, you will be able to build an actor system that has a router actor. This actor system you build can easily be called anywhere in your program without having to pass a reference around for your actor system. You will also be able to build a supervisor heartbeat system that will keep track of other actors and force a restart of those actors if they fail to ping the supervisor past a time threshold. To start on this journey, you need to understand how to build basic actors.

Building a Basic Actor

The most basic actor we can build is an async function that is stuck in an infinite loop listening for messages:

```
use tokio::sync::{
    mpsc::channel,
    mpsc::{Receiver, Sender},
    oneshot
};

struct Message {
    value: i64
}

async fn basic_actor(mut rx: Receiver<Message>) {
    let mut state = 0;
```

```
    while let Some(msg) = rx.recv().await {
        state += msg.value;
        println!("Received: {}", msg.value);
        println!("State: {}", state);
    }
}
```

The actor listens to incoming messages by using a multiproducer, single-consumer channel (mpsc), updates the state, and then prints it out. We can test our actor as follows:

```
#[tokio::main]
async fn main() {
    let (tx, rx) = channel::<Message>(100);

    let _actor_handle = tokio::spawn(
        basic_actor(rx)
    );
    for i in 0..10 {
        let msg = Message { value: i };
        tx.send(msg).await.unwrap();
    }
}
```

But what if we want to receive a response? Right now, we are sending a message into the void and looking at the printout in the terminal. We can facilitate a response by packaging oneshot::Sender in the message that we are sending to the actor. The receiving actor can then use that oneshot::Sender to send a response. We can define our responding actor with the following code:

```
struct RespMessage {
    value: i32,
    responder: oneshot::Sender<i64>
}

async fn resp_actor(mut rx: Receiver<RespMessage>) {
    let mut state = 0;

    while let Some(msg) = rx.recv().await {
        state += msg.value;
        if msg.responder.send(state).is_err() {
            eprintln!("Failed to send response");
        }
    }
}
```

If we wanted to send a message to our responding actor, we would have to construct a oneshot channel, use it to construct a message, send over the message, and then wait for the response. The following code depicts a basic example of how to achieve this:

```
let (tx, rx) = channel::<RespMessage>(100);

let _resp_actor_handle = tokio::spawn(async {
    resp_actor(rx).await;
});
for i in 0..10 {
    let (resp_tx, resp_rx) = oneshot::channel::<i64>();
    let msg = RespMessage {
        value: i,
        responder: resp_tx
    };
    tx.send(msg).await.unwrap();
    println!("Response: {}", resp_rx.await.unwrap());
}
```

Here, we are using a oneshot channel because we need the response to be sent only once, and then the client code can go about doing other things. This is the best choice for our use case because oneshot channels are optimized in terms of memory and synchronization for the use case of sending just one message back and then closing.

Considering that we are sending structs over the channel to our actor, you can see that our functionality can increase in complexity. For instance, sending an enum that encapsulates multiple messages could instruct the actor to do a range of actions based on the type of message being sent. Actors can also create new actors or send messages to other actors.

From the example we have shown, we could just use a mutex and acquire it for the mutation of the state. The mutex would be simple to code, but how would it match up to the actor?

Working with Actors Versus Mutexes

For this exercise, we need these additional imports:

```
use std::sync::Arc;
use tokio::sync::Mutex;
use tokio::sync::mpsc::error::TryRecvError;
```

To re-create what our actor in the previous section did with a mutex, we have a function that takes the following form:

```
async fn actor_replacement(state: Arc<Mutex<i64>>, value: i64) -> i64 {
    let mut state = state.lock().await;
    *state += value;
    return *state
}
```

While this is simple to write, how does this measure up in terms of performance? We can devise a simple test:

```
let state = Arc::new(Mutex::new(0));
let mut handles = Vec::new();

let now = tokio::time::Instant::now();

for i in 0..100000000 {
    let state_ref = state.clone();
    let future = async move {
        let handle = tokio::spawn(async move {
            actor_replacement(state_ref, i).await
        });
        let _ = handle.await.unwrap();
    };
    handles.push(tokio::spawn(future));
}
for handle in handles {
    let _ = handle.await.unwrap();
}
println!("Elapsed: {:?}", now.elapsed());
```

We have spawned a lot of tasks at once, trying to gain access to the mutex, and then waited on them. If we spawned one task at a time, we would not get the true effect that the concurrency of our mutex has on the outcome. Instead, we would just be getting the speed of individual transactions. We are running a large number of tasks because we want to see a statistically significant difference between the approaches.

These tests take a long time to run, but the results cannot be misinterpreted. At the time of this writing on an M2 MacBook with high specs, the time taken for all the mutex tasks to complete is 155 seconds when running the code in --release mode.

To run the same test using our actor in the previous section, we need this code:

```
let (tx, rx) = channel::<RespMessage>(100000000);
let _resp_actor_handle = tokio::spawn(async {
    resp_actor(rx).await;
});
let mut handles = Vec::new();

let now = tokio::time::Instant::now();
for i in 0..100000000 {
    let tx_ref = tx.clone();

    let future = async move {
        let (resp_tx, resp_rx) = oneshot::channel::<i64>();
        let msg = RespMessage {
            value: i,
            responder: resp_tx
        };
        tx_ref.send(msg).await.unwrap();
        let _ = resp_rx.await.unwrap();
    };
    handles.push(tokio::spawn(future));
```

```
    }
    for handle in handles {
        let _ = handle.await.unwrap();
    }
    println!("Elapsed: {:?}", now.elapsed());
```

Running this test takes 103 seconds at the time of this writing. Note that we ran the tests in --release mode to see what the compiler optimizations would do to the system. The actor is faster by 52 seconds. One reason is the overhead of acquiring the mutex. When placing a message in a channel, we have to check whether the channel is full or has been closed. When acquiring a mutex, the checks are more complicated. These checks typically involve checking whether the lock is held by another task. If it is, the task trying to acquire the lock then needs to register interest and wait to be notified.

> Generally, passing messages through channels can scale better than mutexes in concurrent environments because the senders do not have to wait for other tasks to finish what they are doing. They may have to wait to put a message on the queue of the channel, but waiting for a message to be put on a queue is quicker than waiting for an operation to finish what it is doing with the mutex, yield the lock, and then for the awaiting task to acquire the lock. As a result, channels can result in higher throughput.

To drive our point home, let's explore a scenario in which the transaction is more complex than just increasing the value by one. Maybe we have a few checks and a calculation before committing the final result to the state and returning the number. As efficient engineers, we may want to do other things while that process is happening. Because we are sending a message and waiting for the response, we already have that luxury with our actor code, as you can see here:

```
let future = async move {
    let (resp_tx, resp_rx) = oneshot::channel::<i32>();
    let msg = RespMessage {
        value: i,
        responder: resp_tx
    };
    tx_ref.send(msg).await.unwrap();
    // do something else
    let _ = resp_rx.await.unwrap();
};
```

However, our mutex implementation would merely yield the control back to the scheduler. If we wanted to progress our mutex task while waiting for the complex transaction to complete, we would have to spawn another async task as follows:

```
async fn actor_replacement(state: Arc<Mutex<i32>>, value: i32) -> i32 {
    let update_handle = tokio::spawn(async move {
```

```
        let mut state = state.lock().await;
        *state += value;
        return *state
    });
    // do something else
    update_handle.await.unwrap()
}
```

However, the overhead of spawning those extra async tasks shoots up the time elapsed in our test to 174 seconds. That is 73 seconds more than the actor for the same functionality. This is not surprising, as we are sending an async task to the runtime and getting a handle back just to allow us to progress a wait for our transaction result later in our task.

With our test results in mind, you can see why we would want to use actors. Actors are more complex to write. You need to pass messages over a channel and package a oneshot channel for the actor to respond just to get the result. This is more complex than acquiring a lock. However, the flexibility of choosing when to wait for the result of that message comes for free with actors. Mutexes, on the other hand, have a big penalty if that flexibility is desired.

We can also argue that actors are easier to conceptualize. If we think about this, actors contain their state. If you want to see all interactions with that state, you look in the actor code. However, with mutex codebases, we do not know where all the interactions with the state are. The distributed interactions with the mutex also increase the risk of it being highly coupled throughout the system, making refactoring a headache.

Now that we have gotten our actors working, we need to be able to utilize them in our system. The easiest way to implement actors into the system with a minimal footprint is the router pattern.

Implementing the Router Pattern

For our routing, we construct a router actor that accepts messages. These messages can be wrapped in enums to help our router locate the correct actor. For our example, we are going to implement a basic key-value store. We must stress that although we are building the key-value store in Rust, you should not use this educational example in production. Established solutions like RocksDB and Redis have put a lot of work and expertise into making their key-value stores robust and scalable.

For our key-value store, we need to set, get, and delete keys. We can signal all these operations with the message layout defined in Figure 8-1.

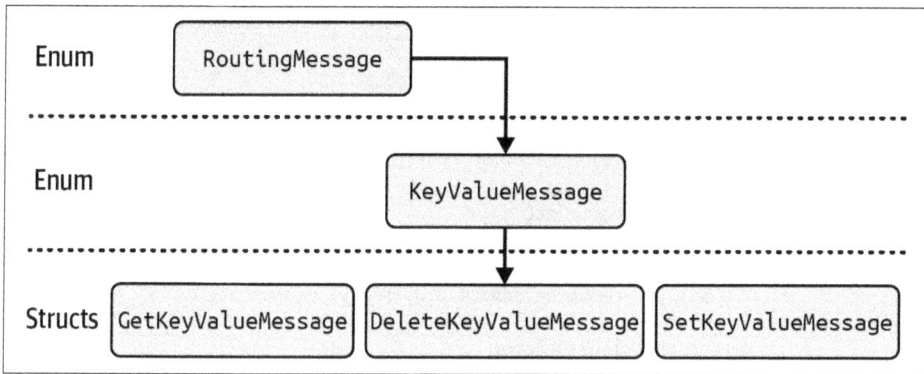

Figure 8-1. The enum structure of the router actor message

Before we code anything, we need the imports defined here:

```
use tokio::sync::{
    mpsc::channel,
    mpsc::{Receiver, Sender},
    oneshot,
};
use std::sync::OnceLock;
```

We also need to define our message layout shown in Figure 8-1:

```
struct SetKeyValueMessage {
    key: String,
    value: Vec<u8>,
    response: oneshot::Sender<()>,
}
struct GetKeyValueMessage {
    key: String,
    response: oneshot::Sender<Option<Vec<u8>>>,
}
struct DeleteKeyValueMessage {
    key: String,
    response: oneshot::Sender<()>,
}
enum KeyValueMessage {
    Get(GetKeyValueMessage),
    Delete(DeleteKeyValueMessage),
    Set(SetKeyValueMessage),
}
enum RoutingMessage {
    KeyValue(KeyValueMessage),
}
```

We now have a message that can be routed to the key-value actor, and this message signals the correct operation with the data needed to perform the operation. For our key-value actor, we accept the `KeyValueMessage`, match the variant, and perform the operation as follows:

```
async fn key_value_actor(mut receiver: Receiver<KeyValueMessage>) {
    let mut map = std::collections::HashMap::new();
    while let Some(message) = receiver.recv().await {
        match message {
            KeyValueMessage::Get(
                GetKeyValueMessage { key, response }
            ) => {
                let _ = response.send(map.get(&key).cloned());
            }
            KeyValueMessage::Delete(
                DeleteKeyValueMessage { key, response }
            ) => {
                map.remove(&key);
                let _ = response.send(());
            }
            KeyValueMessage::Set(
                SetKeyValueMessage { key, value, response }
            ) => {
                map.insert(key, value);
                let _ = response.send(());
            }
        }
    }
}
```

With our handling of the key-value message, we need to connect our key-value actor with a router actor:

```
async fn router(mut receiver: Receiver<RoutingMessage>) {
    let (key_value_sender, key_value_receiver) = channel(32);
    tokio::spawn(key_value_actor(key_value_receiver));

    while let Some(message) = receiver.recv().await {
        match message {
            RoutingMessage::KeyValue(message) => {
                let _ = key_value_sender.send(message).await;
            }
        }
    }
}
```

We create the key-value actor in our router actor. Actors can create other actors. Putting the creation of the key-value actor in the router actor ensures that there will never be a mistake in setting up the system. It also reduces the footprint of our actor system's setup in our program. Our router is our interface, so everything will go through the router to get to the other actors.

Now that the router is defined, we must turn our attention to the channel for that router. All the messages being sent into our actor system will go through that channel. We have chosen the number 32 arbitrarily; this means that the channel can hold up to 32 messages at a time. This buffer size gives us some flexibility.

The system would not be very useful if we had to keep track of references to the sender of that channel. If a developer wants to send a message to our actor system and they are four levels deep, imagine the frustration that developer will feel if they have to trace the function they are using back to `main`, opening up a parameter for the channel sender for each function leading to the function that they are working on. Making changes later would be equally frustrating. To avoid such frustrations, we define the sender as a global `static`:

```
static ROUTER_SENDER: OnceLock<Sender<RoutingMessage>> = OnceLock::new(
);
```

When we create the main channel for the router, we will set the sender. You might be wondering whether it would be more ergonomic to construct the main channel and set `ROUTER_SENDER` inside the router actor function. However, you could get some concurrency issues if functions try to send messages down the main channel before the channel is set. Remember, async runtimes can span multiple threads, so it's possible that an async task could be trying to call the channel while the router actor is trying to set up the channel. Therefore, it is better to set up the channel at the start of the `main` function before spawning anything. Then, even if the router actor is not the first task to be polled on the async runtime, it can still access the messages sent to the channel before it was polled.

Be Aware of Static Globals

We are using a global variable (`ROUTER_SENDER`) with `OnceLock` to simplify the example and avoid cluttering the chapter with additional setup code. While this approach keeps the code simple and straightforward, it's important to be aware of the potential drawbacks of using global state in asynchronous Rust code:

Fragility
    Global state can lead to bugs that are hard to track down, especially in larger or more complex applications. If the global state is modified unexpectedly, unintended side effects can result.

Testing difficulty
    Testing code that relies on global state can be more challenging. Tests may become dependent on the order in which they are run or may interfere with one another.

Resource management
    Managing the lifecycle of resources (like the sender channel) becomes more complex when using global state.

To protect against this, you can create the channel at the start of your `main` function and pass the `Sender` to your actors, which can then pass a `Sender` to other actors, because we can clone `Sender` structs as shown here:

```
#[tokio::main]
async fn main() -> Result<(), std::io::Error> {
    let (sender, receiver) = channel(32);
    tokio::spawn(router(receiver, sender.clone()));
        . . .
}
```

We will omit this approach for the global in this chapter because we have a lot of moving parts to keep track of as it is.

Our router actor is now ready to receive messages and route them to our key-value store. We need some functions that enable us to send key-value messages. We can start with our **set** function, which is defined by the following code:

```
pub async fn set(key: String, value: Vec<u8>)  -> Result<(), std::io::Error> {
    let (tx, rx) = oneshot::channel();
    ROUTER_SENDER.get().unwrap().send(
        RoutingMessage::KeyValue(KeyValueMessage::Set(
            SetKeyValueMessage {
            key,
            value,
            response: tx,
        }))).await.unwrap();
    rx.await.unwrap();
    Ok(())
}
```

This code has a fair number of unwraps, but if our system is failing because of channel errors, we have bigger problems. These unwraps merely avoid code bloat in the chapter. We cover handling errors later in "Creating Actor Supervision" on page 170. We can see that our routing message is self-explanatory. We know it is a routing message and that the message is routed to the key-value actor. We then know which method we are calling in the key-value actor and the data being passed in. The routing message enums are just enough information to tell us the route intended for the function.

Now that our **set** function is defined, you can probably build the **get** function by yourself. Give that a try.

Hopefully, your **get** function goes along the same lines as this:

```
pub async fn get(key: String) -> Result<Option<Vec<u8>>, std::io::Error> {
    let (tx, rx) = oneshot::channel();
    ROUTER_SENDER.get().unwrap().send(
        RoutingMessage::KeyValue(KeyValueMessage::Get(
            GetKeyValueMessage {
```

```
        key,
        response: tx,
    }))).await.unwrap();
    Ok(rx.await.unwrap())
}
```

Our delete function is pretty much identical to get, apart from the different route and the fact that the delete function does not return anything:

```
pub async fn delete(key: String) -> Result<(), std::io::Error> {
    let (tx, rx) = oneshot::channel();
    ROUTER_SENDER.get().unwrap().send(
        RoutingMessage::KeyValue(KeyValueMessage::Delete(
            DeleteKeyValueMessage {
        key,
        response: tx,
    }))).await.unwrap();
    rx.await.unwrap();
    Ok(())
}
```

And our system is ready. We can test our router and key-value store with the main function:

```
#[tokio::main]
async fn main() -> Result<(), std::io::Error> {
    let (sender, receiver) = channel(32);
    ROUTER_SENDER.set(sender).unwrap();
    tokio::spawn(router(receiver));

    let _ = set("hello".to_owned(), b"world".to_vec()).await?;
    let value = get("hello".to_owned()).await?;
    println!("value: {:?}", String::from_utf8(value.unwrap()));
    let _ = delete("hello".to_owned()).await?;
    let value = get("hello".to_owned()).await?;
    println!("value: {:?}", value);
    Ok(())
}
```

The code gives us the following printout:

```
value: Ok("world")
value: None
```

Our key-value store is working and operational. However, what happens when our system closes down or crashes? We need an actor that can keep track of the state and recover it when restarting the system.

Implementing State Recovery for Actors

Right now our system has a key-value store actor. However, our system might be stopped and started again, or an actor could crash. If this happens, we could lose all our data, which is not good. To reduce the risk of data loss, we will create another actor that writes our data to a file. The outline of our new system is defined in Figure 8-2.

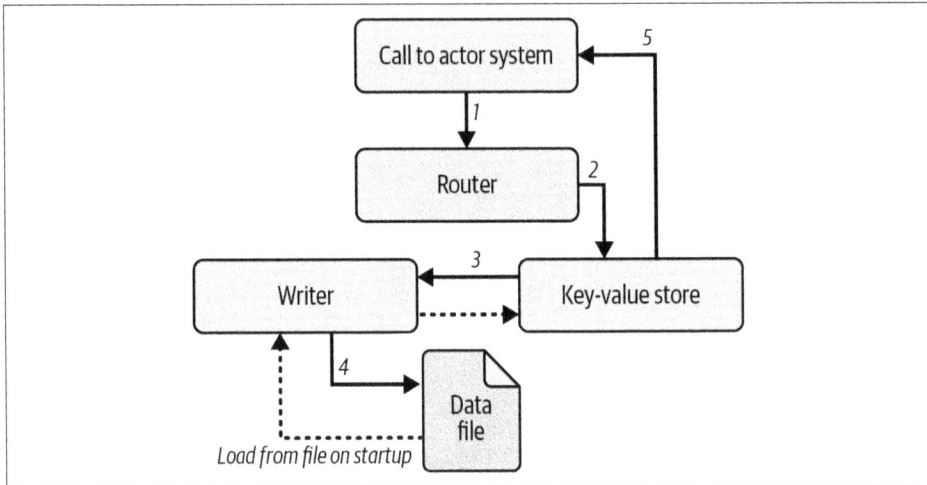

Figure 8-2. A writer backup actor system

From Figure 8-2, we can see the following steps that are carried out:

1. A call is made to our actor system.
2. The router sends the message to the key-value store actor.
3. Our key-value store actor clones the operation and sends that operation to the writer actor.
4. The writer actor performs the operation on its own map and writes the map to the datafile.
5. The key-value store performs the operation on its own map and returns the result to the code that called the actor system.

When our actor system starts up, we will have this sequence:

1. Our router actor starts, creating our key-value store actor.
2. Our key-value store actor creates our write actor.
3. When our writer actor starts, it reads the data from the file, populates itself, and also sends the data to the key-value store actor.

We have given our writer actor exclusive access to the datafile. This will avoid concurrency issues because the writer actor can process only one transaction at a time, and no other resources will be altering the file. The writer's exclusivity to the file can also give us performance gains because the writer actor can keep the file handle to the datafile open for the entire duration of its lifetime instead of opening the file for each write. This drastically reduces the number of calls to the OS for permissions and checks for file availability.

For this system, we need to update the initialization code for the key-value actor. We also need to build the writer actor and add a new message for the writer actor that can be constructed from the key-value message.

Before we write any new code, we need the following imports:

```
use serde_json;
use tokio::fs::File;
use tokio::io::{
    self,
    AsyncReadExt,
    AsyncWriteExt,
    AsyncSeekExt
};
use std::collections::HashMap;
```

For our writer message, we need the writer to set and delete values. However, we also need our writer to return the full state that has been read from the file, giving us the following definition:

```
enum WriterLogMessage {
    Set(String, Vec<u8>),
    Delete(String),
    Get(oneshot::Sender<HashMap<String, Vec<u8>>>),
}
```

We need to construct this message from the key-value message without consuming it:

```
impl WriterLogMessage {
    fn from_key_value_message(message: &KeyValueMessage)
        -> Option<WriterLogMessage> {
        match message {
            KeyValueMessage::Get(_) => None,
            KeyValueMessage::Delete(message) => Some(
                WriterLogMessage::Delete(message.key.clone())
            ),
            KeyValueMessage::Set(message) => Some(
                WriterLogMessage::Set(
                    message.key.clone(),
                    message.value.clone()
                )
            ),
```

```
        }
    }
}
```

Our message definitions are now complete. We need only one more piece of functionality before we can write our writer actor: the loading of the state. We need both
actors to load the state on startup, so our file loading is defined by the following
isolated function:

```
async fn read_data_from_file(file_path: &str)
    -> io::Result<HashMap<String, Vec<u8>>> {
    let mut file = File::open(file_path).await?;
    let mut contents = String::new();
    file.read_to_string(&mut contents).await?;
    let data: HashMap<String, Vec<u8>> = serde_json::from_str(
        &contents
    )?;
    Ok(data)
}
```

Although this works, we need the loading of the state to be fault-tolerant. It is nice to
recover the state of the actors before they were shut down, but our system wouldn't be
very good if our actors failed to run at all because they could not load from a missing
or corrupted state file. Therefore, we wrap our loading in a function that will return
an empty hashmap if a problem occurs when loading the state:

```
async fn load_map(file_path: &str) -> HashMap<String, Vec<u8>> {
    match read_data_from_file(file_path).await {
        Ok(data) => {
            println!("Data loaded from file: {:?}", data);
            return data
        },
        Err(e) => {
            println!("Failed to read from file: {:?}", e);
            println!("Starting with an empty hashmap.");
            return HashMap::new()
        }
    }
}
```

We print this out so we can check the logs of the system if we are not getting the
results we expect.

We are now ready to build our writer actor. Our writer actor needs to load data from
the file and then listen to incoming messages:

```
async fn writer_actor(mut receiver: Receiver<WriterLogMessage>)
    -> io::Result<()> {
    let mut map = load_map("./data.json").await;
    let mut file = File::create("./data.json").await.unwrap();

    while let Some(message) = receiver.recv().await {
```

```
    match message {
        . . .
    }
    let contents = serde_json::to_string(&map).unwrap();
    file.set_len(0).await?;
    file.seek(std::io::SeekFrom::Start(0)).await?;
    file.write_all(contents.as_bytes()).await?;
    file.flush().await?;
}
Ok(())
}
```

> You can see that we wipe the file and write the entire map between
> each message cycle. This is not an efficient way of writing to the
> file. However, this chapter is focused on actors and how to use
> them. Trade-offs around writing transactions to files is a big subject
> involving various file types, batch writing, and garbage collection to
> clean up data. If this interests you, *Database Internals* by Alex Pet-
> rov (O'Reilly, 2019) provides comprehensive coverage on writing
> transactions to files.

Inside our matching of the message in the writer actor, we insert, remove, or clone
and then return the entire map:

```
match message {
    WriterLogMessage::Set(key, value) => {
        map.insert(key, value);
    }
    WriterLogMessage::Delete(key) => {
        map.remove(&key);
    },
    WriterLogMessage::Get(response) => {
        let _ = response.send(map.clone());
    }
}
```

While our router actor remains untouched, our key-value actor needs to create the
writer actor before it does anything else:

```
let (writer_key_value_sender, writer_key_value_receiver) = channel(32);
tokio::spawn(writer_actor(writer_key_value_receiver));
```

Our key-value actor then needs to get the state of the map from our writer actor:

```
let (get_sender, get_receiver) = oneshot::channel();
let _ = writer_key_value_sender.send(WriterLogMessage::Get(
    get_sender
)).await;
let mut map = get_receiver.await.unwrap();
```

Finally, the key-value actor can construct a writer message and send that message to the writer actor before handling the transaction itself:

```
while let Some(message) = receiver.recv().await {
    if let Some(
        write_message
    ) = WriterLogMessage::from_key_value_message(
    &message) {
        let _ = writer_key_value_sender.send(
            write_message
        ).await;
    }
    match message {
        . . .
    }
}
```

And with this, our system supports writing and loading from a file while all the key-value transactions are handled in memory. If you play around with your code in the main function, commenting bits out and inspecting the *data.json* file, you will see that it works. However, if your system is running on something like a server, you may not be manually monitoring the file to see what is going on. Now that our actor system has gotten more complex, our writer actor could have crashed and not be running, but we would be none the wiser because our key-value actor could still be running. This is where supervision comes in, as we need to keep track of the state of our actors.

Creating Actor Supervision

Right now we have two actors: the writer and key-value store actors. In this section, we are going to build a supervisor actor that keeps track of every actor in our system. This is where we'll be grateful that we have implemented the router pattern. Creating a supervisor actor and then passing the sender of the supervisor actor channel through to every actor would be a headache. Instead, we can send update messages to the supervisor actor through the router, as every actor has direct access to ROUTER_SENDER. The supervisor can also send reset requests to the correct actor through the browser, as depicted in Figure 8-3.

You can see in Figure 8-3 that if we do not get an update from either the key-value actor or the writer actor, we can reset the key-value actor. Because we can get the key-value actor to hold the handle of the writer actor when the key-value actor creates the writer actor, the writer actor will die if the key-value actor dies. When the key-value actor is created again, the writer actor will also be created.

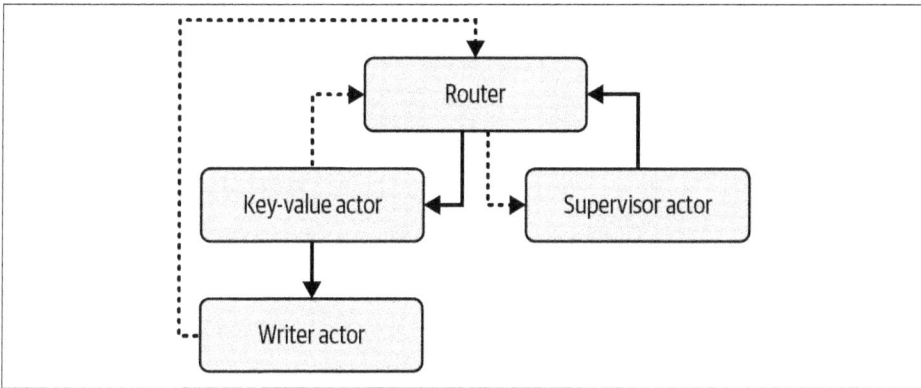

Figure 8-3. A supervisor actor system

To achieve this heartbeat supervisor mechanism, we must refactor our actors a bit, but this will illustrate how a little trade-off in complexity enables us to keep track of and manage our long-running actors. Before we code anything, however, we do need the following import to handle the time checks for our actors:

```
use tokio::time::{self, Duration, Instant};
```

We also need to support the resetting of actors and registering of heartbeats. Therefore, we must expand our `RoutingMessage`:

```
enum RoutingMessage {
    KeyValue(KeyValueMessage),
    Heartbeat(ActorType),
    Reset(ActorType),
}
#[derive(Clone, Copy, PartialEq, Eq, Hash, Debug)]
enum ActorType {
    KeyValue,
    Writer
}
```

Here, we can request a reset or register a heartbeat of any actor that we want to declare in the `ActorType` enum.

Our first refactor can be our key-value actor. First, we define a handle for the writer actor:

```
let (writer_key_value_sender, writer_key_value_receiver) = channel(32);
let _writer_handle = tokio::spawn(
    writer_actor(writer_key_value_receiver
));
```

We still send a `get` message to the writer actor to populate the map, but then we lift our message-handling code into an infinite loop so we can implement a timeout:

```
let timeout_duration = Duration::from_millis(200);
let router_sender = ROUTER_SENDER.get().unwrap().clone();

loop {
    match time::timeout(timeout_duration, receiver.recv()).await {
        Ok(Some(message)) => {
            if let Some(
                write_message
            ) = WriterLogMessage::from_key_value_message(&message) {
                let _ = writer_key_value_sender.send(
                    write_message
                ).await;
            }
            match message {
                . . .
            }
        },
        Ok(None) => break,
        Err(_) => {
            router_sender.send(
                RoutingMessage::Heartbeat(ActorType::KeyValue)
            ).await.unwrap();
        }
    };
}
```

At the end of the cycle, we send a heartbeat message to the router to say that our
key-value store is still alive. We also have a timeout, so if 200 ms passes, we still run
a cycle because we do not want the lack of incoming messages to be the reason our
supervisor thinks that our actor is dead or stuck.

We need a similar approach for our writer actor. We encourage you to try to code this
yourself. Hopefully, your attempt will be similar to the following code:

```
let timeout_duration = Duration::from_millis(200);
let router_sender = ROUTER_SENDER.get().unwrap().clone();

loop {
    match time::timeout(timeout_duration, receiver.recv()).await {
        Ok(Some(message)) => {
            match message {
                . . .
            }
            let contents = serde_json::to_string(&map).unwrap();
            file.set_len(0).await?;
            file.seek(std::io::SeekFrom::Start(0)).await?;
            file.write_all(contents.as_bytes()).await?;
            file.flush().await?;
        },
        Ok(None) => break,
        Err(_) => {
            router_sender.send(
```

```
                    RoutingMessage::Heartbeat(ActorType::Writer)
                ).await.unwrap();
            }
        };
    }
```

Our actors now support sending heartbeats to the router for the supervisor to keep track of. Next we need to build our supervisor actor. Our supervisor actor has a similar approach to the rest of the actors. It has an infinite loop containing a timeout because the lack of heartbeat messages should not stop the supervisor actor from checking on the state of the actors it is tracking. In fact, the lack of heartbeat messages would suggest that the system is in need of checking. However, instead of sending a message at the end of the infinite loop cycle, the supervisor actor loops through its own state to check for any actors that have not checked in. If the actor is out of date, the supervisor actor sends a reset request to the router. The outline of this process is laid out in the following code:

```
async fn heartbeat_actor(mut receiver: Receiver<ActorType>) {
    let mut map = HashMap::new();
    let timeout_duration = Duration::from_millis(200);
    loop {
        match time::timeout(timeout_duration, receiver.recv()).await {
            Ok(Some(actor_name)) => map.insert(
                actor_name, Instant::now()
            ),
            Ok(None) => break,
            Err(_) => {
                continue;
            }
        };
        let half_second_ago = Instant::now() -
                            Duration::from_millis(500);
        for (key, &value) in map.iter() {
            . . .
        }
    }
}
```

We have decided that we are going to have a cutoff of half a second. The smaller the cutoff, the quicker the actor is restarted after failure. However, this increases work as the timeouts in the actors waiting for messages also have to be smaller to keep the supervisor satisfied.

When we are looping through our state keys to check the actors, we send a request for a reset if the cutoff is exceeded:

```
if value < half_second_ago {
    match key {
        ActorType::KeyValue | ActorType::Writer => {

            ROUTER_SENDER.get().unwrap().send(
```

```
            RoutingMessage::Reset(ActorType::KeyValue)
        ).await.unwrap();

        map.remove(&ActorType::KeyValue);
        map.remove(&ActorType::Writer);

        break;
      }
    }
  }
```

You might notice that we reset the key-value actor even if the writer actor is failing. This is because the key-value actor will restart the writer actor. We also remove the keys from the map because when the key-value actor starts again, it will send a heartbeat message causing the keys to be checked again. However, the writer key might still be out of date, causing a second unnecessary fire. We can start checking those actors after they have registered again.

Our router actor now must support all our changes. First of all, we need to set our key-value channel and handle to be mutable:

```
let (mut key_value_sender, mut key_value_receiver) = channel(32);
let mut key_value_handle = tokio::spawn(
    key_value_actor(key_value_receiver)
);
```

This is because we need to reallocate a new handle and channel if the key-value actor is reset. We then spawn the heartbeat actor to supervise our other actors:

```
let (heartbeat_sender, heartbeat_receiver) = channel(32);
tokio::spawn(heartbeat_actor(heartbeat_receiver));
```

Now that our actor system is running, our router actor can handle incoming messages:

```
while let Some(message) = receiver.recv().await {
    match message {
        RoutingMessage::KeyValue(message) => {
            let _ = key_value_sender.send(message).await;
        },
        RoutingMessage::Heartbeat(message) => {
            let _ = heartbeat_sender.send(message).await;
        },
        RoutingMessage::Reset(message) => {
            . . .
        }
    }
}
```

For our reset, we must carry out a couple of steps. First, we create a new channel. We abort the key-value actor, reallocate the sender and receiver to the new channel, and then spawn a new key-value actor:

```
match message {
    ActorType::KeyValue | ActorType::Writer => {
        let (new_key_value_sender, new_key_value_receiver) = channel(
            32
        );
        key_value_handle.abort();
        key_value_sender = new_key_value_sender;
        key_value_receiver = new_key_value_receiver;
        key_value_handle = tokio::spawn(
            key_value_actor(key_value_receiver)
        );
        time::sleep(Duration::from_millis(100)).await;
    },
}
```

You can see that we have a small sleep to ensure that the task has spawned and is running on the async runtime. You may worry that more requests to the key-value actor might be being sent during this transition, which may error. However, all requests go through the router actor. If these messages are being sent to the router for the key-value actor, they will just queue up in the channel of the router. With this, you can see how actor systems are very fault-tolerant.

Since this code has a lot of moving parts, let's run this all together with the main function:

Before you run the following code, make sure that your *data.json* file has a set of empty curly braces like the following:

```
{}
```

```
#[tokio::main]
async fn main() -> Result<(), std::io::Error> {
    let (sender, receiver) = channel(32);
    ROUTER_SENDER.set(sender).unwrap();
    tokio::spawn(router(receiver));
    let _ = set("hello".to_string(), b"world".to_vec()).await?;
    let value = get("hello".to_string()).await?;
    println!("value: {:?}", value);
    let value = get("hello".to_string()).await?;
    println!("value: {:?}", value);
    ROUTER_SENDER.get().unwrap().send(
        RoutingMessage::Reset(ActorType::KeyValue)
    ).await.unwrap();
    let value = get("hello".to_string()).await?;
    println!("value: {:?}", value);
    let _ = set("test".to_string(), b"world".to_vec()).await?;
    std::thread::sleep(std::time::Duration::from_secs(1));
    Ok(())
}
```

Running our `main` gives us this printout:

```
Data loaded from file: {}
value: Some([119, 111, 114, 108, 100])
value: Some([119, 111, 114, 108, 100])
Data loaded from file: {"hello": [119, 111, 114, 108, 100]}
value: Some([119, 111, 114, 108, 100])
```

We can see that the data was loaded by the writer actor initially when setting up the system. Our `get` functions work after the setting of the `hello` value. We then manually forced a reset. Here we can see that the data is loaded again, meaning that the writer actor is being restarted. We know that the previous writer actor died because the writer actor gets the file handle and keeps hold of it. We would get an error as the file descriptor would already be held.

If you want to sleep soundly at night, you can add a timestamp before the loop of the writer actor and print out the timestamp at the start of every iteration of the loop so the printout of the timestamp is not dependent on any incoming messages. This would give a printout like the following:

```
Data loaded from file: {}
writer instance: Instant { tv_sec: 1627237, tv_nsec: 669830291 }
value: Some([119, 111, 114, 108, 100])
writer instance: Instant { tv_sec: 1627237, tv_nsec: 669830291 }
value: Some([119, 111, 114, 108, 100])
Starting key_value_actor
writer instance: Instant { tv_sec: 1627237, tv_nsec: 669830291 }
Data loaded from file: {"hello": [119, 111, 114, 108, 100]}
writer instance: Instant { tv_sec: 1627237, tv_nsec: 773026500 }
value: Some([119, 111, 114, 108, 100])
writer instance: Instant { tv_sec: 1627237, tv_nsec: 773026500 }
writer instance: Instant { tv_sec: 1627237, tv_nsec: 773026500 }
writer instance: Instant { tv_sec: 1627237, tv_nsec: 773026500 }
writer instance: Instant { tv_sec: 1627237, tv_nsec: 773026500 }
writer instance: Instant { tv_sec: 1627237, tv_nsec: 773026500 }
writer instance: Instant { tv_sec: 1627237, tv_nsec: 773026500 }
```

We can see that the instance before and after the reset is different, and there's no trace of the existing writer instance after the reset. We can sleep well knowing that our reset works and there isn't a lonely actor out there without a purpose (in our system, that is—we cannot vouch for Hollywood).

Summary

In this chapter, we built a system that accepts key-value transactions, backs them up with a writer actor, and is monitored via a heartbeat mechanism. Even though this system has a lot of moving parts, the implementation was simplified by the router pattern. The router pattern is not as efficient as directly calling an actor, as the message has to go through one actor before hitting its mark. However, the router pattern is an excellent starting point. You can lean on the router pattern when figuring out the actors you need to solve your problem. Once the solution has taken form, you can then move toward actors directly calling each other as opposed to going through the router actor.

While we focused on building our entire system by using actors, we must remember that they are running on an async runtime. Because actors are isolated and easy to test because they communicate only with messages, we can take a hybrid approach with actors. This means that we can add additional functionality to our normal async system using actors. The actor channel can be accessed anywhere. As with the migration from the router actor to actors directly calling one another, you can slowly migrate your new async code from actors to standard async code when the overall form of the new async addition takes form. You can also use actors to break out functionality in legacy code when trying to isolate dependencies to get the legacy code into a testing harness.

In general, because of their isolated nature, actors are a useful tool that you can implement in a range of settings. Actors can also act as code limbo when you are still in your discovery phase. We've both reached for actors when having to come up with solutions in tight deadlines such as caching and buffering chatbot messages in a microservices cluster.

In Chapter 9, we continue our exploration of how to approach and structure solutions with our coverage of design patterns.

CHAPTER 9

Design Patterns

Throughout the book, we have covered various async concepts and how to implement async code in multiple ways to solve problems. However, we know that software engineering does not exist in a vacuum. When applying your newfound knowledge of async programming in the wild, you will not be able to apply isolated async code in a perfect environment. You might be applying async code to an existing codebase that is not async. You might be interacting with a third-party service like a server, where you will need to handle variances in the response to the server. In this chapter, we cover design patterns that help you implement async code when solving a range of problems.

By the end of this chapter, you will be able to implement async code in an existing codebase that previously did not support async programming. You will also be able to implement the waterfall design pattern to enable the building of pathways with reusable async components. Instead of altering the code of our async tasks to add features, you will be able to implement the decorator pattern so you can easily slot in extra functionality such as logging by just adding a compilation flag when running or building your program. Finally, you will be able to get the entire async system to adapt to errors by implementing the retry and circuit-breaker patterns.

First of all, we need to be able to implement async code in our system before implementing design patterns. So we should start with building an isolated module.

Building an Isolated Module

Let's imagine that we have a Rust codebase that does not have any async code, and we would like to integrate some async Rust into this existing codebase. Instead of rewriting the entire codebase to incorporate async Rust, we advise keeping the blast radius of the interactions small. Massive rewrites rarely keep to deadlines, and as the rewrite is delayed, more features get added to the existing codebase, threatening the completion of the rewrite. We can thus start small by writing our async code in its own module and then offering synchronous entry points into it. The synchronous entry points enable our async module to be implemented anywhere in the existing codebase. The synchronous entry points also enable other developers to use our async module without having to read up on async programming. This eases the integration, and other developers can get to grips with async programming in their own time.

But how can we offer the benefits of async programming with synchronous entry points? Figure 9-1 depicts a high-level flow for offering async benefits to the non-async codebase.

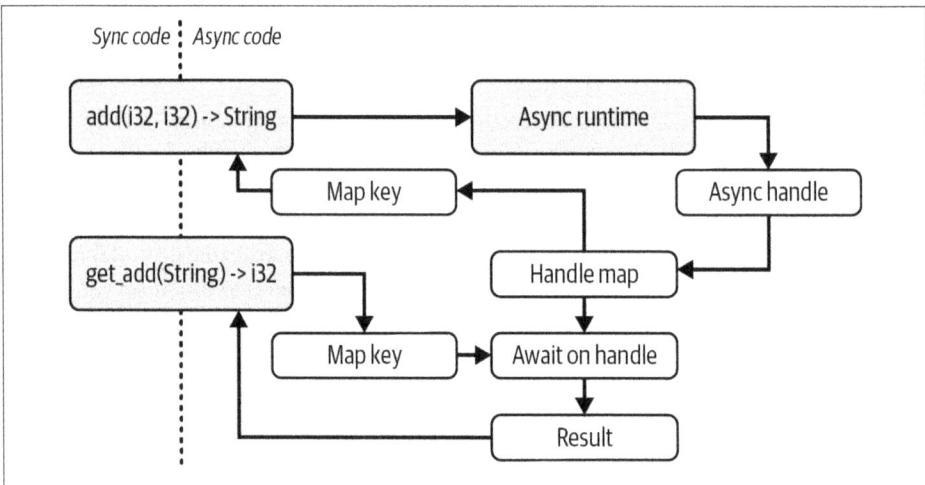

Figure 9-1. Overview of our isolated async module

As Figure 9-1 lays out, we send an async task to the runtime, put the handle in a map for those async tasks, and return a key that corresponds to the handle in the map. The developer using the module calls a normal blocking function and receives a unique ID back. The task is being progressed in the async runtime, and the developer can write some more synchronous code. When the developer needs the result, they pass the unique ID through the `get_add` function, which will block the synchronous code until the result is yielded. The developer is treating the unique ID like an async handle but does not have to directly interact with any async code. Before we can implement this approach, we need the following dependencies:

```
tokio = { version = "1.33.0", features = ["full"] }
uuid = { version = "1.5.0", features = ["v4"] }
```

With these dependencies, we can create our *async_mod.rs* file next to our *main.rs*. Our *async_mod.rs* file is going to house our async module code. Inside this file, we need these imports:

```
use std::sync::LazyLock;
use tokio::runtime::{Runtime, Builder};
use tokio::task::JoinHandle;
use std::collections::HashMap;
use std::sync::{Arc, Mutex};

pub type AddFutMap = LazyLock<Arc<Mutex<HashMap<String, JoinHandle<i32>>>>>;
```

For our runtime, we are going to use the following:

```
static TOKIO_RUNTIME: LazyLock<Runtime> = LazyLock::new(|| {
    Builder::new_multi_thread()
        .enable_all()
        .build()
        .expect("Failed to create Tokio runtime")
});
```

We define our trivial `async_add` function with a sleep to represent an async task:

```
async fn async_add(a: i32, b: i32) -> i32 {
    println!("starting async_add");
    tokio::time::sleep(tokio::time::Duration::from_secs(3)).await;
    println!("finished async_add");
    a + b
}
```

This is the core async task that we are going to expose to the async runtime but not outside the module, which is why the runtime and the `async_add` function are not public.

Now that we have defined our async runtime and `async_add` task, we can build our handler. As shown in Figure 9-2, our handler is essentially a router for our entry points to interact with the runtime and map.

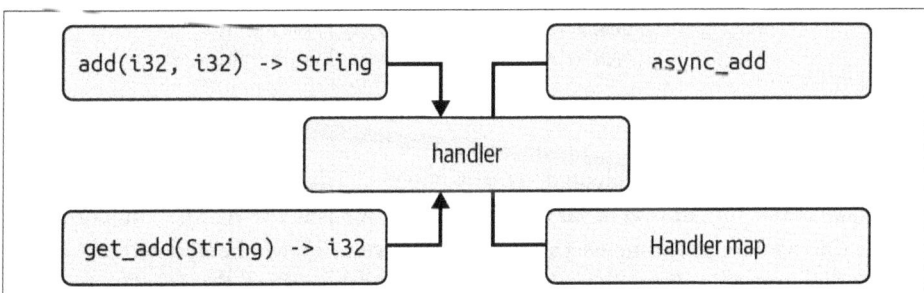

Figure 9-2. Links to our async handle map

Our handler needs to be a function that accepts either the numbers to be added or the unique ID to get the result:

```
fn add_handler(a: Option<i32>, b: Option<i32>, id: Option<String>)
    -> Result<(Option<i32>, Option<String>), String> {
    static MAP: AddFutMap = LazyLock::new(|| Arc::new(
                                    Mutex::new(HashMap::new())
                              ));
    match (a, b, id) {
        (Some(a), Some(b), None) => {
            . . .
        },
        (None, None, Some(id)) => {
            . . .
        },
        _ => Err(
            "either a or b need to be provided or a
            handle_id".to_string()
        )
    }
}
```

For our example, the Option<i32> input works for the add_han dler function because the users will not be directly interacting with it. However, if you plan for add_handler to support more operations such as subtraction or multiplication, it is better to pass in an enum to the add_handler function list:

```
enum Operation {
    Add { a: i32, b: i32 },
    Multiply { a: i32, b: i32 },
    Subtract { a: i32, b: i32 },
}

fn perform_operation(op: Operation) -> i32 {
    match op {
        Operation::Add { a, b } => a + b,
        Operation::Multiply { a, b } => a * b,
        Operation::Subtract { a, b } => a - b,
    }
}
```

Our future map is lazily evaluated, as in Chapter 3 when we defined the queue in the spawn_task function as a lazy evaluation. If we call the handler function and update the MAP, the next time we call the handler, we will have the updated MAP within the handler function. Even though we are going to be calling the handler function only from the main thread in synchronous code, we cannot guarantee that another developer won't spin up a thread and call this function.

If you are 100% certain that the handler will be called only in the main thread, you can get rid of the Arc and Mutex, make the MAP mutable, and access the MAP in the rest of the function with unsafe code. However, as you have probably guessed, it is unsafe. You could also use thread_local to get rid of the Arc and Mutex. This can be safe as long as the developer gets the result in the same thread that the task was spawned. A developer does not need access to the entire map of the program. The developer needs access only to the map that holds their async handle for their task.

In our first match branch of our handler function, we are providing the numbers to be added, so we spawn a task, tether it to a unique ID in our MAP, and return the unique ID:

```
let handle = TOKIO_RUNTIME.spawn(async_add(a, b));
let id = uuid::Uuid::new_v4().to_string();
MAP.lock().unwrap().insert(id.clone(), handle);
Ok((None, Some(id)))
```

We can now define our branch that handles the unique ID for getting the result of the task. Here, we get the task handle from the MAP, pass the handle into the async runtime to block the current thread until the result has been yielded, and return the result:

```
let handle = match MAP.lock().unwrap().remove(&id) {
    Some(handle) => handle,
    None => return Err("No handle found".to_string())
};
let result: i32 = match TOKIO_RUNTIME.block_on(async {
    handle.await
}){
    Ok(result) => result,
    Err(e) => return Err(e.to_string())
};
Ok((Some(result), None))
```

Our handler now works. However, note that our handler is not public. This is because the interface is not ergonomic. A developer using our module could pass in the wrong combination of inputs. We can start with our first public interface:

```
pub fn send_add(a: i32, b: i32) -> Result<String, String> {
    match add_handler(Some(a), Some(b), None) {
        Ok((None, Some(id))) => Ok(id),
        Ok(_) => Err(
            "Something went wrong, please contact author".to_string()
        ),
        Err(e) => Err(e)
    }
}
```

We give the developer no option but to provide two integers that are passed into our handler. We then return the ID. However, if we return any other variant that is not an error, something is seriously wrong with our implementation. To help the developer using our module save time trying to debug what they did wrong, we tell them to contact us because it is our issue to solve.

The get-result interface is similar to our send interface, just inverted, taking the following form:

```rust
pub fn get_add(id: String) -> Result<i32, String> {
    match add_handler(None, None, Some(id)) {
        Ok((Some(result), None)) => Ok(result),
        Ok(_) => Err(
            "Something went wrong, please contact author".to_string()
        ),
        Err(e) => Err(e)
    }
}
```

Now that our async module is complete, we can use it in our *main.rs*:

```rust
mod async_mod;

fn main() {
    println!("Hello, world!");
    let id = async_mod::send_add(1, 2).unwrap();
    println!("id: {}", id);
    std::thread::sleep(std::time::Duration::from_secs(4));
    println!("main sleep done");
    let result = async_mod::get_add(id).unwrap();
    println!("result: {}", result);
}
```

Running the code gives us output similar to the following printout:

```
Hello, world!
starting async_add
id: e2a2f3e1-2a77-432c-b0b8-923483ae637f
finished async_add
main sleep done
result: 3
```

Your ID will be different, but the order should be the same. Here, we can see that our async task is being processed as our main thread continues, and we can get the result. We can see how isolated our async code is. We now have the freedom to experiment. For instance, you will be able to experiment with different runtimes and runtime configurations. Recall in Chapter 7 we could switch over to local sets and start using local thread states to cache recently calculated values if the computational needs increase for our calculations. However, our interface is completely decoupled from async primitives, so other developers using our module will not notice the difference, and thus their implementations of our interface will not break.

Now that we have covered how to implement an async module with a minimal footprint on the rest of the codebase, we can implement other design patterns in our codebases. We can start with the waterfall design pattern.

Waterfall Design Pattern

The *waterfall design pattern* (also known as the *chain of responsibility pattern* (*https://oreil.ly/K2mdw*)) is a chain of async tasks that feed values directly into one another, as laid out in Figure 9-3.

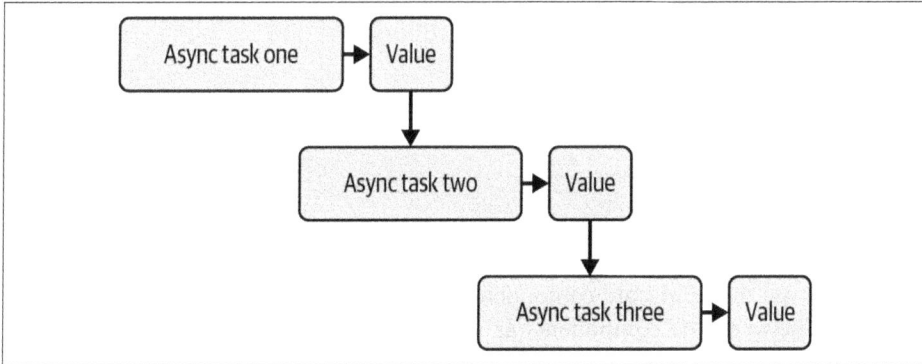

Figure 9-3. Waterfall async design pattern

Implementing a basic waterfall design pattern is straightforward. With Rust, we can exploit the error-handling system for safe and concise code. We can demonstrate this with the following three async tasks:

```
type WaterFallResult = Result<String, Box<dyn std::error::Error>>;

async fn task1() -> WaterFallResult {
    Ok("Task 1 completed".to_string())
}
async fn task2(input: String) -> WaterFallResult {
    Ok(format!("{} then Task 2 completed", input))
}
async fn task3(input: String) -> WaterFallResult {
    Ok(format!("{} and finally Task 3 completed", input))
}
```

Because they all return the same error type, they all lock into one another, with the ? operator:

```
#[tokio::main]
async fn main() -> Result<(), Box<dyn std::error::Error>> {
    let output1 = task1().await?;
    let output2 = task2(output1).await?;
    let result = task3(output2).await?;
    println!("{}", result);
```

```
        Ok(())
    }
```

The waterfall approach is simple and predictable. It also enables us to reuse our async tasks for building blocks. For instance, our three async tasks could be accepting i32 data types. We could add logic around these async tasks as follows:

```
#[tokio::main]
async fn main() -> Result<(), Box<dyn std::error::Error>> {
    let output1 = task1().await?;
    let output2: i32;
    if output1 > 10 {
        output2 = task2(output1).await?;
    } else {
        output2 = task3(output1).await?;
    }
    println!("{}", output2);
    Ok(())
}
```

Considering how we can use logic to direct the flow of the waterfall, we can see where the waterfall implementation might be useful for building pathways that differ slightly but use the same core components. We can also easily slot metrics into these workflows between the components as needed. Although inserting metrics/logging between the components can be useful, we can also use the decorator pattern to add functionality to our tasks.

The Decorator Pattern

The *decorator pattern* (*https://oreil.ly/2Upon*) is a wrapper around a functionality that either adds to that functionality or executes logic before or after the main execution. Classic examples of decorators are fixtures: a unit test sets up the state of some data storage before the test and then destroys the state after the test. The setup and destroying of state between tests ensures that tests are atomic, and a failed test will not alter the outcome of other tests. This state management can be wrapped around code that we are testing. Logging is also a classic use because we can easily switch off the logging without having to change our core logic. Decorators are also used for session management.

Before we look at implementing the decorator pattern in an async context, let's look at how to implement a basic decorator for a struct. Our decorator will add to a string. The functionality that we are going to decorate will yield a string with the following code:

```
trait Greeting {
    fn greet(&self) -> String;
}
```

We then define a struct that implements our trait:

```
struct HelloWorld;
impl Greeting for HelloWorld {
    fn greet(&self) -> String {
        "Hello, World!".to_string()
    }
}
```

We can define a decorator struct that implements our trait, and it contains an inner component that similarly embodies our trait:

```
struct ExcitedGreeting<T> {
    inner: T,
}

impl<T> ExcitedGreeting<T> {
    fn greet(&self) -> String
    where
        T: Greeting,
    {
        let mut greeting = self.inner.greet();
        greeting.push_str(" I'm so excited to be in Rust!");
        greeting
    }
}
```

Here, we are calling the trait from the inner struct and adding to the string, returning the altered string. We can test our decorator pattern easily:

```
fn main() {
    let raw_one = HelloWorld;
    let raw_two = HelloWorld;
    let decorated = ExcitedGreeting { inner: raw_two };
    println!("{}", raw_one.greet());
    println!("{}", decorated.greet());
}
```

We can easily wrap functionality around our struct. Because we are implementing the same trait for the wrapper, we can also pass our wrapped struct into functions that expect structs that have implemented our trait. Therefore, we don't need to change any code in our codebase if we are expecting traits as opposed to structs.

We can even make our implementation of the decorator pattern dependent on the compilation features. For example, we can add a feature in our *Cargo.toml*:

```
[features]
logging_decorator = []
```

We can then rewrite our main function to compile with the decorated logic (or not), depending on the feature flags:

```
fn main() {
    #[cfg(feature = "logging_decorator")]
    let hello = ExcitedGreeting { inner: HelloWorld };

    #[cfg(not(feature = "logging_decorator"))]
    let hello = HelloWorld;

    println!("{}", hello.greet());
}
```

To run our decorator, we need to call the following terminal command:

```
cargo run --features "logging_decorator"
```

We can set this feature to be the default if needed and can also add extra dependencies to the feature if it relies on any dependencies.

Now that you understand the basics of a decorator, we can implement the same functionality in a future. Instead of a struct, we have an inner future. Before we build our future, we need these imports:

```
use std::future::Future;
use std::pin::Pin;
use std::task::{Context, Poll};
```

For this decorator, we are going to implement a logging trait, and our example is going to call a log function before we poll the inner future. Our logging trait takes the following form:

```
trait Logging {
    fn log(&self);
}
```

We then define our logging struct that contains an inner future:

```
struct LoggingFuture<F: Future + Logging> {
    inner: F,
}

impl<F: Future + Logging> Future for LoggingFuture<F> {
    type Output = F::Output;

    fn poll(self: Pin<&mut Self>, cx: &mut Context<'_>)
        -> Poll<Self::Output> {
        let inner = unsafe { self.map_unchecked_mut(|s| &mut s.inner) };
        inner.log();
        inner.poll(cx)
    }
}
```

Although we are using unsafe code in our poll, our code is safe. We have to use the unsafe block because the Rust compiler cannot check projections of the pin. We are not moving the value out of the pin.

While the unsafe block is safe, we can negate the need for the unsafe tag by pinning our inner future with the following code:

```
struct LoggingFuture<F: Future + Logging> {
    inner: Pin<Box<F>>,
}

impl<F: Future + Logging> Future for LoggingFuture<F> {
    type Output = F::Output;

    fn poll(self: Pin<&mut Self>, cx: &mut Context<'_>)
        -> Poll<Self::Output> {
        let this = self.get_mut();
        let inner = this.inner.as_mut();
        inner.log();
        inner.poll(cx)
    }
}
```

We now need to implement the Logging trait for any type that also implements the future:

```
impl<F: Future> Logging for F {
    fn log(&self) {
        println!("Polling the future!");
    }
}
```

This means that whatever future is held by our decorator, we can call the log function. We could get creative with combining other traits so that our futures being passed into the decorator can yield specific values about the future, but for this example, we are merely demonstrating how to implement an async decorator. We can now define a simple future, wrap it, and call it:

```
async fn my_async_function() -> String {
    "Result of async computation".to_string()
}

#[tokio::main]
async fn main() {
    let logged_future = LoggingFuture { inner: my_async_function() };
    let result = logged_future.await;
    println!("{}", result);
}
```

Running our code results in the following printout:

```
Polling the future!
Result of async computation
```

Here, we can see that our logging decorator works. We can use the same compilation feature approaches for our decorator.

Because decorators are designed to be slotted in with minimal friction and have the same type signature, they should not affect the logic of the program too much. If we want to alter the flow of our program based on certain conditions, we can consider using the state machine pattern.

The State Machine Pattern

State machines hold a particular state as well as logic around how that state is changed. Other processes can reference that state to inform the way they act; this is the *state machine pattern* (*https://oreil.ly/npoSz*). A simple real-world example of a state machine is a set of traffic lights. Depending on the country, traffic lights can vary, but they all have at least two states: red and green. Depending on the system, a range of inputs and hardcoded logic can change the state of each traffic light through time. What is important to note is that drivers directly observe the state of the traffic lights and act accordingly. We can have as many or as few drivers as we want, but the contract stays the same. The lights focus on maintaining the state and changing it depending on inputs, and the drivers merely observe and react to that state.

With this analogy, it is not surprising that state machines (*https://oreil.ly/A1_q-*) can be used for scheduling tasks and managing job queues, networking, creating workflows and pipelines, and controlling machinery/systems with distinct states that respond to a combination of async inputs and timed events.

In fact, to drive it home further, the concept of state machines isn't just limited to specific examples like traffic lights. Rust's `async`/`await` model also relies on the idea of futures being state machines. A future represents a value that may not be available yet, and as it progresses, it transitions through different states (e.g., `Pending`, `Ready`) until it produces a result or error.

For our example, we can build a basic switch state that is either on or off. Enums are great for managing states because we have the match pattern, and enum variants can also house data. Our simple state takes the following form:

```
enum State {
    On,
    Off,
}
```

We define the event state that our state machine consumes to change the state:

```
enum Event {
    SwitchOn,
    SwitchOff,
}
```

We now have events and the state. The interface between the events and state can be defined with the following code:

```
impl State {
    async fn transition(self, event: Event) -> Self {
        match (&self, event) {
            (State::On, Event::SwitchOff) => {
                println!("Transitioning to the Off state");
                State::Off
            },
            (State::Off, Event::SwitchOn) => {
                println!("Transitioning to the On state");
                State::On
            },
            _ => {
                println!(
                    "No transition possible,
                    staying in the current state"
                );
                self
            },
        }
    }
}
```

Here, we can see that if the state of the switch is on, the event of turning off our switch would turn the state to off, and vice versa. We can test our state machine:

```
#[tokio::main]
async fn main() {
    let mut state = State::On;

    state = state.transition(Event::SwitchOff).await;
    state = state.transition(Event::SwitchOn).await;
    state = state.transition(Event::SwitchOn).await;

    match state {
        State::On => println!("State machine is in the On state"),
        _ => println!("State machine is not in the expected state"),
    }
}
```

Running this code gives the following printout:

```
Transitioning to the Off state
Transitioning to the On state
No transition possible, staying in the current state
State machine is in the On state
```

In our example, async code is not essential, but this is because our example is simple. We could use async code, for example, to access a state through a mutex or to listen to events through an async channel. As in our traffic light example, our state machine decouples the logic behind the state, with the async tasks being processed in the runtime. For instance, our state machine would be a struct with a count and enum of on or off. Other tasks when starting could send an event to our state machine via a channel to increase the count. When the count is over a certain threshold, the state machine could switch the state to off. If new tasks are required to check the state machine for the switch to be on before starting, we have implemented a simple signal system that throttles the progression of new async tasks if the task count is too high. However, we could replace this switch with a counter by using an `AtomicUsize`, as opposed to an `AtomicBool`, if we wanted. But our state machine example sets us up to implement more complex logic if needed.

Our state machine can also poll different futures depending on its state. The following code is an example of how we can poll different futures based on the state of our switch:

```
struct StateFuture<F: Future, X: Future> {
    pub state: State,
    pub on_future: F,
    pub off_future: X,
}
```

Now that the state machine has the state and the two futures to poll, we can implement the polling logic:

```
impl<F: Future, X: Future> Future for StateFuture<F, X> {
    type Output = State;

    fn poll(mut self: Pin<&mut Self>, cx: &mut Context<'_>)
        -> Poll<Self::Output> {
        match self.state {
            State::On => {
                let inner = unsafe {
                    self.map_unchecked_mut(|s| &mut s.on_future)
                };
                let _ = inner.poll(cx);
                cx.waker().wake_by_ref();
                Poll::Pending
            },
            State::Off => {
                let inner = unsafe {
                    self.map_unchecked_mut(|s| &mut s.off_future)
                };
                let _ = inner.poll(cx);
                cx.waker().wake_by_ref();
                Poll::Pending
            },
        }
    }
}
```

In this example, the future will constantly poll in the background. This enables our state machine to switch its continuous operations based on the state. Adding extra functionality such as listening to events through a channel to potentially change the state before polling the futures can easily be done.

Going back to our example of our state machine throttling the progression of new tasks if the count is too high, how should the async tasks checking the state machine handle the off state? This is where the retry pattern comes in.

The Retry Pattern

We might be in a situation where our async tasks are blocked when trying to access something. This could be our state machine saying that there are too many tasks or a server could be overloaded. We do not want our async task to give up, so a retry might yield the result we want. However, we also do not want to hammer our target relentlessly. If a server, mutex, or database is overloaded, the last thing we want to do is flood the overloaded target with back-to-back requests.

The retry pattern (*https://oreil.ly/EMMW8*) allows the async task to retry the request. However, within each retry, there is a delay, and this delay doubles every attempt. This backing off will allow our target to get a drop in the frequency of requests to catch up on tasks that the target is processing.

To explore the retry pattern, we initially define a `get_data` function that will always return an error:

```
async fn get_data() -> Result<String, Box<dyn std::error::Error>> {
    Err("Error".into())
}
```

We then define an async task that implements the retry function:

```
async fn do_something() -> Result<(), Box<dyn std::error::Error>> {
    let mut miliseconds = 1000;
    let total_count = 5;
    let mut count = 0;
    let result: String;
    loop {
        match get_data().await {
            Ok(data) => {
                result = data;
                break;
            },
            Err(err) => {
                println!("Error: {}", err);
                count += 1;
                if count == total_count {
                    return Err(err);
                }
            }
        }
    }
    tokio::time::sleep(
        tokio::time::Duration::from_millis(miliseconds)
    ).await;
    miliseconds *= 2;
```

```
        }
        Ok(())
    }
```

We run our retry pattern:

```
#[tokio::main]
async fn main() {
    let outcome = do_something().await;
    println!("Outcome: {:?}", outcome);
}
```

And we get the following printout:

```
Error: Error
Error: Error
Error: Error
Error: Error
Error: Error
Outcome: Err("Error")
```

Our retry works. Retry patterns are more of a utility than a design choice for an entire application. Sprinkling the retry pattern throughout the application when an async task needs to access a target will give your system more flexibility if the system handles spikes in traffic due to reducing pressure on the targets.

However, what if we keep getting errors? Surely, if a threshold is passed, continuing to spawn tasks doesn't make sense. For instance, if a server has completely crashed, there has to be a state where we no longer waste CPU resources by sending further requests. This is where the circuit-breaker pattern helps us.

The Circuit-Breaker Pattern

The circuit-breaker pattern (*https://oreil.ly/I6z0n*) stops tasks from being spawned if the number of errors exceeds the threshold. Instead of defining our own state machine that is either on or off, we can replicate the same effect with two simple atomic values that are defined here:

```
use std::sync::atomic::{AtomicBool, AtomicUsize, Ordering};
use std::future::Future;
use tokio::task::JoinHandle;

static OPEN: AtomicBool = AtomicBool::new(false);
static COUNT : AtomicUsize = AtomicUsize::new(0);
```

The premise is fairly simple. If OPEN is true, we state that the circuit is open, and we can no longer spawn new tasks. If an error occurs, we increase COUNT by one and set OPEN to true if COUNT exceeds the threshold. We also need to write our own spawn_task function that checks OPEN before spawning a task. Our spawn_task function takes the following form:

```
fn spawn_task<F, T>(future: F) -> Result<JoinHandle<T>, String>
where
    F: Future<Output = T> + Send + 'static,
    T: Send + 'static,
{
    let open = OPEN.load(Ordering::SeqCst);
    if open == false {
        return Ok(tokio::task::spawn(future))
    }
    Err("Circuit Open".to_string())
}
```

We can now define two simple async tasks—one task to throw an error and another to just pass:

```
async fn error_task() {
    println!("error task running");
    let count = COUNT.fetch_add(1, Ordering::SeqCst);
    if count == 2 {
        println!("opening circuit");
        OPEN.store(true, Ordering::SeqCst);
    }
}
async fn passing_task() {
    println!("passing task running");
}
```

With these tasks, we can determine when our system is going to break. We can test that our system breaks when it reaches three errors:

```
#[tokio::main]
async fn main() -> Result<(), String> {
    let _ = spawn_task(passing_task())?.await;
    let _ = spawn_task(error_task())?.await;
    let _ = spawn_task(error_task())?.await;
    let _ = spawn_task(error_task())?.await;
    let _ = spawn_task(passing_task())?.await;
    Ok(())
}
```

This gives us the following printout:

```
passing task running
error task running
error task running
error task running
opening circuit
Error: "Circuit Open"
```

We can no longer spawn tasks after the threshold is reached. We can get creative with what we do when the threshold is reached. Maybe we keep track of all tasks and block only certain types of tasks if their own individual thresholds were broken. We could stop the program altogether with a graceful shutdown and trigger an alert system so developers and IT staff are informed of the shutdown. We could also take time snapshots and close the circuit after a certain amount of time has passed. These variances all depend on the problem you are solving and the solution that's needed. And with this circuit-breaker pattern, we have covered enough design patterns to aid your implementation of async code into a codebase.

Summary

In this chapter, we covered a range of design patterns to enable you to implement the async code that you learned throughout the book. Thinking about the codebase as a whole is key. If you are integrating into an existing codebase with no async code, the isolated module is the obvious first step. All the design patterns in this chapter were chosen with simple code examples. Small, simple steps are best for implementing async code. This approach makes testing easier and enables you to roll back if the recent implementation is no longer needed or is breaking something else in the code.

While it can be tempting to preemptively apply design patterns, overengineering seems to be the number one criticism of design patterns in general. Write your code as you would, and consider implementing a design pattern when it presents itself. Setting out to force a design pattern increases the risk of your implementation, resulting in overengineering. Understanding your design patterns is crucial to knowing when and where to implement them.

In Chapter 10, we cover async approaches to networking by using just the standard library and no external dependencies to build our own async TCP server.

CHAPTER 10

Building an Async Server with No Dependencies

We are now at the penultimate chapter of this book. Therefore, we need to focus on understanding how async interacts in a system. To do this, we are going to build an async server completely from the standard library with no third-party dependencies. This will solidify your understanding of the fundamentals of async programming and how it fits into the bigger picture of a software system. Packages, programming languages, and API documentation will change over time. While understanding the current tools of async is important, and we have covered them throughout the book, knowing the fundamentals of async programming will enable you to read new documentation/tools/frameworks/languages you come across with ease.

By the end of this chapter, you will be able to build a multithreaded TCP server that will accept incoming requests and send these requests to an async executor to be processed asynchronously. Because we are only using the standard library, you will also be able to build your own async executor that accepts tasks and keeps polling them to completion. Finally, you will also be able to implement this async functionality to a client that sends requests to the server. This will give you the ability and confidence to build basic async solutions with minimal dependencies to solve lightweight problems. So, let's get started with setting up the basics of this project.

Setting Up the Basics

For our project, we are going to use four workspaces which are defined in the root directory *Cargo.toml*:

```
[workspace]
members = [
    "client",
```

```
    "server",
    "data_layer",
    "async_runtime"
]
```

The reason why we have four workspaces is that these modules have a fair amount of crossover use. The client and server are going to be separate in order to call them separately. Both server and client are going to use our async runtime, so this needs to be separate. The data_layer is merely a message struct that serializes and deserializes itself. It needs to be in a separate workspace because both client and server are going to reference the data struct. We can write our boilerplate code in *data_layer/src/data.rs*, with the following layout:

```rust
use std::io::{self, Cursor, Read, Write};

#[derive(Debug)]
pub struct Data {
    pub field1: u32,
    pub field2: u16,
    pub field3: String,
}
impl Data {
    pub fn serialize(&self) -> io::Result<Vec<u8>> {
        . . .
    }
    pub fn deserialize(cursor: &mut Cursor<&[u8]>) -> io::Result<Data> {
        . . .
    }
}
```

The serialize and deserialize functions enable us to send the Data struct over TCP connections. We can use serde if we want to do more complicated structs, but in the spirit of this chapter, we are writing our own serialization logic because our entire application is not going to have any dependencies. Do not worry, this is the only part of non-async boilerplate code that we are going to write. Our serialize function takes the following form:

```rust
let mut bytes = Vec::new();
bytes.write(&self.field1.to_ne_bytes())?;
bytes.write(&self.field2.to_ne_bytes())?;
let field3_len = self.field3.len() as u32;
bytes.write(&field3_len.to_ne_bytes())?;
bytes.extend_from_slice(self.field3.as_bytes());
Ok(bytes)
```

We use 4 bytes for each number, and another 4-byte integer to dictate the length of the string, as the length of strings can vary.

For our deserialize function, we pass in arrays and vectors with the correct capacity into the array of bytes to read and convert them to the right format:

```
// Initialize buffers for the fields, using arrays of the appropriate size
let mut field1_bytes = [0u8; 4];
let mut field2_bytes = [0u8; 2];

// Read the first field (4 bytes) from the cursor into the buffer.
// Do the same for second field.
cursor.read_exact(&mut field1_bytes)?;
cursor.read_exact(&mut field2_bytes)?;

// Convert the byte arrays into the appropriate data types (u32 and u16)
let field1 = u32::from_ne_bytes(field1_bytes);
let field2 = u16::from_ne_bytes(field2_bytes);

// Initialize a buffer to read the length of the third field,
// which is 4 bytes long
let mut len_bytes = [0u8; 4];

// Read the length from the cursor into the buffer
cursor.read_exact(&mut len_bytes)?;

// Convert the length bytes into a usize
let len = u32::from_ne_bytes(len_bytes) as usize;

// Initialize a buffer with the specified length to hold the third field's data
let mut field3_bytes = vec![0u8; len];

// Read the third field's data from the cursor into the buffer
cursor.read_exact(&mut field3_bytes)?;

// Convert the third field's bytes into a UTF-8 string, or
// return an error if this cannot be done.
let field3 = String::from_utf8(field3_bytes)
    .map_err(|_| io::Error::new(
        io::ErrorKind::InvalidData, "Invalid UTF-8"
    ))?;

//  Return the structured data
Ok(Data { field1, field2, field3 })
```

With our data layer logic completed, we make our Data struct public in the *data_layer/src/lib.rs* file:

```
pub mod data;
```

With our data layer completed, we can move on to the interesting stuff: building our async runtime from just the standard library.

Building Our std Async Runtime

To build the async components for our server, we need the following components in order:

1. Waker: waking up futures to be resumed

2. Executor: processing futures to completion

3. Sender: async future enabling async sending of data

4. Receiver: async future enabling async receiving of data

5. Sleeper: async future enabling async sleeping of a task

Seeing as we need the waker to help the executor reanimate tasks to be polled again, we will start with building our waker.

Building Our Waker

We have used the waker throughout the book when implementing the `Future` trait, and we know instinctively that the `wake` or `wake_by_ref` function is required to allow the future to be polled again. Therefore, the waker is our obvious first choice because futures and the executor will handle the waker. To build our waker, we start with the following import in our *async_runtime/src/waker.rs* file:

```
use std::task::{RawWaker, RawWakerVTable};
```

We then build our waker table:

```
static VTABLE: RawWakerVTable = RawWakerVTable::new(
    my_clone,
    my_wake,
    my_wake_by_ref,
    my_drop,
);
```

We can call the functions whatever we want as long as they have the correct function signatures. `RawWakerTable` is a virtual function pointer table that `RawWaker` points to and calls to perform operations throughout its lifecycle. For instance, if the `clone` function is called on `RawWaker`, the `my_clone` function in `RawWakerTable` will be called. We are going to keep the implementation of these functions as basic as possible, but we can see how `RawWakerTable` can be utilized. For instance, data structures that have static lifetimes and are thread-safe could keep track of the wakers in our system by interacting with the functions in `RawWakerTable`.

We can start with our `clone` function. This usually gets called when we poll a function, as we need to clone an atomic reference of our waker in our executor to wrap in a context and pass into the future being polled. Our clone implementation takes the following form:

```
unsafe fn my_clone(raw_waker: *const ()) -> RawWaker {
    RawWaker::new(raw_waker, &VTABLE)
}
```

Our wake and wake_by_ref functions are called when the future should be polled again because the future that is being waited on is ready. For our project, we are going to be polling our futures without being prompted by the waker to see if they are ready, so our simple implementation is defined here:

```
unsafe fn my_wake(raw_waker: *const ()) {
    drop(Box::from_raw(raw_waker as *mut u32));
}
unsafe fn my_wake_by_ref(_raw_waker: *const ()) {
}
```

The my_wake function converts the raw pointer back to a box and drops it. This makes sense because my_wake is supposed to consume the waker. The my_wake_by_ref function does nothing. It is the same as the my_wake function but does not consume the waker. If we wanted to experiment with notifying the executor, we could have an AtomicBool that we set to true in these functions. Then we can come up with some form of executor mechanism to check the AtomicBool before bothering to poll the future, as checking an AtomicBool is less computationally expensive than polling a future. We could also have another queue where a notification could be sent for task readiness, but for our server implementation, we are going to stick with polling without checking before the poll is performed.

When our task has finished or has been canceled, we no longer need to poll our task, and our waker is dropped. Our drop function takes the following form:

```
unsafe fn my_drop(raw_waker: *const ()) {
    drop(Box::from_raw(raw_waker as *mut u32));
}
```

This is where we convert the box back to a raw pointer and drop it.

We have now defined all the functions for our waker. All we need is a function to create the waker:

```
pub fn create_raw_waker() -> RawWaker {
    let data = Box::into_raw(Box::new(42u32));
    RawWaker::new(data as *const (), &VTABLE)
}
```

We pass in some dummy data and create RawWaker with a reference to our function table. We can see the customization that we have with this raw approach. We could have multiple RawWakerTable definitions, and we could construct different function tables than RawWaker, depending on what we pass into the create_raw_waker function. In our executor, we could vary the input depending on the type of future we are processing. We could also pass in a reference to a data structure that our executor is holding instead of the u32 number 42. The number 42 has no significance; it is just an example of data being passed in. The data structure passed in could then be referenced in our functions bound to the table.

Even though we have built the bare bones of a waker, we can appreciate the power and customization that we have for choosing to build our own. Considering we need to use our waker to execute tasks in our executor, we can now move on to building our executor.

Building Our Executor

At a high level, our executor is going to consume futures, turn them into tasks so they can be run by our executor, return a handle, and put the task on a queue. Periodically, our executor is also going to poll tasks on that queue. We are going to house our executor in our *async_runtime/src/executor.rs* file. First, we need the following imports:

```
use std::{
    future::Future,
    sync::{Arc, mpsc},
    task::{Context, Poll, Waker},
    pin::Pin,
    collections::VecDeque
};
use crate::waker::create_raw_waker;
```

Before we begin to write our executor, we need to define our task struct that is going to be passed around the executor:

```
pub struct Task {
    future: Pin<Box<dyn Future<Output = ()> + Send>>,
    waker: Arc<Waker>,
}
```

Something might seem off to you when looking at the Task struct, and you would be right. Our future in our Task struct returns a (). However, we want to be able to run tasks that return different data types. The runtime would be terrible if we could only return one data type. You might feel the need to pass in a generic parameter, resulting in the following code:

```
pub struct Task<T> {
    future: Pin<Box<dyn Future<Output = T> + Send>>,
    waker: Arc<Waker>,
}
```

However, what happens with generics is that the compiler will look at all the instances of Task<T> and generate structs for every variance of T. Also, our executor will need the T generic argument to process Task<T>. This will result in multiple executors for each variance of T, which would result in a mess. Instead, we wrap our future in an async block, get the result of the future, and send that result over a channel. Therefore, our signature of all tasks return (), but we can still extract the result from the future. We will see how this is implemented in the spawn function on our executor. Here is the outline for our executor:

```
pub struct Executor {
    pub polling: VecDeque<Task>,
}
impl Executor {
    pub fn new() -> Self {
        Executor {
            polling: VecDeque::new(),
        }
    }
    pub fn spawn<F, T>(&mut self, future: F) -> mpsc::Receiver<T>
    where
        F: Future<Output = T> + 'static + Send,
        T: Send + 'static,
    {
        . . .
    }
    pub fn poll(&mut self) {
        . . .
    }
    pub fn create_waker(&self) -> Arc<Waker> {
        Arc::new(unsafe{Waker::from_raw(create_raw_waker())})
    }
}
```

The `polling` field of the `Executor` is where we are going to put our spawned tasks to be polled.

> Take note of our `create_waker` function in our `Executor`. Remember, our `Executor` is running on one thread and can only process one future at a time. If our `Executor` houses a data collection, we can pass a reference through to the `create_raw_waker` function if we have configured `create_raw_waker` to handle it. Our waker can have `unsafe` access to the data collection because only one future is being processed at a time, so there is not going to be more than one mutable reference from a future at a time.

Once a task is polled, if the task is still pending, we will put the task back on the polling queue to be polled again. To initially put the task on the queue, we use the spawn function:

```
pub fn spawn<F, T>(&mut self, future: F) -> mpsc::Receiver<T>
where
    F: Future<Output = T> + 'static + Send,
    T: Send + 'static,
{
    let (tx, rx) = mpsc::channel();
    let future: Pin<Box<dyn Future<Output = ()> + Send>> = Box::pin(
        async move {
            let result = future.await;
            let _ = tx.send(result);
```

```
    });
    let task = Task {
        future,
        waker: self.create_waker(),
    };
    self.polling.push_back(task);
    rx
}
```

We use the channel to return a handle and convert the return value of the future to
().

> If exposing the internal channel is not your style, you can create the
> following JoinHandle struct for the spawn task to return:
>
> ```
> pub struct JoinHandle<T> {
>     receiver: mpsc::Receiver<T>,
> }
> ```
>
> ```
> impl<T> JoinHandle<T> {
>     pub fn await(self) -> Result<T, mpsc::RecvError> {
>         self.receiver.recv()
>     }
> }
> ```
>
> Give your return handle the following await syntax:
>
> ```
> match handle.await() {
>     Ok(result) => println!("Received: {}", result),
>     Err(e) => println!("Error receiving result: {}", e),
> }
> ```

Now that we have our task on our polling queue, we can poll it with the Executor's
polling function:

```
pub fn poll(&mut self) {
    let mut task = match self.polling.pop_front() {
        Some(task) => task,
        None => return,
    };
    let waker = task.waker.clone();
    let context = &mut Context::from_waker(&waker);
    match task.future.as_mut().poll(context) {
        Poll::Ready(()) => {}
        Poll::Pending => {
            self.polling.push_back(task);
        }
    }
}
```

We just pop the task from the front of the queue, wrap a reference of our waker in a
context, and pass that into the poll function of the future. If the future is ready, we

do not need to do anything, as we are sending the result back via a channel so the future is dropped. If our future is pending, we just put it back on the queue.

The backbone of our async runtime is now done, and we can run async code. Before we build the rest of our `async_runtime` module, we should take a detour and run our executor. Not only must you be excited to see it work, but you may want to play around with customizing how futures are processed. Now is a good time to get a feel for how our system works.

Running Our Executor

Running our async runtime is fairly straightforward. In the *main.rs* file of our `async_runtime` module, we import the following:

```
use std::{
    future::Future,
    task::{Context, Poll},
    pin::Pin
};
mod executor;
mod waker;
```

We need a basic future to trace how our system is running. We have been using the counting future throughout the book, as it is such an easy implementation of a future that returns either `Pending` or `Ready` depending on the state. For quick reference (hopefully you can code this from memory now), the counting future takes this form:

```
pub struct CountingFuture {
    pub count: i32,
}
impl Future for CountingFuture {
    type Output = i32;
    fn poll(mut self: Pin<&mut Self>, cx: &mut Context<'_>)
        -> Poll<Self::Output> {
        self.count += 1;
        if self.count == 4 {
            println!("CountingFuture is done!");
            Poll::Ready(self.count)
        } else {
            cx.waker().wake_by_ref();
            println!(
                "CountingFuture is not done yet! {}",
                self.count
            );
            Poll::Pending
        }
    }
}
```

We define our futures, define our executor, spawn our futures, and then run them with the following code:

```
fn main() {
    let counter = CountingFuture { count: 0 };
    let counter_two = CountingFuture { count: 0 };
    let mut executor = executor::Executor::new();
    let handle = executor.spawn(counter);
    let _handle_two = executor.spawn(counter_two);
    std::thread::spawn(move || {
        loop {
            executor.poll();
        }
    });
    let result = handle.recv().unwrap();
    println!("Result: {}", result);
}
```

We spawn a thread and run an infinite loop polling the futures in the executor. While this loop is happening, we wait for the result of one of the futures. In our server, we will implement our executors properly so they can continue to receive futures throughout the entire lifetime of the program. This quick implementation gives us the following printout:

```
CountingFuture is not done yet! 1
CountingFuture is not done yet! 1
CountingFuture is not done yet! 2
CountingFuture is not done yet! 2
CountingFuture is not done yet! 3
CountingFuture is not done yet! 3
CountingFuture is done!
CountingFuture is done!
Result: 4
```

We can see that it works! We have an async runtime running with just the standard library!

> Remember that our waker does not really do anything. We are polling our futures in our executor queue regardless. If you comment out the cx.waker().wake_by_ref(); line in the poll function of CountingFuture, you will get the exact same result, which is different from what happens in runtimes like *smol* or *Tokio*. This tells us that established runtimes are using the waker to only poll futures that are to be woken. This means that established runtimes are more efficient with their polling.

Now that we have our async runtime running, we can drag the rest of our async processes over the finish line. We can start with a sender.

Building Our Sender

When it comes to sending data over a TCP socket, we must allow our executor to switch over to another async task if the connection is currently blocked. If the connection is not blocked, we can write the bytes to the stream. In our *async_runtime/src/sender.rs* file, we start by importing the following:

```
use std::{
    future::Future,
    task::{Context, Poll},
    pin::Pin,
    net::TcpStream,
    io::{self, Write},
    sync::{Arc, Mutex}
};
```

Our sender is essentially a future. During the `poll` function, if the stream is blocking, we will return `Pending`; if the stream is not blocking, we write the bytes to the stream. Our sender structure is defined here:

```
pub struct TcpSender {
    pub stream: Arc<Mutex<TcpStream>>,
    pub buffer: Vec<u8>
}
impl Future for TcpSender {

    type Output = io::Result<()>;

    fn poll(self: Pin<&mut Self>, cx: &mut Context<'_>)
        -> Poll<Self::Output> {
        . . .
    }
}
```

Our `TcpStream` is wrapped in `Arc<Mutex<T>>`. We use `Arc<Mutex<T>>` so we can pass `TcpStream` into `Sender` and `Receiver`. Once we have sent the bytes over the stream, we will want to employ a `Receiver` future to await for the response.

For our `poll` function in the `TcpSender` struct, we initially try to get the lock of the stream:

```
let mut stream = match self.stream.try_lock() {
    Ok(stream) => stream,
    Err(_) => {
        cx.waker().wake_by_ref();
        return Poll::Pending;
    }
};
```

If we cannot get the lock, we return `Pending` so we are not blocking the executor, and the task will be put back on the queue to be polled again. Once we have it, we set it to nonblocking:

```
stream.set_nonblocking(true)?;
```

The `set_nonblocking` function makes the stream return a result immediately from the `write`, `recv`, `read`, or `send` functions. If the I/O operation was successful, the result will be `Ok`. If the I/O operation returns an `io::ErrorKind::WouldBlock` error, the IO operation needs to be retried because the stream was blocking. We handle these I/O operation outcomes as follows:

```
match stream.write_all(&self.buffer) {
    Ok(_) => {
        Poll::Ready(Ok(()))
    },
    Err(ref e) if e.kind() == io::ErrorKind::WouldBlock => {
        cx.waker().wake_by_ref();
        Poll::Pending
    },
    Err(e) => Poll::Ready(Err(e))
}
```

We now have a sender future defined, so we can move on to our receiver future.

Building Our Receiver

Our receiver will wait for the data in the stream, returning `Pending` if the bytes are not in the stream to be read. To build this future, we import the following in the *async_runtime/src/receiver.rs* file:

```
use std::{
    future::Future,
    task::{Context, Poll},
    pin::Pin,
    net::TcpStream,
    io::{self, Read},
    sync::{Arc, Mutex}
};
```

Seeing as we are returning bytes, it will not be a surprise that our receiver future takes this form:

```
pub struct TcpReceiver {
    pub stream: Arc<Mutex<TcpStream>>,
    pub buffer: Vec<u8>
}
impl Future for TcpReceiver {

    type Output = io::Result<Vec<u8>>;
```

```
    fn poll(mut self: Pin<&mut Self>, cx: &mut Context<'_>)
        -> Poll<Self::Output> {
        . . .
    }
}
```

In our poll function, we acquire the lock of the stream and set it to nonblocking, just like we did in our sender future:

```
let mut stream = match self.stream.try_lock() {
    Ok(stream) => stream,
    Err(_) => {
        cx.waker().wake_by_ref();
        return Poll::Pending;
    }
};
stream.set_nonblocking(true)?;
```

Next we handle the read of the stream:

```
let mut local_buf = [0; 1024];

match stream.read(&mut local_buf) {
    Ok(0) => {
        Poll::Ready(Ok(self.buffer.to_vec()))
    },
    Ok(n) => {
        std::mem::drop(stream);
        self.buffer.extend_from_slice(&local_buf[..n]);
        cx.waker().wake_by_ref();
        Poll::Pending
    },
    Err(ref e) if e.kind() == io::ErrorKind::WouldBlock => {
        cx.waker().wake_by_ref();
        Poll::Pending
    },
    Err(e) => Poll::Ready(Err(e))
}
```

We now have all the async functionality to get our server running. However, there is one basic future that we can build to allow sync code to also have async properties: the sleep future.

Building Our Sleep

We covered this before, so hopefully you are able to implement this yourself. However, for reference, our *async_runtime/src/sleep.rs* file will house our sleep future. We import the following:

```
use std::{
    future::Future,
    pin::Pin,
```

```
        task::{Context, Poll},
        time::{Duration, Instant},
    };
```

Our Sleep struct takes this form:

```
pub struct Sleep {
    when: Instant,
}
impl Sleep {
    pub fn new(duration: Duration) -> Self {
        Sleep {
            when: Instant::now() + duration,
        }
    }
}
```

And our Sleep future implements the Future trait:

```
impl Future for Sleep {
    type Output = ();
    fn poll(self: Pin<&mut Self>, cx: &mut Context<'_>)
        -> Poll<Self::Output> {
        let now = Instant::now();
        if now >= self.when {
            Poll::Ready(())
        } else {
            cx.waker().wake_by_ref();
            Poll::Pending
        }
    }
}
```

Now our async system has everything we need. To make our async runtime components public, we have the following code in our *async_runtime/src/lib.rs* file:

```
pub mod executor;
pub mod waker;
pub mod receiver;
pub mod sleep;
pub mod sender;
```

We can now import our components into our server. Considering that all the functionality is completed, we should use it to build our server.

Building Our Server

To build our server, we need the data and async modules that we coded. To install these, the *Cargo.toml* file dependencies take the following form:

```
[dependencies]
data_layer = { path = "../data_layer" }
async_runtime = { path = "../async_runtime" }
```

```
[profile.release]
opt-level = 'z'
```

We are optimizing for binary size with opt-level.

The entire code for our server can be in our *main.rs* file, which needs these imports:

```
use std::{
    thread,
    sync::{mpsc::channel, atomic::{AtomicBool, Ordering}},
    io::{self, Read, Write, ErrorKind, Cursor},
    net::{TcpListener, TcpStream}
};
use data_layer::data::Data;
use async_runtime::{
    executor::Executor,
    sleep::Sleep
};
```

Now that we have everything we need, we can build out the code that will accept our requests.

Accepting Requests

We can have our main thread listening to incoming TCP requests. Then our main thread distributes the requests along three threads and executors, as depicted in Figure 10-1.

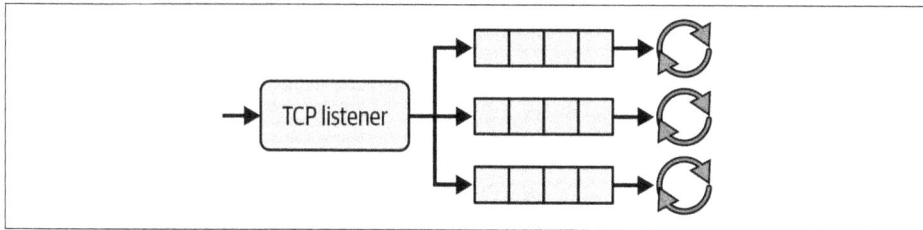

Figure 10-1. Handling incoming requests

We also want our threads to park if there are no requests to process. To communicate with the threads for parking, we have an AtomicBool for each thread:

```
static FLAGS: [AtomicBool; 3] = [
    AtomicBool::new(false),
    AtomicBool::new(false),
    AtomicBool::new(false),
];
```

Each AtomicBool represents a thread. If the AtomicBool is false, the thread is not parked. If the AtomicBool is true, then our router knows that our thread is parked and that we have to wake it up before sending the thread a request.

Now that we have our FLAGS, we must handle our incoming requests for each thread. Inside our threads, we create an executor and then try to receive a message in the channel for the thread. If there is a request in the channel, we spawn a task on that executor. If there is no incoming request, we check for tasks waiting to be polled. If there are no tasks, then the thread sets FLAG to true and parks the thread. If there are any tasks to be polled, then we poll the task at the end of the loop. We can carry out this process with this macro:

```
macro_rules! spawn_worker {
    ($name:expr, $rx:expr, $flag:expr) => {
        thread::spawn(move || {
            let mut executor = Executor::new();
            loop {
                if let Ok(stream) = $rx.try_recv() {
                    println!(
                        "{} Received connection: {}",
                        $name,
                        stream.peer_addr().unwrap()
                    );
                    executor.spawn(handle_client(stream));
                } else {
                    if executor.polling.len() == 0 {
                        println!("{} is sleeping", $name);
                        $flag.store(true, Ordering::SeqCst);
                        thread::park();
                    }
                }
                executor.poll();
            }
        })
    };
}
```

Here in our macro, we accept the name of our thread for logging purposes, the receiver of a channel to accept incoming requests, and the flag to inform the rest of the system when the thread parks.

> You can read more about creating complex macros in "Writing Complex Macros in Rust" (*https://oreil.ly/xinnm*) by Ingvar Stepanyan.

We can orchestrate the accepting of our requests in the main function:

```
fn main() -> io::Result<()> {
    . . .
    Ok(())
}
```

First, we define the channels that we will use to send requests to our threads:

```
let (one_tx, one_rx) = channel::<TcpStream>();
let (two_tx, two_rx) = channel::<TcpStream>();
let (three_tx, three_rx) = channel::<TcpStream>();
```

We then create our threads for our requests to be handled:

```
let one = spawn_worker!("One", one_rx, &FLAGS[0]);
let two = spawn_worker!("Two", two_rx, &FLAGS[1]);
let three = spawn_worker!("Three", three_rx, &FLAGS[2]);
```

Now our executors are running in their own threads and waiting for our TCP listener to send them requests. We need to keep and reference the thread handles and thread channel transmitters so we can wake and send requests to individual threads. We can interact with the threads by using the following code:

```
let router = [one_tx, two_tx, three_tx];
let threads = [one, two, three];
let mut index = 0;

let listener = TcpListener::bind("127.0.0.1:7878")?;
println!("Server listening on port 7878");

for stream in listener.incoming() {
    . . .
}
```

All we need to do now is handle our incoming TCP requests:

```
for stream in listener.incoming() {
    match stream {
        Ok(stream) => {
            let _ = router[index].send(stream);
            if FLAGS[index].load(Ordering::SeqCst) {
                FLAGS[index].store(false, Ordering::SeqCst);
                threads[index].thread().unpark();
            }
            index += 1;  // cycle through the index of threads
            if index == 3 {
                index = 0;
            }
        }
        Err(e) => {
            println!("Connection failed: {}", e);
        }
    }
}
```

Once we receive the TCP request, we send the TCP stream to a thread, check whether the thread is parked, and unpark the thread if needed. Next, we move the index over to the next thread so we can distribute the requests evenly across all our threads.

So what do we do with the requests once we have sent the request to an executor? We handle them.

Handling Requests

When it comes to handling our requests, we recall that our `handle_stream` function is called in the executor. Our handle async function takes the following form:

```
async fn handle_client(mut stream: TcpStream) -> std::io::Result<()> {
    stream.set_nonblocking(true)?;
    let mut buffer = Vec::new();
    let mut local_buf = [0; 1024];
    loop {
        . . .
    }
    match Data::deserialize(&mut Cursor::new(buffer.as_slice())) {
        Ok(message) => {
            println!("Received message: {:?}", message);
        },
        Err(e) => {
            println!("Failed to decode message: {}", e);
        }
    }
    Sleep::new(std::time::Duration::from_secs(1)).await;
    stream.write_all(b"Hello, client!")?;
    Ok(())
}
```

This should look similar to the sender and receiver futures that we built in the async runtime. Here, we add our async sleep for 1 second. This is just to simulate work being done. This will also ensure that our async is working. If our async is not properly working and we send 10 requests, then the total time will be above 10 seconds.

Inside our loop, we process the incoming stream:

```
match stream.read(&mut local_buf) {
    Ok(0) => {
        break;
    },
    Ok(len) => {
        buffer.extend_from_slice(&local_buf[..len]);
    },
    Err(ref e) if e.kind() == ErrorKind::WouldBlock => {
        if buffer.len() > 0 {
            break;
        }
        Sleep::new(std::time::Duration::from_millis(10)).await;
        continue;
    },
    Err(e) => {
```

```
            println!("Failed to read from connection: {}", e);
        }
    }
```

If blocking occurs, we introduce a tiny async sleep so the executor will put the request handle back on the queue to poll other request handles.

Our server is now fully functioning. The only piece left that we need to code is our client.

Building Our Async Client

Because our client also relies on the same dependencies, it will not be surprising that the client *Cargo.toml* has the following dependencies:

```
[dependencies]
data_layer = { path = "../data_layer" }
async_runtime = { path = "../async_runtime" }
```

In our *main.rs* file, we need the following imports:

```
use std::{
    io,
    sync::{Arc, Mutex},
    net::TcpStream,
    time::Instant
};
use data_layer::data::Data;
use async_runtime::{
    executor::Executor,
    receiver::TcpReceiver,
    sender::TcpSender,
};
```

To send, we implement the sending and receiving futures from our async runtime:

```
async fn send_data(field1: u32, field2: u16, field3: String)
    -> io::Result<String> {
    let stream = Arc::new(Mutex::new(TcpStream::connect(
                                        "127.0.0.1:7878")?
                          ));
    let message = Data {field1, field2, field3};
    TcpSender {
        stream: stream.clone(),
        buffer: message.serialize()?
    }.await?;
    let receiver = TcpReceiver {
        stream: stream.clone(),
        buffer: Vec::new()
    };
    String::from_utf8(receiver.await?).map_err(|_|
        io::Error::new(io::ErrorKind::InvalidData, "Invalid UTF-8")
```

```
        )
    }
```

We can now call our async `send_data` function 4,000 times and wait on all those handles:

```
fn main() -> io::Result<()> {
    let mut executor = Executor::new();
    let mut handles = Vec::new();
    let start = Instant::now();
    for i in 0..4000 {
        let handle = executor.spawn(send_data(
            i, i as u16, format!("Hello, server! {}", i)
        ));
        handles.push(handle);
    }
    std::thread::spawn(move || {
        loop {
            executor.poll();
        }
    });
    println!("Waiting for result...");
    for handle in handles {
        match handle.recv().unwrap() {
            Ok(result) => println!("Result: {}", result),
            Err(e) => println!("Error: {}", e)
        };
    }
    let duration = start.elapsed();
    println!("Time elapsed in expensive_function() is: {:?}", duration);
    Ok(())
}
```

And our test is ready. If you run the server and client in different terminals, you will see that all the printouts display that the requests are being handled. The entire client process takes roughly 1.2 seconds, meaning that our async system is running. And there you have it! We have built an async server with zero third-party dependencies!

Summary

In this chapter, we used only the standard library to build an async runtime that is fairly efficient. Part of this performance is a result of us coding our server in Rust. Another factor is that the async module increases the utilization of our resources for I/O bound tasks like connections. Sure, our server is not going to be as efficient as runtimes like *Tokio*, but it is usable.

We do not advise that you start ripping *Tokio* and web frameworks out of your projects since a lot of crates have been built to integrate with runtimes like *Tokio*. You would lose a lot of integration with third-party crates, and your runtime would not be as efficient. However, you can also have another runtime active in your program at the same time. For instance, we can use *Tokio* channels to send tasks to our custom async runtime. This means that *Tokio* can juggle other async *Tokio* tasks while awaiting the completion of the task in our custom async runtime. This approach is useful when you need an established runtime like *Tokio* to handle standard async tasks like incoming requests, but you also have specific need to handle tasks in a very particular way for a niche problem. For instance, you may have built a key-value store and have read up on the latest computer science papers on how to handle transactions on it. You then want to directly implement that logic in your custom async runtime.

We can conclude that building our own async runtime isn't the best or worst approach. Knowing established runtimes and being able to build your own is the best of both worlds. Having both tools at hand and knowing where and when to apply them is way better than being an evangelist for one tool. However, you need to practice these tools before you whip them out and use them to solve a problem. We suggest that you continue pushing yourself with custom async runtimes on a range of projects. Experimenting with different types of data around the waker is a good start to explore multiple approaches.

Testing is a big part of exploring and refining your approaches. Testing enables you to get in-depth, direct feedback on your async code and implementation. In Chapter 11, we will cover how to test your async code so you can continue exploring async concepts and implementations.

CHAPTER 11

Testing

We know by now how powerful writing async systems in Rust can be. However, when building big async systems in Rust, we need to know how to test our async code. This is because the complexity of the system grows as the size of the system increases.

Testing increases the feedback of the code that we are implementing, making our code faster to write and safer. For instance, if we have a big codebase and need to alter or add functionality into a piece of code, it would be slow and dangerous if we had to spin up the entire system and run it to see if our code works. Instead, altering or adding the code we need and running the specific tests for that piece of code not only provides a faster feedback loop, but also enables us to test more edge cases, making our code safer. In this chapter, we explore various approaches to testing async and the interfaces between our code and external systems.

By the end of this chapter, you will be able to build isolated tests where you can mock interfaces and inspect the calls to those interfaces. This gives you the ability to build truly isolated atomic tests. You will also be able to test for synchronization pitfalls like deadlocks, race conditions, and channel capacity issues that block async tasks. Finally, you will also learn how to mock interactions with networks such as servers, obtain fine-grained testing control of all futures, and know when to poll them to see how your system progresses under different polling conditions.

We can start our testing journey by covering the basics of synchronous testing.

Performing Basic Sync Testing

In "Building an Isolated Module" on page 179, we built an async runtime environment that has a synchronous interface. Unsurprisingly, because the interface includes just a couple of functions that are synchronous, the isolated module is one of the easiest to test. We can start our testing journey by performing synchronous testing.

Before we build our tests, we need the following dependency in our *Cargo.toml*:

```
[dev-dependencies]
mockall = "0.11.4"
```

The *mockall* dependency will enable us to mock traits and their functions so we can inspect inputs and mock outputs.

For the interface of our isolated module, we recall that the two functions are spawn, which returns a key, and get_result, which returns the result of the async task we spawn. We can define the following trait for these interactions:

```rust
pub trait AsyncProcess<X, Y, Z> {
    fn spawn(&self, input: X) -> Result<Y, String>;
    fn get_result(&self, key: Y) -> Result<Z, String>;
}
```

Here, we have generic parameters so we can vary the inputs, outputs, and the type of key that is used. We can now move on to our async function where we spawn a task, print something out, and then get the result from the async function and handle the result:

```rust
fn do_something<T>(async_handle: T, input: i32)
    -> Result<i32, String>
    where T: AsyncProcess<i32, String, i32>
{
    let key = async_handle.spawn(input)?;
    println!("something is happening");
    let result = async_handle.get_result(key)?;
    if result > 10 {
        return Err("result is too big".to_string());
    }
    if result == 8 {
        return Ok(result * 2)
    }
    Ok(result * 3)
}
```

Here, we are relying on dependency injection. In a *dependency injection*, we pass a struct, object, or function into another function as a parameter. What we pass into the function then performs a computation.

For us, we pass in a struct that has implemented the trait, and then we call that trait. This is powerful. For example, we could implement a read trait for a struct that accesses a database for the read function. However, we could get a different struct that handles the reading from files and also implement the read trait. Depending on the storage solution we want, we can just feed that handle into the function. As you have probably guessed, we can create a mock struct and implement whatever functionality we want for the trait implemented on that mock struct, and then pass the mock struct into the function that we are testing. However, if we properly mock our struct by using *mockall*, we can also assert certain conditions, such as what is passed into our functions for the handler. Our test layout takes the following form:

```
#[cfg(test)]
mod get_team_processes_tests {
    use super::*;
    use mockall::predicate::*;
    use mockall::mock;


    mock! {
        DatabaseHandler {}
        impl AsyncProcess<i32, String, i32> for DatabaseHandler {
            fn spawn(&self, input: i32) -> Result<String, String>;


            fn get_result(&self, key: String) -> Result<i32, String>;
        }
    }
    #[test]
    fn do_something_fail() {
        . . .
    }
}
```

Inside our do_something_fail test function, we define the mock handler and assert that 4 is passed into the spawn function, which will then return a test_key:

```
let mut handle = MockDatabaseHandler::new();
handle.expect_spawn()
        .with(eq(4))
        .returning(|_|{Ok("test_key".to_string())});
```

Now that we have the test_key, we can assume that it is going to be passed into our get_result function, and we state that get_result will return an 11:

```
handle.expect_get_result().with(eq("test_key".to_string()))
                        .returning(|_|{Ok(11)});
```

We can assume that the function we are testing will return an error, so we assert this

```
let outcome = do_something(handle, 4);
assert_eq!(outcome, Err("result is too big".to_string()));
```

We are following the industry standard of *arrange*, *act*, and *assert* in our testing process:

Arrange

We set up our test environment and define the expected behavior of our mocks. (This is done when we create the mock handler and specify the expected inputs and outputs.)

Act

> We execute the function under test with the arranged conditions. (This happens when we call `do_something(handle, 4)`.)

Assert

> We verify that the outcome matches our expectations. (This is where we use `assert_eq!` to check the result.)

Our test is now defined, as we can run it with a `cargo test` command, resulting in the following printout:

```
running 1 test
test get_team_processes_tests::do_something_fail ... ok
```

And there we have it: our test is passing. Even though we will not define every possible outcome in this book for the sake of brevity, it is a good opportunity for you to practice unit testing by attempting all edge cases.

> Mocking is powerful because it enables us to isolate our logic. Let's imagine that our `do_something` function is in an application requring the database to be in a certain state. For instance, if `do_something` processes the number of team members in a database, the teams probably need to be in the database. However, if we want to run `do_something`, we would not want to have to populate the database and ensure that everything is lined up before we run the code. There are several reasons for this. If we wanted to redefine the parameters for another edge case, we would have to reshuffle the database. This would take a long time, and every time we run the code, we would have to fiddle with the database again. Mocking makes our test atomic. We can run our code again and again without needing to set up the environment. Developers who employ test-driven development generally develop at a faster pace with fewer bugs.

So we have the basic mocking defined for our program, but we are not going to be using the isolated module on everything. Your code might be fully async. This is especially true if you are doing web development. You may want to test async functions in your async module. To do this, we need to cover async mocking.

Mocking Async Code

To test our async traits, we need an async runtime in our test functions. You are free to pick whichever runtime you are comfortable with, but for our examples, we are going to stick with *Tokio*, giving us the following dependencies:

```
[dependencies]
tokio = { version = "1.34.0", features = ["full"] }

[dev-dependencies]
mockall = "0.11.4"
```

We no longer need two functions for our trait because our trait is async; the async function will return a handle that we can wait on. So we have just the `get_result` function since the handle is managed in the async code:

```
use std::future::Future;

pub trait AsyncProcess<X, Z> {
    fn get_result(&self, key: X) -> impl Future<
    Output = Result<Z, String>> + Send + 'static;
}
```

The `get_result` function within our `AsyncProcess` trait returns a future as opposed to `get_result` just being an async function. This desugaring enables us to have more control over the traits that the future has implemented on them.

Our `do_something` function is also redefined:

```
async fn do_something<T>(async_handle: T, input: i32)
    -> Result<i32, String>
where
    T: AsyncProcess<i32, i32> + Send + Sync + 'static
{
    println!("something is happening");
    let result: i32 = async_handle.get_result(input).await?;
    if result > 10 {
        return Err("result is too big".to_string());
    }
    if result == 8 {
        return Ok(result * 2)
    }
    Ok(result * 3)
}
```

The logic of how we handle the result stays the same: we spawn the task before the print statement and get the result after the print statement. Before we do any mocks, however, we must ensure that we have the following imports for our tests module:

```
use super::*;
use mockall::predicate::*;
use mockall::mock;
use std::boxed::Box;
```

Because our trait now has only one function, our mock is redefined with the following code:

```
mock! {
    DatabaseHandler {}
```

```
impl AsyncProcess<i32, i32> for DatabaseHandler {
    fn get_result(&self, key: i32) -> impl Future<
    Output = Result<i32, String>> + Send + 'static;
}
}
```

Now that our function is async, we need to define a runtime inside our test and then block on it. Our tests are not going to all run on one thread, so we can ensure that our tests are atomic by defining the runtime in each individual test:

```
#[test]
fn do_something_fail() {
    let mut handle = MockDatabaseHandler::new();
    handle.expect_get_result()
            .with(eq(4))
            .returning(
                |_|{
                    Box::pin(async move { Ok(11) })
                }
            );
    let runtime = tokio::runtime::Builder::new_current_thread()
                                        .enable_all()
                                        .build()
                                        .unwrap();
    let outcome = runtime.block_on(do_something(handle, 4));
    assert_eq!(outcome, Err("result is too big".to_string()));
}
```

We now have mocking for our async code. We advise that you have isolated async functions for processes that interact with other sources such as HTTP requests or database connections. This makes them easier to mock, which makes our code easier to test. However, we know with async that making calls to external resources is not the only thing we need to keep in mind when testing async code. Remember, we can also get syncing problems such as deadlocks with our async code, so we need to test for these.

Testing For Deadlocks

In a *deadlock*, an async task is held up with no way out of completing because of a lock. Not all the examples throughout the book expose the async system to deadlocks, but they can happen. A simple example of creating a deadlock is having two async tasks trying to access the same two locks but in opposite order (Figure 11-1).

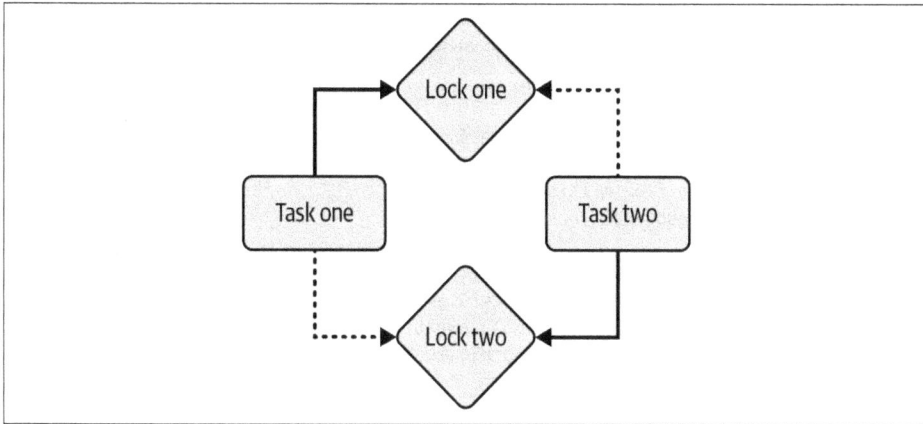

Figure 11-1. A deadlock

In Figure 11-1, task one acquires lock one. Task two acquires lock two. However, neither task has given up its lock, but each tries to acquire the other lock that is already held while still keeping hold of their own. This results in a deadlock: the two tasks will never finish because they can never acquire the second lock that they are trying to acquire.

This deadlock does not just hold up the two tasks. If other tasks require access to these locks, they will also be blocked when spawned; before we know it, our entire system will grind to a halt. Testing for deadlocks is important. With unit testing, we can try to catch these deadlocks before we integrate our code into the rest of the system. For our test, we have the following output:

```
#[cfg(test)]
mod tests {
    use tokio::sync::Mutex;
    use std::sync::Arc;
    use tokio::time::{sleep, Duration, timeout};

    #[tokio::test]
    async fn test_deadlock_detection() {
        . . .
    }
}
```

We are using the #[tokio::test] macro for our test. This is essentially the same as creating an async runtime inside the test function. Inside our test function, we create two mutexes and references to these mutexes, where both tasks can access both mutexes:

```
let resource1 = Arc::new(Mutex::new(0));
let resource2 = Arc::new(Mutex::new(0));
```

```
let resource1_clone = Arc::clone(&resource1);
let resource2_clone = Arc::clone(&resource2);
```

We then spawn two tasks:

```
let handle1 = tokio::spawn(async move {
    let _lock1 = resource1.lock().await;
    sleep(Duration::from_millis(100)).await;
    let _lock2 = resource2.lock().await;
});
let handle2 = tokio::spawn(async move {
    let _lock2 = resource2_clone.lock().await;
    sleep(Duration::from_millis(100)).await;
    let _lock1 = resource1_clone.lock().await;
});
```

Our first task goes for the first mutex, and the second mutex after a sleep. The second task reverses the order to locks that they are trying to acquire. The sleep functions will give both tasks the time to acquire their first locks before trying to acquire the second lock. We now want to wait on these tasks that are spawned, but we are testing for a deadlock. If a deadlock occurs and we do not set a timeout, the test will hang indefinitely. To avoid this, we can set a timeout:

```
let result = timeout(Duration::from_secs(5), async {
    let _ = handle1.await;
    let _ = handle2.await;
}).await;
```

The timeout is fairly big, but if the two async tasks have not finished after 5 seconds, we can conclude that the deadlock has occurred. Now that we have set our timeout, we can check it with the following code:

```
assert!(result.is_ok(), "A potential deadlock detected!");
```

Running our test gives this printout:

```
thread 'tests::test_deadlock_detection'
panicked at 'A potential deadlock detected!', src/main.rs:43:9
note: run with `RUST_BACKTRACE=1` environment variable to
display a backtrace
test tests::test_deadlock_detection ... FAILED

failures:
    tests::test_deadlock_detection

test result: FAILED. 0 passed; 1 failed; 0 ignored;
0 measured; 0 filtered out; finished in 5.01s
```

The time is just over 5 seconds, and we get a helpful message that a potential deadlock has been detected. We have not only caught a deadlock but also isolated the specific function causing the deadlock.

Another locking issue, called *livelocks*, has the same overall effect as deadlocks: livelocks can grind the system to a halt. In a livelock, two or more async tasks get held up. However, instead of two or more async tasks holding and not progressing, the two or more async tasks are responding to each other but not progressing. A simple example is two async tasks echoing the same message to each other in a constant loop. A classic but clear analogy of the difference between deadlocks and livelocks is that a deadlock is like two people in a corridor standing still, waiting for the other one to move but neither of them moving. Livelocks, on the other hand, are two people trying to constantly sidestep each other, but both stepping in the wrong way, resulting in a constant block so neither person passes.

Although we should avoid deadlocks at all costs, their occurrences are generally obvious because the system usually grinds to a halt. However, our code can silently cause errors without us knowing. This is why we need to test for race conditions.

Testing for Race Conditions

In a *race condition*, the state of data gets changed, but the reference to that state is out of date. A simple example of a data race is depicted in Figure 11-2.

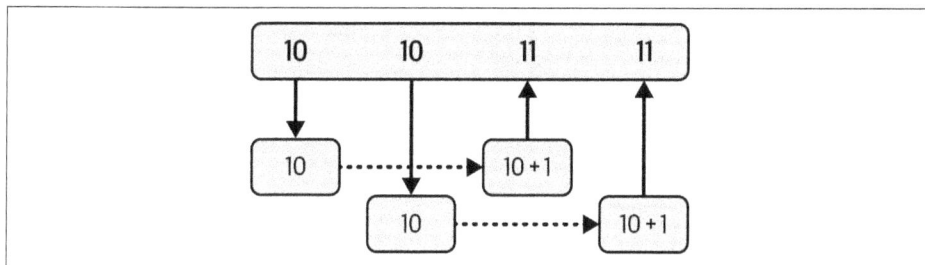

Figure 11-2. A race condition

Figure 11-2 shows two async tasks that are getting a number from a data store and increasing the number by one. Because the second task gets the data before the first task has updated the data store, both tasks increase from 10, which results in the data being 11 when it should be 12. Throughout this book, we have protected against this with mutexes or specific atomic operations that prevent data races from happening. The compare and update atomic operations are the simplest way of preventing this race condition example from happening. However, although preventing race conditions is the best approach, the way to do so is not always clear, and we need to explore how to test our code for data races. The outline of our test takes the following form:

```
#[cfg(test)]
mod tests {
```

```
use std::sync::atomic::{AtomicUsize, Ordering};
use tokio::time::{sleep, Duration};
use tokio::runtime::Builder;

static COUNTER: AtomicUsize = AtomicUsize::new(0);

async fn unsafe_add() {
    let value = COUNTER.load(Ordering::SeqCst);
    COUNTER.store(value + 1, Ordering::SeqCst);
}
#[test]
fn test_data_race() {
    . . .
}
}
```

Instead of doing an atomic add, we get the number, increase the number, and then set the new value so we have the chance of a race condition as shown in Figure 11-2. In our test function, we can build a single-threaded runtime and spawn 10,000 unsafe_add tasks. Once we have handled those tasks, we can assert that the COUNTER is 10,000:

```
let runtime = Builder::new_current_thread().enable_all()
                                           .build()
                                           .unwrap();
let mut handles = vec![];
let total = 100000;

for _ in 0..total {
    let handle = runtime.spawn(unsafe_add());
    handles.push(handle);
}
for handle in handles {
    runtime.block_on(handle).unwrap();
}
assert_eq!(
    COUNTER.load(Ordering::SeqCst),
    total,
    "race condition occurred!"
);
```

If we run our test, we can see that it passes. This is because the runtime has only one thread, and there is no async between the get and the set. However, say we change our runtime to have multiple threads:

```
let runtime = tokio::runtime::Runtime::new().unwrap();
```

We get the following error:

```
thread 'tests::test_data_race' panicked at
'assertion failed: `(left == right)`
  left: `99410`,
 right: `100000`: race condition occurred!'
```

Some of these tasks have been the victims of a race condition. Say we were to put another async function between the set and get, such as a sleep function:

```
let value = COUNTER.load(Ordering::SeqCst);
sleep(Duration::from_secs(1)).await;
COUNTER.store(value + 1, Ordering::SeqCst);
```

We would get the following error:

```
thread 'tests::test_data_race' panicked at
'assertion failed: `(left == right)`
  left: `1`,
 right: `100000`: Race Condition occurred!'
```

All our tasks are victims of race conditions. This is because all the tasks initially read the COUNTER before any of the tasks had written to it because of the async sleep yielding control back to the executor for other async tasks to read the COUNTER.

This result would also happen in the single-threaded environment if the sleep is nonblocking. This highlights the need to use multithreaded test environments if we are concerned about race conditions. We can also appreciate the speed at which we changed the parameters surrounding our task and can test the effect of the parameter changes on our tasks.

We know mutexes and atomic values are not the only way to enable multiple tasks to access data. We can use channels to send data between async tasks. Therefore, we need to test our channel capacity.

Testing Channel Capacity

We have used unbound channels for some of our examples, but we sometimes want to restrict the maximum size of the channel to prevent excessive memory consumption. However, if the channel reaches its maximum limit, senders cannot send more messages to the channel. We may have a system such as a collection of actors, and we need to see whether our system clogs up if we send too many messages into the system. Depending on the needs, we may require the system to slow down until all the messages are processed, but it is good to test the system so we know how it works for our use cases.

For our tests, we have the following layout:

```
#[cfg(test)]
mod tests {
    use tokio::sync::mpsc;
    use tokio::time::{Duration, timeout};
    use tokio::runtime::Builder;

    #[test]
    fn test_channel_capacity() {
```

```
        . . .
    }
}
```

Inside our test function, we define our async runtime and channel with a capacity of five:

```
let runtime = Builder::new_current_thread().enable_all()
                                           .build()
                                           .unwrap();
let (sender, mut receiver) = mpsc::channel::<i32>(5);
```

We then spawn a task that sends messages above the capacity of our channel:

```
let sender = runtime.spawn(async move {
    for i in 0..10 {
        sender.send(i).await.expect("Failed to send message");
    }
});
```

We want to see whether our system will break down with a timeout test:

```
let result = runtime.block_on(async {
    timeout(Duration::from_secs(5), async {
        sender.await.unwrap();
    }).await
});
assert!(result.is_ok(),  "A potential filled channel is not handled correctly");
```

Right now, our test will fail because the sender future will never complete, so our timeout is exceeded. To make our tests pass, we need to put in a receiver future before the timeout test:

```
let receiver = runtime.spawn(async move {
    let mut i = 0;
    while let Some(msg) = receiver.recv().await {
        assert_eq!(msg, i);
        i += 1;
        println!("Got message: {}", msg);
    }
});
```

Now when we run our test, it passes. Although we have tested a simple system of a sender and receiver, we must appreciate that our tests highlighted that our system will grind to a halt because we were not handling our messages properly. Channels can also result in deadlocks, just like our mutexes, and our timeout test will also highlight deadlocks if our testing is sufficient enough.

As we know, channels enable us to share data across the system asynchronously. When it comes to sharing data across processes and computers, we can use network protocols. No doubt in the wild, you will write async code that will interact with a server using a protocol. Our interactions also need to be tested.

Testing Network Interactions

When it comes to running network interactions in development and testing them, it might be tempting to spin up the server locally and rely on that server. However, this can be bad for testing. For instance, if we have an operation that deletes a row on the server after we have run the test once, we cannot run it again right away because the row is deleted. We could build a step that inserts the row, but this gets more complicated if the row has dependencies. Also, the `cargo test` command runs over multiple processes. If a couple of tests are hitting the same server, we can get data race conditions on the server. This is where we use *mockito*. This crate enables us to mock servers in the test directly and assert that the server endpoint was called with certain parameters. For our example of network testing, we need the following dependencies:

```
[dependencies]
tokio = { version = "1.34.0", features = ["full"] }
reqwest = { version = "0.11.22", features = ["json"] }

[dev-dependencies]
mockito = "1.2.0"
```

And our test outline takes the following form:

```
#[cfg(test)]
mod tests {
    use tokio::runtime::Builder;
    use mockito::Matcher;
    use reqwest;

    #[test]
    fn test_networking() {
        . . .
    }
}
```

Inside our test function, we spin up our test server:

```
let mut server = mockito::Server::new();
let url = server.url();
```

Here, *mockito* is finding a port that is not currently in use on the computer. If we send requests to the URL, our mock server can track them. Remember, our server is in the scope of the test function, so after the test is finished, the mock server will be terminated. With *mockito*, our tests remain truly atomic.

We then define a mock for a server endpoint:

```
let mock = server.mock("GET", "/my-endpoint")
.match_query(Matcher::AllOf(vec![
    Matcher::UrlEncoded("param1".into(), "value1".into()),
    Matcher::UrlEncoded("param2".into(), "value2".into()),
]))
```

```
.with_status(201)
.with_body("world")
.expect(5)
.create();
```

Our mock has the endpoint /my-endpoint. Our mock also expects certain parameters in the URL. Our mock will return the response code of 201 with a body of world. We also expect our server to be hit five times. We can add more endpoints if we want, but for this example we are using only one to avoid bloating the chapter.

Now that our mock server is built, we define our runtime environment:

```
let runtime = Builder::new_current_thread()
            .enable_io()
            .enable_time()
            .build()
            .unwrap();
let mut handles = vec![];
```

Everything is ready, so we send five async tasks to our runtime:

```
for _ in 0..5 {
    let url_clone = url.clone();
    handles.push(runtime.spawn(async move {
        let client = reqwest::Client::new();
        client.get(&format!(
            "{}/my-endpoint?param1=value1&param2=value2",
        url_clone)).send().await.unwrap()
    }));
}
```

Finally, we can block the thread for the async tasks and then assert the mock:

```
for handle in handles {
    runtime.block_on(handle).unwrap();
}
mock.assert();
```

We can assert that all our async tasks achieved their goal of hitting the server. If one of our tasks was unsuccessful, our test will fail.

When defining a URL for requests, it is best to have the definition dynamic as opposed to hardcoded. This enables us to change the host of the URL depending on whether we are making requests to a live server, local server, or mock server. Using environment variables is tempting. However, in testing, this can cause problems in the multithreaded environment of `cargo test`. Instead, it is best to define a trait that extracts configuration variables. We then pass structs that implement this extracted config variable trait. When binding our view functions to a live server, we can pass in a struct that extracts config variables from the environment. However, we can also just pass the *mockito* URL into the extracted config variable trait implementation when testing functions and views that make calls to other servers.

There is more functionality to *mockito*. For instance, JSON bodies, functions determining the response of the request, and other features are available when reading the API docs of *mockito*. Now that we can mock servers and traits, we can test our systems in an isolated environment. However, what about isolating futures and testing these futures in a fine-grained way, inspecting what the future is like between polling? This is where async testing crates help us out.

Fine-Grained Future Testing

For this section, we will use the *Tokio* testing tool. However, the concepts covered here can be applied when testing futures in any async runtime. For our tests, we need the following dependencies:

```
[dependencies]
tokio = { version = "1.34.0", features = ["full"] }

[dev-dependencies]
tokio-test = "0.4.3"
```

For our fine-grained testing, we will have two futures acquire the same mutex, increase the count by one, and then finish. Because some indirect interaction occurs between two futures through acquiring the same mutex, we can poll the futures individually and determine the state of the future at the time the future is polled.

Initially, our tests have the following layout:

```
#[cfg(test)]
mod tests {

    use tokio::sync::Mutex;
    use tokio::time::{sleep, Duration};
    use tokio_test::{task::spawn, assert_pending};
    use std::sync::Arc;
    use std::task::Poll;
```

```
async fn async_mutex_locker(mutex: Arc<Mutex<i32>>) -> () {
    let mut lock = mutex.lock().await;
    *lock += 1;
    sleep(Duration::from_millis(1)).await;
}
#[tokio::test]
async fn test_monitor_file_metadata() {
    . . .
}
```

Inside our test, we define our mutex with the references for the futures:

```
let mutex = Arc::new(Mutex::new(0));
let mutex_clone1 = mutex.clone();
let mutex_clone2 = mutex.clone();
```

We can now spawn the futures with the mutex references by using the tokio_test::spawn function:

```
let mut future1 = spawn(async_mutex_locker(mutex_clone1));
let mut future2 = spawn(async_mutex_locker(mutex_clone2));
```

We then poll our futures, asserting that both should be pending:

```
assert_pending!(future1.poll());
assert_pending!(future2.poll());
```

Although both futures are pending, we know that the first future will acquire the mutex first because it was polled first. We could have swapped the order of polling, and we would get the opposite effect. This is where we can see the power of this testing approach. It enables us to inspect what happens to futures if we change the order of polling. We can then test edge cases at a deeper level since we cannot ensure the order of polling in our live system unless we purposely design our system to do so.

As we have seen in our deadlock example, as long as our first future has acquired the lock of the mutex, we know that no matter how many times we poll the second future, the second future will always be pending. We ensure that our assumption is correct as follows:

```
for _ in 0..10 {
    assert_pending!(future2.poll());
    sleep(Duration::from_millis(1)).await;
}
```

Here we can see with our assert_pending trait, if our assumption is incorrect, our test will fail. Adequate time has elapsed, so we can assume that if we poll the first future now, it will be ready. We define the following assertion:

```
assert_eq!(future1.poll(), Poll::Ready(()));
```

However, we have not dropped our first future, and we do not give up the lock for the entirety of the future. Therefore, we can conclude that even if we wait for a time that would allow the second future to complete, the second future will still be pending since the first future is still keeping hold of the mutex guard. We can assert this assumption with this code:

```
sleep(Duration::from_millis(3)).await;
assert_pending!(future2.poll());
```

We can assert that our theory around holding onto the mutex is correct by dropping the first future, waiting, and then asserting that the second future is now finished:

```
drop(future1);
sleep(Duration::from_millis(1)).await;
assert_eq!(future2.poll(), Poll::Ready(()));
```

We can then assert that our mutex has the value we expect:

```
let lock = mutex.lock().await;
assert_eq!(*lock, 2);
```

If we run our test, we can see that it will pass.

Here, we have managed to freeze our async system, inspect the state, and then poll again, progressing our futures one step at a time. We can even swap around the order of the polling whenever we want in the test. This gives us a lot of power in testing results when the order of polling changes.

Summary

We covered a range of testing methods to async problems in a test-driven approach. We highly recommend that if you are starting a new async Rust project, you build the tests as you write the async code. You will maintain a fast development pace as a result.

We are now at the end of our journey together. We hope you are excited about using async Rust. It is a powerful and evolving field. With your new skills and async knowledge, you now have another tool that you can bring to your solutions. You can break problems into async concepts and implement powerful, fast solutions. We hope you have experienced joy at the beauty of async and in the way Rust implements async systems. We honestly are excited about what you will build with async Rust.

Index

Symbols
? operator for error handling, 185

A
actor model
 actor supervision, 170-176
 actors defined, 155
 building a basic actor, 155
  refactored for heartbeat mechanism,
   171-176
 documentation link, 155
 mutexes versus actors, 157-160
 router pattern, 160-165
  actor supervision, 170-176
  sender as global static, 163
  sender as global static caution, 163
 sending a message to an actor, 156
  multiproducer, single-consumer channel
   (mpsc), 156
  oneshot::Sender for response, 156
 state of actors, 155, 160
  fault-tolerant state recovery, 168
  state recovery for actors, 165-170
 testing actors, 156
  isolation simplifying testing, 155
anyhow library, 72
API calls via reqwest package, 20
Arc (atomic reference counting), 13
 basic asynchronous code, 14
async closure in static lifetime, 51
 async closure documentation link, 51
async move, 51
async programming
 about, vii, 1, 10

async described, 2-4
 basic asynchronous code, 3
async programming in the wild, 179
 (see also design patterns)
async Rust (see async Rust)
computationally heavy tasks, 58
coroutines mimicking async behavior, 90,
 100-103
deadlocks, 104, 224
examples of using async, 16-22
 file I/O, 16-20
 HTTP request performance, 20-22
futures, 26, 29
 (see also futures)
generators, 94
 (see also generators)
ownership
 AsyncRead execution, 78
 shared data, 14
 variables in static lifetime, 51
processes, 5-10
 (see also processes)
 async Rust, 7
 basic asynchronous code, 7
 definition, 5
 drawbacks, 9
reactive programming (see reactive programming)
runtime summary, 56
synchronous code mix issues, 110
tasks, 23-28
 (see also tasks)
 definition, 28
 flow control via coroutines, 104-108

futures, 26, 29
  (see also futures)
  nonblocking sleep allowing async, 27,
    54, 145
threads, 10-16
  basic asynchronous code, 11, 14
  Condvar for interaction, 13
  definition, 10
  JoinHandle, 11
  JoinHandle return result, 12
  multiple Condvars, 15
  parked while waiting, 14, 62
async queues
  building your own, 50-57
    about, 49
    async runtime summary, 56
    background processes, 68
    CPU tasks offloaded to new thread pool,
      34, 58
    increasing threads and queues, 57
    join macro created, 65
    networking (see networking integrated
      into async runtime)
    Runnable handle, 52
    runtime configured, 66-68
    runtime rebuilt, 141
    static keyword, 51
    task stealing, 61-63
    task-spawning function, 51
    task-spawning function refactored,
      63-64
    tasks to different queues, 59-61
  lazy in evaluation, 63
    runtime configured for, 66-68
  multiple queues, 59-61
    task stealing, 61-63
    Tokio for task distribution, 61
async runtime (see runtime)
async Rust
  about, vii
  function colors, 110
  global state drawbacks, 163
  Rust learning resources, vii
  tasks, 23-28
    (see also tasks)
    futures, 26, 29
      (see also futures)
    nonblocking sleep allowing async, 27,
      54, 145

async server built
  about, 197
  basics set up, 197-199
    Data struct public, 199
    four workspaces, 197
    serialize and deserialize functions, 198
  client built, 215
  receiver built, 208
  runtime components, 199-210
    executor built, 202-205
    executor run, 205-206
    waker, 200-202
  sender built, 207
  server built, 210
    accepting requests, 211-214
    handling requests, 214
  sleep built, 209
async tasks (see tasks)
async-native-tls, 72
async-task, 50
  building an async queue, 50-57
async/await functions
  accessing thread data directly and, 147-149
  await keyword in Tokio, 26, 55
    Tokio runtime for, 143
  building an async queue, 53
  coroutines described, 90, 103
  futures with, 33, 42
AsyncRead trait, 77-79
  documentation link, 77
Atomic Bool
  documentation link, 15
  Relaxed ordering, 15
atomics, 121
  compare and exchange, 120
  documentation link, 115
  event bus, 128-129
  reactive system, 116-117
audit trail example of futures, 44-48
await keyword (Tokio), 26, 55, 143
  accessing thread data directly and, 147-149

B
background processes, 68
backpressure from event buildup, 133
book web page, x
Box<dyn Any + Send>> dynamic trait object,
  12
broadcasting via event bus, 127-135

broadcast channels versus, 127
dependencies and imports, 128
event bus interactions via tasks, 132
handle for event bus, 131-132
    garbage collection for dead IDs, 133
struct for event bus, 128-130

C

caching via local pool, 145
callbacks, 124
    callback guard, 126
    nested callbacks leading to hell, 126
    user input via, 124-127
        event loop for nonblocking, 125
channels
    async file I/O example, 18-20
    flume for building async queue, 50-57
        increasing threads and queues, 57
        task stealing, 61-63
    lazy in evaluation, 63
    testing channel capacity, 229
    waking futures remotely, 35-37
circuit-breaker pattern, 194-196
    documentation link, 194
    spawn_task checking OPEN, 194
clearscreen for heater system display, 116, 118-121, 125
Clone trait
    event bus struct, 128-130
    JoinHandle not implementing, 12
Condvar (conditional variable), 13
    basic asynchronous code, 14
    thread interaction, 13
        multiple Condvars, 15
        parked thread, 14
connectors, 72
    hyper relying on, 74-77
Context in futures, 32-34
cooperative multitasking, 27
Coroutine trait
    formerly Generator trait and Generator-State, 96
    Future trait similarity, 94
        coroutines implementing Future traits, 107
    resume as only required method, 96
coroutines
    about syntax used in book, 89
    async behavior mimicked by, 100-103

coroutines sent over threads, 107
    drawbacks of, 103
    Executor struct created, 102
    struct for coroutines with async runtime, 108
described, 89, 90
    subroutines compared, 90
    threads compared, 91
    trade-offs, 91
    Yield type and Return type, 93
flow control via, 104-108
Future traits implemented by, 107
    struct for coroutines with async runtime, 108
as generators, 94
    async generator documentation link, 94
    calling a coroutine from a coroutine, 98-100
    flow control via coroutines, 105
    implementing a generator, 95, 105
    large file transfer example, 96-98
    stacking coroutines, 96-98
    symmetric coroutines, 98-100
testing coroutines, 109-113
why use, 91
    example uses, 89, 94
    file-writing example, 92-94
    Yielded and Complete states, 93
yielding, 90
CPU
    async described, 2-4
    basic asynchronous code, 3
    processes, 5-10
    processes simple to schedule, 9
    work offloaded to new thread pool, 34, 58
Ctrl-C for graceful shutdown, 149-153
custom asynchronous queue, 50-57
    about, 49

D

data
    sharing across threads, 146
    sharing between futures, 37-41
        high-level data sharing, 41
    streaming via a coroutine generator, 95
    thread data accessed directly, 147
Database Internals (Petrov), 169
deadlocks, 104, 224
    livelocks, 227

testing for, 224-227
decorator pattern, 186-190
    compilation feature flags, 187
    inner futures, 188
deleted records tombstoned, 133
Deserialize trait, 20
design patterns
    about async programming, 179
    circuit-breaker pattern, 194-196
        documentation link, 194
        spawn_task checking OPEN, 194
    decorator pattern, 186-190
        compilation feature flags, 187
        documentation link, 186
    isolated async modules, 179-185
        basic sync testing, 219-222
        synchronous entry points, 180-185
    retry pattern, 193
        documentation link, 193
    router pattern with actor model, 160-165
        actor supervision, 170-176
        sender as global static, 163
        sender as global static caution, 163
    state machine pattern, 190-193
        documentation link, 190
    waterfall pattern, 185
        documentation link, 185
        error handling, 185
detach method, 69
device_query crate for user input, 124-127
    callback guard, 126
documentation (see resources online)

E

errors
    anyhow library, 72
    Box<dyn Any + Send>> dynamic trait
        object, 12
    catch_unwind function to catch, 52
    design pattern error handling
        circuit-breaker pattern, 194-196
        retry pattern, 193
        waterfall pattern, 185
    fault-tolerant state recovery, 168
    isolated async module variant return values,
        183
    process exit value, 8, 10
    segmentation faults, 32
    unwrap, 14

event bus, 127
    backpressure from event buildup, 133
    broadcasting via, 127-135
        broadcast channels versus, 127
        dependencies and imports, 128
        garbage collection for dead IDs, 133
        handle for event bus, 131-132
        interactions via async tasks, 132
        struct for event bus, 128-130
event loops
    callbacks made nonblocking, 125
    mouse and keyboard movements, 126
executors, 72
    coroutines for, 102
    hyper relying on, 73

F

file I/O with async, 16-20
    audit trail example of futures, 44-48
    coroutine file-writing example, 92-94
    file reading API dependent, 18
    large file transfer via coroutines, 96-98
    state recovery for actors, 165-170
    streaming data via a coroutine generator, 95
    writing transactions to files, 169
Flitton, Maxwell, vii
flow control via coroutines, 104-108
flume, 50
    building an async queue, 50-57
        increasing threads and queues, 57
        multiple queues, 60
        task stealing, 61-63
function colors, 110
Future trait
    building an async queue, 51
    Coroutine trait similarity, 94
        coroutines implementing Future traits,
        107
    polls used, 42, 107
    static keyword, 51
futures, 26, 29
    background tasks, 68
    cancel safety, 34
    Context, 32-34
    example audit trail, 44-48
    executors running to completion, 72
    futures-lite, 50
        building an async queue, 50-57
    non-send futures and local thread pool, 145

passed into Tokio join macro, 27
pinning, 30-32
    documentation link, 31
polling, 29
    coroutines integrated with, 107
    depending on state of future, 192
    poll pending, 68
    polling sockets in futures, 83-86
    polling without stopping, 68
    Rust async for polling, 54
    Rust implementation of futures, 42
processing of, 43
Rust implementation, 42
sharing data between, 37-41
    high-level data sharing, 41
testing, 233-235
timeouts, 33
wakers, 32
waking remotely, 35-37
futures-lite, 50
    building an async queue, 50-57

G

garbage collection for dead event bus handles, 133
Generator trait, 96
    (see also Coroutine trait)
generators, 94
    async generators in Rust, 94
        documentation link, 94
    coroutines as, 94
        calling a coroutine from a coroutine, 98-100
        flow control via coroutines, 105
        implementing a generator, 95, 105
        large file transfer example, 96-98
        stacking coroutines, 96-98
        symmetric coroutines, 98-100
GeneratorState, 96
    (see also Coroutine trait)
global state in async Rust, 163
graceful shutdowns, 149-154
    Ctrl-C overridden, 149-153
    SIGHUP signal, 153
green threads, 12
    documentation link, 12

H

handle for event bus, 131-132

garbage collection for dead IDs, 133
heartbeat supervisor mechanism, 170-176
heater reactive system, 115-127
    about, 115
    display observer future built, 118-121
        running all the futures, 123
    display with user input, 125
    feedback simple, 117
    heat-loss observer future built, 123
    heater observer future built, 121-123
    oscillating temperature, 123
    subjects defined, 116
    user input via callbacks, 124-127
HTTP
    about, 74
    basic asynchronous code, 3
        processes, 7
        request performance, 20-22
        reqwest crate, 3
    networking integrated into runtime
        about, 71
        client connection and execution, 81
        dependencies, 71
        HTTP connection built, 74-77
        hyper crate, 71
        Tokio AsyncRead trait, 77-79
        Tokio AsyncWrite trait, 79-81
    port 80 as standard, 77
    testing network interactions, 231-233
HTTPS, 74
    port 443 as standard, 77
Huang, Jensen, 1
hyper, 72
    client feature, 72
    mio versus, 83
    networking integrated into async runtime
        HTTP connection built, 74-77
        hyper connection and execution, 81
        hyper integration, 73
        Tokio AsyncRead trait, 77-79
        Tokio AsyncWrite trait, 79-81
    runtime feature, 72

I

I/O operations
    file I/O with async, 16-20
        audit trail example of futures, 44-48
        coroutine file-writing example, 92-94
        file reading API dependent, 18

large file transfer via coroutines, 96-98
HTTP request performance, 20-22
    (see also HTTP)
state recovery for actors, 165-170
streaming data via a coroutine generator, 95
writing transactions to files, 169
input via device_query crate, 124-127
interior mutability via Mutex, 13
isolated async modules, 179-185
    basic sync testing, 219-222
    synchronous entry points, 180-185

J

join macro
    creating your own, 65
    Tokio
        basic asynchronous code, 4
        futures passed into, 27
JoinHandle, 11
    return result, 12
JSON feature of reqwest enabled, 20

K

key-value store
    commercial products for production, 160
    router pattern for actor messages, 160-165
        actor supervision, 170-176
keyboard keypress event loop, 126
kill -SIGHUP <pid> for graceful shutdown, 153
Klabnik, Steve, vii

L

lazy evaluation
    generators' lazy performance, 94
    isolated async modules, 182
    LazyLock
        graceful shutdown, 151
        reactive system built, 116
        Tokio runtime built, 138
    queues and channels as lazy, 63
        async queue runtime configuration,
            66-68
LazyLock
    graceful shutdown, 151
    reactive system built, 116
    Tokio runtime built, 138
learning Rust books, vii
livelocks, 227

local pools for processing tasks, 142-147
    advantages, 145
    no task stealing, 143, 145
lock function as blocking, 39, 110
lock poisoning, 14
log file example of futures, 44-48

M

Meadows, Donella H., 124
memory
    memory leak when handle dropped, 131
    pinning in futures, 30-32
        documentation link, 31
    processes spawned per connection, 6
    Rust as memory safe, 10
    segmentation faults, 32
messages via channels over mutexes, 159
    multiproducer, single-consumer channel
        (mpsc), 156
    oneshot::Sender in messages to actors, 156
        actor supervision, 171-176
        router pattern, 160-165
        sending a message, 156
messages via event bus, 127-135
milliseconds (ms), 16
mio crate
    about, 82
    hyper versus, 83
    polling sockets in futures, 83-86
    sending data over socket, 86-88
    UnixDatagrams, 88
mocking, 222
    mockall, 219-222
    mocking async code, 222-224
    mocking network interactions, 231-233
    mockito, 231-233
module isolation for async code, 179-185
    basic sync testing, 219-222
    synchronous entry points, 180-185
Moore's law dead, 1
mouse movement event loop, 126
mpsc (multiproducer, single-consumer chan-
    nel), 156
    actors versus mutexes, 157-160
    router pattern for actors, 160-165
ms (milliseconds), 16
multiproducer, single-consumer channel (see
    mpsc)
Mutex (mutual exclusion), 13

actors versus mutexes, 157-160
basic asynchronous code, 14
try_lock for acquiring, 39

N

nanoseconds (ns), 16
networking integrated into async runtime
  about, 71
  client connection and execution, 81
  connectors, 72
  dependencies, 71
  executors, 72
  HTTP connection built, 74-77
  hyper into async runtime, 73
  mio, 82
    hyper versus, 83
    polling sockets in futures, 83-86
    sending data over socket, 86-88
    UnixDatagrams, 88
  testing network interactions, 231-233
  Tokio AsyncRead trait, 77-79
  Tokio AsyncWrite trait, 79-81
Nichols, Carol, vii
non-send futures and local thread pool, 145
ns (nanoseconds), 16

O

observer pattern
  building a basic reactive system, 115-127
    about, 115
    display observer future built, 118-121
    display of all futures running, 123
    display with user input, 125
    feedback simple, 117
    heat-loss observer future built, 123
    heater observer future built, 121-123
    oscillating temperature, 123
    subjects defined, 116
    user input via callbacks, 124-127
  documentation links, 115
oneshot::Sender in messages to actors, 156
  sending a message, 156
oscillations in output, 124
  temperature in reactive system, 123
ownership
  AsyncRead execution, 78
  shared data, 14
  variables in static lifetime, 51

P

parked thread, 14
  task stealing, 62
  Tokio quickly parking threads, 141
pausing execution then resuming (see coroutines)
Petrov, Alex, 169
PID (process ID), 6
  killing a PID, 6
pinning in futures, 30-32
  documentation link, 31
polling futures, 29
  coroutines integrated with, 107
  depending on state of future, 192
  poll pending, 68
  polling sockets in futures, 83-86
  polling without stopping, 68
  Rust async for polling, 54
  Rust implementation, 42
port numbers
  443 for HTTPS, 77
  80 for HTTP, 77
PostgreSQL processes, 5, 6
  connection is a process, 9
procedural macros
  documentation link, 66
  Tokio runtime setup, 66
process ID (see PID)
processes, 5-10
  async described, 2-4
    async Rust, 7
    basic asynchronous code, 7, 9
    drawbacks, 9
    scheduling simple, 9
  definition, 5
  exit value and errors, 8, 10
  PID, 6
    killing a PID, 6
  spawning per connection, 5, 6
  threads versus, 6, 10

Q

question mark (?) operator for error handling, 185
queues (see async queues)

R

race conditions tested for, 227-229

about race conditions, 227
reactive programming
    about, 115
    broadcasting via event bus, 127-135
        broadcast channels versus, 127
        dependencies and imports, 128
        event bus interactions via tasks, 132
        garbage collection for dead IDs, 133
        handle for event bus, 131-132
        struct for event bus, 128-130
    building a basic reactive system, 115-127
        about, 115
        display observer future built, 118-121
        display of all futures running, 123
        display with user input, 125
        feedback simple, 117
        heat-loss observer future built, 123
        heater observer future built, 121-123
        oscillating temperature, 123
        subjects defined, 116
        user input via callbacks, 124-127
real-time responsiveness (see reactive program-
    ming)
Relaxed ordering, 15
reqwest package
    basic asynchronous code, 3
        API calls, 20
        processes, 7
    JSON feature enabled, 20
    testing network interactions, 231-233
resources for learning Rust, vii
resources online
    actor model, 155
    async closure documentation, 51
    AsyncRead trait documentation, 77
    Atomic Bool, 15
    atomics documentation, 115
    book web page, x
    design pattern documentation
        circuit-breaker, 194
        decorator, 186
        retry, 193
        state machine, 190
        waterfall, 185
    green threads documentation, 12
    observer pattern documentation, 115
    pinning and unpinning, 31
    procedural macro documentation, 66
    Rust by Example, vii

Rust RFC Book
    async and await, 26
    async generators, 94
    state machines, 190
retry pattern, 193
    documentation link, 193
router pattern with actor model, 160-165
    actor supervision, 170-176
    sender as global static, 163
    sender as global static caution, 163
Runnable handle, 52
runtime
    building a Tokio runtime, 137-142
        (see also Tokio runtime)
        used for actors, 155
        used in local pools code, 143
    configured for async queue, 66-68
        runtime rebuilt, 141
    coroutine struct for interaction with, 108
    networking integrated into (see networking
        integrated into async runtime)
Rust
    async generators, 94
        Rust RFC Book for information, 94
    async Rust (see async Rust)
    futures implementation, 42
    green threads not implemented, 12
    learning resources, vii
    RFC Book link
        async and await, 26
        async generators, 94
Rust by Example (Rust online community), vii
The Rust Programming Language (Klabnik and
    Nichols), vii
Rust Web Programming (Flitton), vii

S
schedulers
    green threads, 12
        documentation link, 12
    process scheduling simple, 9
    threads independently managed, 10
segmentation faults, 32
Send trait
    building an async queue, 51
        static keyword, 51
    JoinHandle implementing, 12
server built (see async server built)
SIGHUP signal for graceful shutdown, 153

sleep function
    file I/O, 18, 19
    nonblocking sleep functions
        coroutines mimicking, 100-103
        explained, 54
        Tokio sleep function, 19, 25, 145
        Tokio sleep function allowing async, 27,
            54, 145
        when blocking better, 55
    response latency and, 62
    Tokio
        await keyword, 26, 55
        nonblocking, 19, 25, 145
        nonblocking allowing async, 27, 54, 145
smol, 72
sockets
    HTTP connection built, 74-77
    mio, 82
        hyper versus mio, 83
        polling sockets in futures, 83-86
        sending data over socket, 86-88
        UnixDatagrams, 88
    tokens identifying, 83
spawn_blocking function (Tokio), 146
spawn_task function, 51
    calling custom Tokio runtime, 140
    circuit-breaker pattern, 194
    refactored, 63-64
    running background processes, 68
    runtime configuration, 67
        custom executor for, 73
    socket continually polled, 85
state
    actors, 155, 160
        fault-tolerant state recovery, 168
        state recovery for actors, 165-170
    coroutines
        storing and resuming state, 90
        Yielded and Complete states, 93
    graceful shutdowns, 151-154
    sharing data across threads, 146
    state isolation of processes spawned per
        connection, 6
    state machine design pattern, 190-193
        documentation link, 190
    state machine documentation link, 190
    state of future from other threads, 35
state machine documentation link, 190
state machine pattern, 190-193

documentation link, 190
streaming data via a coroutine generator, 95
subroutines compared to coroutines, 90
subscribers to event bus messaging, 127-135
supply chain oscillations, 124
suspending execution then resuming (see
    coroutines)
symmetric coroutines, 98-100
Sync trait implemented by JoinHandle, 12

T
TAP (task-based asynchronous pattern), 23-28
task stealing, 61-63
    local pools can't, 143, 145
task-based asynchronous pattern (TAP), 23-28
task-spawning function (see spawn_task func-
    tion)
tasks, 23-28
    background processes, 68
    coroutines compared to async tasks, 91
        flow control via coroutines, 104-108
    deadlocks, 104, 224
    definition, 28
    event bus interactions, 132
    futures, 26
        cancel safety, 34
        Context, 32-34
        example audit trail, 44-48
        high-level data sharing between, 41
        passed into join macro, 27
        pinning, 30-32
        pinning documentation link, 31
        poll pending, 68
        polling, 29, 42
        polling via Rust async, 54
        polling without stopping, 68
        processing of, 43
        sharing data between, 37-41
        static keyword, 51
        timeouts, 33
        waking remotely, 35-37
    laziness of queues and channels, 63
        runtime configured for, 66-68
    multiple queues, 59-61
        task stealing, 61-63
        Tokio for task distribution, 61
    Runnable handle, 52
    spawn_task function, 51
        refactored, 63-64

wakers, 32
    Context, 32-34
TCP
    about, 74
    client connection and execution, 81
    HTTP connection built, 74-77
    mio, 82
        hyper versus, 83
        polling sockets in futures, 83-86
        sending data over socket, 86-88
        UnixDatagrams, 88
    Tokio AsyncRead trait, 77-79
    Tokio AsyncWrite trait, 79-81
TCP server built
    about, 197
    basics set up, 197-199
        Data struct public, 199
        four workspaces, 197
        serialize and deserialize functions, 198
    client built, 215
    receiver built, 208
    runtime components, 199-210
        executor built, 202-205
        executor run, 205-206
        waker, 200-202
    sender built, 207
    server built, 210
        accepting requests, 211-214
        handling requests, 214
    sleep built, 209
temperature reactive system, 115-127
testing
    about, 219
    actors, 156
        isolation simplifying testing, 155
    arrange, act, assert, 221
    basic sync testing, 219-222
    channel capacity, 229
    coroutines tested easily, 108
        simple generator implementation, 105
        testing coroutines, 109-113
    for deadlocks, 224-227
    fine-grained future testing, 233-235
    fixtures as decorator pattern, 186
    global state in async Rust, 163
    mocking, 222
        mockall, 219-222
        mocking async code, 222-224
        mocking network interactions, 231-233

    mockito, 231-233
    race conditions, 227-229
Thinking in Systems (Meadows), 124
thread pools
    CPU-intensive work offloaded, 34, 58
    local pools for processing tasks, 142-147
        advantages, 145
        no task stealing, 143, 145
    Rust web servers, 5
threads, 10-16
    async described, 2-4
        basic asynchronous code, 11, 14
        Condvar for interaction, 13
        JoinHandle, 11
        JoinHandle return result, 12
        multiple Condvars, 15
        parked while waiting, 14, 62
    coroutines compared, 91
        coroutines sent over threads, 107
    definition, 10
    green threads, 12
        documentation link, 12
    local pool thread affinity, 145
    processes versus, 6, 10
    thread data accessed directly, 147
timeouts, 33
    future cancel safety, 34
timing the running of scripts, 9
Tokio runtime
    AsyncRead trait, 77-79
    AsyncWrite trait, 79-81
    basic asynchronous code, 3
        #[tokio::main] macro, 137
        file I/O, 17-20
        HTTP request performance, 20-22
        processes, 7, 9
    broadcast channels, 127
    building a runtime, 137-142
        #[tokio::main] macro, 137
        calling function signature, 140
        calling the runtime, 140
        configuration options, 138-140
        LazyLock, 138
        used for actors, 155
        used in local pools code, 143
    graceful shutdowns, 149-154
        Ctrl-C overridden, 149-153
        SIGHUP signal, 153
    green threads implemented, 12

join macro
    basic asynchronous code, 4
    futures passed into, 27
local pools for processing tasks, 142-147
mio crate as foundation, 82
networking (see networking integrated into
    async runtime)
parking threads quickly, 141
reactive heater system, 116
runtime struct, 66
sleep function
    await keyword, 26, 55, 143
    nonblocking, 19, 25, 145
    nonblocking allowing async, 27, 54, 145
spawn_blocking function, 146
tasks, 25-28
    distribution to different queues, 61
    futures, 26
        (see also futures)
    test macro, 225
    fine-grained future testing, 233-235
    timeouts, 33
    UnsafeCell for thread data, 147
tombstoning deleted records, 133
traits
    AsyncRead trait, 77-79
        documentation link, 77
    Box<dyn Any + Send>> dynamic trait
        object, 12
    Clone trait
        event bus struct, 128-130
        JoinHandle not implementing, 12
    Coroutine trait
        coroutines implementing Future traits,
            107
        formerly Generator trait and Generator-
            State, 96
        Future trait similarity, 94
        resume as only required method, 96
    Deserialize trait, 20
    future trait
        polls used, 42
    Future trait
        building an async queue, 51
        Coroutine trait similarity, 94

coroutines implementing Future traits,
    107
polls used, 107
static keyword, 51
JoinHandle
    Clone trait not implemented, 12
    Send and Sync traits implemented, 12
Send trait
    building an async queue, 51
    JoinHandle implementing, 12
    static keyword, 51
SymmetricCoroutine trait created, 99
Sync trait implemented by JoinHandle, 12
Unpin trait, 31
    documentation link, 31
transactions written to files, 169
try_lock
    acquiring Mutex, 39
    nonblocking, 39, 110

U

UnixDatagrams via mio, 88
Unpin trait, 31
    documentation link, 31
UnsafeCell (Tokio) for thread data, 147
unwrap, 14
user input via device_query crate, 124-127

V

variables
    LazyLock for lazy initialization, 116
    ownership in static lifetime, 51

W

wakers, 32
    waking futures remotely, 35-37
waterfall pattern, 185
    documentation link, 185
    error handling, 185

Y

yielding by a coroutine, 90

About the Authors

Maxwell Flitton is a software engineer at the Rust open source database SurrealDB and an honorary researcher at King's College London in surgical robotics, where he builds GPU streaming in Rust. In 2011, Maxwell achieved his bachelor of science degree in nursing from the University of Lincoln, UK, and a degree in physics from the Open University with a postgraduate diploma in physics and engineering in medicine from UCL in London while working as a nurse at Charing Cross A&E. He has worked on numerous projects, such as building the medical simulation software Clinical Metrics and supervising computational medicine students at Imperial College London. He also has experience in financial tech working on financial loss modeling engines used by companies like Nasdaq and Monolith AI. While building the medical simulation software, Maxwell and Caroline had to build Rust async systems in the Kubernetes cluster to create real-time events and caching mechanisms. Maxwell has written the Packt textbooks *Rust Web Programming* and *Speed Up Your Python with Rust*.

Caroline Morton studied medicine and international health at the University of Birmingham in the UK before moving to London to work as a doctor. She is a qualified general practitioner and completed a master's degree in epidemiology at the London School of Hygiene and Tropical Medicine. Caroline later set up the first course in the UK training doctors and medical students to learn programming (Coding for Medicine), which later developed into a 10-week module, and wrote a textbook covering the same topic called *Computational Medicine* (Elsevier, 2018). In 2019, she moved to the University of Oxford to work as an epidemiologist and software developer and was key in developing OpenSAFELY, a trusted research environment that processed COVID-19 data during the pandemic. This resulted in over 60 peer-reviewed papers in journals such as *Nature*, *The Lancet*, and *The BMJ*. Together with Maxwell, she has developed cutting-edge techniques in Rust to solve problems in developing Clinical Metrics, a simulation product for training new doctors, the backend of which is built entirely using Rust. In 2024, Caroline started a part-time PhD in medical statistics, exploring ways to generate realistic synthetic data for electronic health research using Rust.

Colophon

The animal on the cover of *Async Rust* is a rufous hare-wallaby (*Lagorchestes hirsutus*), also known as the mala. It is the smallest of the hare-wallabies, weighing 800 to 1,600 grams, with a body length of 12 to 15 inches and tail length of 10 to 12 inches. Females are slightly larger than males. Its fur is a light grayish- to reddish-brown with a lighter belly, and like kangaroos and other wallabies, it is capable of maneuvering on all fours or hopping on its powerful hind legs.

Rufous hare-wallabies are solitary and nocturnal, dwelling in burrows beneath grass hummocks that provide shelter from the heat of the day. They live on a diet of seeds, fruits, and plants. The rufous hare-wallaby was once widespread in the western half of Australia, though habitat loss and predation by introduced animals such as cats and foxes caused it to go extinct in mainland Australia in the 1990s.

The rufous hare-wallaby is classified as vulnerable, and current populations are primarily restricted to a few islands off the coast of Western Australia. However, programs are in place to protect current populations, and it is being reintroduced in parts of Northern Territory. Many of the animals on O'Reilly covers are endangered; all of them are important to the world.

The cover illustration is by Karen Montgomery, based on an antique line engraving from Lydekker's *Royal Natural History*. The cover fonts are Gilroy Semibold and Guardian Sans. The text font is Adobe Minion Pro; the heading font is Adobe Myriad Condensed; and the code font is Dalton Maag's Ubuntu Mono.

O'REILLY®

Learn from experts.
Become one yourself.

60,000+ titles | Live events with experts | Role-based courses
Interactive learning | Certification preparation

**Try the O'Reilly learning platform
free for 10 days.**

www.ingramcontent.com/pod-product-compliance
Lightning Source LLC
Chambersburg PA
CBHW061359210326
41598CB00035B/6031